This story is for the people who are scared of dogs, that making friends with one will release them from their fear. It is dedicated to those Friends who know that every adventure is better with a dog. It is also for those who think that adventure is scary, and dedicated to those who know that all lives are an adventure.

~Oscar the Pooch, Fall 2019

Oscar and the Intruder

My name is Oscar, and I'm a charming man-dog with a nose for adventure. I have a lustrous black pelt that catches the sun, and rippling muscles that catch the ladies' eyes everywhere I go. I know how to make anyone feel like the most important person in the world, so I'm a pretty popular guy, and of course I'm the hero of this story. Every hero needs a sidekick, and mine's named Mom. I have spent most of my life running right behind Mom, or listening to the *pa-dump, pa-dump* of her footsteps behind me, so her stride is a part of me too, like a heartbeat.

Before our lives changed, I used to spend most of my days sitting at home and waiting for things to happen. Sometimes bad guys like the mailman or the UPS guy came through my front gate to murder me. I would hear their trucks growling for blood at the end of the drive and sit up on high alert to find out who the murderers were coming to massacre today. Then I would listen to their hungry bootsteps prowling down the row of houses to see which dog would make the best meal. Some days they were desperate enough to come all the way to the end where I live, and I could hear the clink-creek of them opening my gate to get me. I always scared them off by barking mean things through the front door before they broke in, and so survived to nap another day.

But one day a man I'd never seen before came in the gate. "You go away, or you're really gonna be sorry!" I shouted through the door. And then, "Hey, booger brain!

I'm talking to you! Turn around now or else I'm going to open a can of whoop-sass on your butt!" But despite me using my most terrifying barking voice, this psycho pulled out a key and tried to open the front door and come into my house! I didn't know if he was a dog-eating man or what. I growled and barked at him and did other manly things to show him how tough I am. Luckily my show of ferocity and toughness was scary enough to convince him to take a hike.

The Dog-Eating Man had gotten me real upset, and I had barked with such venom and ferocity that I accidentally pooped and peed in my bed. Now I had a different problem. Mom also sleeps in my bed, so I wasn't really sure where to nap now, or where either of us were going to sleep tonight... I was so worried between the intruder and soiling my bed that I just had to tear a hole in Mom's favorite sweatshirt to help relieve my anxiety about it all.

But my nightmare wasn't over yet. Even though the Dog-Eating Man went away, Some Lady tried to come into my house a little while later! I'd met this lady once before, but Mom had been home back then. I wasn't sure what business Some Lady had coming in without Mom to escort her. It was very suspicious so soon after the Dog-Eating Man left. What if they were in cahoots?

Then I remembered that when Mom and I met Some Lady for the first time, Mom had looked like she wanted the lady to like her. Maybe Mom wanted Some Lady to like me too, and Mom would want me to do what

Some Lady said. So after more barking and thuggish cowering, I let her put a leash on me. Big mistake! Never, ever let a stranger put a leash on you. Once she had the leash on, she forced me out of my house! Who would protect my home from dog-eating intruders if I was going to be with this lady now? What would Mom do without me?! Would she be upset if she came home and I wasn't there to greet her with wiggles and squirms? This had to be the most stressful day ever!

This part of the story has a happy ending though, because it turned out that Some Lady was going to the dog beach where I made lots of new friends. We ran and ran in the sand, and I showed all my new friends the trick I learned about how to chase the waves and bite them before they go back into the ocean. I also saw The Dog-Eating Man at the beach, probably looking for some innocent dog to eat for lunch. I barked at him to let him know he wasn't fooling me. He was way too scared to murder me in front of so many witnesses, so he gave me treats to pretend that we were friends.

When it was all over, Some Lady was very nice and took me back to my house rather than making me live with her at her house, so I would be there to greet Mom like normal when she got home. Before she left, The Dognapper filled my water bowl all the way to the tippity top, which was also nice of her because something about the beach always makes me really thirsty.

While I waited for Mom to come home, I drank all of my water in just a few big gulps, and then lay down to sleep off all of the excitement. When I woke up, the sun

4

was looking straight into the window, which meant that Mom would be home soon. I hoped that she would hurry because I really had to go potty. I stood by the door and waited and waited and waited for her to come home. But after at least two long minutes of waiting, I couldn't hold it anymore, and I crouched down and went potty on the floor. I went potty until my piddle puddle was a lake, and then an ocean that went all the way into the kitchen. Then I went back to bed to wait for Mom.

When Mom finally came home, I burst through the door to tell her about my day. "Mom," I said. "You'll never guess what happened while you were out! First, a man tried to break into the house and kill me, but I scared him away. And then this lady came and dognapped me and took me to the beach, and it was horrible…" (it wasn't really horrible, but I didn't want Mom to be jealous), "…and when I came home the man had broken in while I was away and peed and pooped on the bed and ripped up your sweatshirt. Then, he went potty all over the floor so that we would know that he was here. Also, where do you think we should sleep tonight?"

Swiping Right on Mom

    I was pretty lucky that I met and adopted the human that I did. I was just a baby at the time, so I didn't really know what I was doing. I wagged my tail and kissed every human I met because I thought they were *all* great. Of all the people who I wagged at and kissed that day, the one I named Mom was the one that signed up to be my service human and life partner. I was Mom's first posting as a service human, but it was also my first time being a dog, so we've been learning how to do life together ever since. Mostly, we run.

    A good sidekick needs a few quirks, or else they wouldn't need a hero following them around to keep things interesting, and that's why Mom's stride has a hitch in it. There's nothing really wrong with her. Everybody has hitches and glitches that make them just right. So one of the things that makes Mom herself is that one of her legs swings ascrew when she runs, like it's avoiding something that's not there, and cowering toward the other leg for comfort.

    Mom says that I have trouble making friends because I'm a "sasshole." But that's silly, because I always make lots of friends at the dog park. Whenever we go there, I have a wonderful time barking at all the New Friends I appoint. They don't know we're friends yet, so I have to tell them. I get all up in their faces and bark, "Come at me, bro!" over and over until they curl up into a submissive ball, or get mad and nip at me. That's when the serious fun begins, because that's when the humans join in on the barking and chase me around the park. The humans growl and bark, and I bark and dodge, and we play tag like that until Mom finally catches me and it's Game Over. Then I have to go on the leash and Mom has to say her lecture about how we're never going to the dog park again.

Mom is my only live-in family, but I have other family, too. I also have a twin sister named Bodø Maile Galaxy Moyer Salz, who is my soulmate. Bodie and I were separated at birth, but our parents found each other through the adoption agency and introduced us when we were grown. We've been soulmates ever since, and she is the only one other than Mom and me that thinks I'm great just the way I am.

When Bodie and I go to the dog park together, she actually thinks that my barking is fun. Bodie also likes to chase me, which is all I ever wanted to begin with. Since Mom doesn't have to do the chasing and barking, we get to stay at the dog park until *everyone* is "sick of this crap," not just Mom. Being "sick of this crap" together is what being a family is all about.

Bodie is a better runner than I am, and can run faster and longer, but I'm a better coach because I make Mom scream a lot less. When we run together, Mom and I run straight down the path, and Bodie runs from side to side as far as her leash will stretch muttering, "Oh boy! Oh boy! Long-eared cat place!"

Bodie lives to chase bunnies, which is a real shame because Mom is scared of bunnies and screams and howls every time we run after one. Cats too. And squirrels. And bags that get caught in the wind. And stumps that look like they might be critters. Since we're all tied together, it comes down to a vote about whether we chase critters or no. Since Mom is outnumbered, she has to chase too, whether she likes it or not. That's called democracy.

I'm a gentleman, so when I run, I like to run right behind a lady. When it's just me and Mom, that means that Mom is the leader. But when the three of us run together, I follow Bodie close enough that her butt smacks my face, and Mom is the caboose. Usually Bodie slows down a bit after she poops, but one morning she didn't stop going full gas for miles and miles. Mom had been whining and pulling on the leash that whole time, and it was starting to get annoying. We were all a little irritable. "Why don't you have patience and slow down a bit so that Mom can keep up?" I asked Bodie.

"It's cool, I'm an expert at patience," said Bodie. "I have to practice it all the time."

"You're the least patient dog I know! You're always trying to get down the trail as fast as you can!"

"And what would you call that feeling when you want to move along but everyone else is going slower than you if not 'patience'?"

"But we run faster than this when you're not here. I think you're actually slowing us down by pulling her."

"That's ridiculous! The harder we pull, the faster she's going to go. Watch this..." Bodie waited until Mom was in mid-air, and then floored it with a full-speed bunny sprint. For a few seconds we were running like the wind, if the wind howled like a terrified and angry human. But after about a hundred yards, Mom finally got all of her feet on the ground and planted herself, growling fiercely and pulling on our leashes.

"See? Now we're stopped," I told Bodie once our collars had given our breath back. "I rest my case. I think she's actually slowing down on purpose."

"Don't be a pudding-head, Oscar! I bet she's just sniffing around for a good place to poop."

"Why don't you slow down and get to know Mom? Sometimes she says some pretty mind-blowing stuff."

"Because long-eared cats, Oscar! And feather-cats. And stripey stink-cats. Duh."

"I think that if you really try to force something, that maybe life makes it so that it's harder and harder for you to get it. Maybe that's why Mom never lets you get the bunnies, and we always have to stop when we see one."

"I think that's just because she only runs on half of her legs, so she can't run as fast as us..."

"No, I'm pretty sure that it's because you're trying to force it. If you just stopped trying to control the run all the time, I bet Mom would let you run faster and we could chase the bunnies all the way into the ocean."

"Oscar, you're obnoxious when you're coaching. Your lady may like this life coach claptrap, but I think you're full of baloney. Obviously if you want something, you should just keep trying harder and harder until you get it. That's why I keep pulling the leash so hard. Sure, I have trouble breathing… but you can't win if you don't make sacrifices. You gotta really **want** it!"

I'm a smart gentleman, so I know never to tell a lady she's wrong. Instead I asked, "What are you always in such a hurry to see anyway?"

"All the things, Dummy! There are long-eared cats, and ground cats, and feather cats, and tree cats, and other dogs, and peemail, and puddles…"

"But those things will still be there if you take your time. If you hurry, you might even miss them because they will be behind you. Don't you want to just look for one thing and then find it?"

Bodie looked perturbed. "Are you saying I should look behind us too? Oh god, I hadn't thought of that! I should be checking in all directions, not just front and sides! Oh no, Oscar! What if I missed something awesome because I forgot to look behind me?!"

"Relax," I told her. "Let me show you how to make Mom run faster. You smell those people who came through here a minute or two ago? I wanna catch them."

"Oh yeah! Me too! I like racing…"

"Well it's not exactly like racing. It's not a competition. It's like a competition against yourself called 'goal setting.' We're going to pull mom just a little bit faster than she wants to go – Not so fast that she gets scared and makes us slow down, but just enough that you always feel her on the end of the leash, okay? If she makes noise, then that means she's going to impose a time penalty and that's bad because we might not catch them."

"Okay. Gotcha. Just a little bit of pressure on the leash so we don't overwhelm the Howling Lady. Got it. But what about the stuff in the back and sides?"

"That's what makes it hard. You've got to ignore all the stuff that's not in front of you. Distractions are bad for goals. That's called 'focus'."

"Oscar! Look! I can see them. They stopped to look at something!"

"See? They don't have focus, and now we're going to pass them."

"Oh boy! Oh boy! Oh boy! We're going to win this run! Hashtag goals! Hashtag focus!"

"Um... I don't think you're using those right..."

"You're a social media dog and you don't know about hashtags?"

"Never mind. Focus," I told her.

Slowly but surely we caught up to the people and passed them. "What pretty dogs!" they told Mom when we went by. And then we relaxed and started running at Mom pace, looking around for the first time in about a mile.

"What?! *Now* you guys slow down?!" said Mom. "It's not a race!"

No, it's training, suckah, and we just won!

"Race?! Did somebody say 'race'?" Bodie said, starting to speed up.

"Hashtag focus, Bodie!" I reminded her. "Go easy!"

"Aren't we supposed to be coaches?" Bodie asked, exasperated. "I thought we settled this, she needs to run fast to learn how to be fast. It's because she's so slow that we never catch the long-eared cats."

"Yeah, but this year she doesn't want to race, so now we're life coaches instead."

"What does that even mean?"

"I don't know, mostly I think I'm supposed to watch her runs and say insightful things about how it's a metaphor for her bad habits."

"That's the stupidest thing I've ever heard," said Bodie. And then she said, "OMG! DID YOU SMELL THAT?!" And then we had to chase a bunny in all the directions because we weren't sure what direction the real bunny was in. Mom squawked and howled behind us until she managed to stick her feet to the ground and squat down like a surfer to make herself an anchor and call off the hunt.

So I guess we'll never know if you can get the bunny if you stop trying to control things, because Bodie will never stop trying. Some dogs just aren't ready to change.

Schrödinger's Dog

There may be no help for Bodie, but Mom and I have a different approach to life than my sister does. I'm a "difficult dog," according to my puppy school professor. That means that I have great self confidence, and am not afraid to bark my mind. It also means that sometimes I know better than humans, and I pick and choose when I want to be the leader and when I want to be the sidekick. That's why I'm so lucky that I found Mom, because she's a "difficult dog" too and understands that not all rules are for following.

I need to follow some rules no matter what. Mom insists that we always be nice and polite to people and never, ever scare them on purpose. This is easier for Mom, who is a tiny and unimpressive human that keeps her thoughts inside her head. But I have a big, boxy head like an elegant anvil, and the brain underneath makes such intense feelings that they can't be held inside, and need to burst out of my mouth and tail and hackles. Not all humans understand barking, so if a human hears me bellowing a friendly hello like a fire and brimstone preacher, and sees my supple and hulking muscles charging at them like a bowling ball, then they may get dangerous and attack me. Dog-dangerous humans are like t-rexes, they can't see you if you don't make any sudden and excited movements, so Mom and I practice being peaceful and polite every day, for safety.

But not all rules are like respect and politeness. Some kinds of rules are confusing because there is no good reason for them and they are always changing, so you have to memorize every single one of them. If a dog sneaks into the park when no one is there to be scared of him, and his assistant picks up his poop and distracts him from the scent of baby nesting owls, then is he still a criminal? According to Mom, if we leave no trace then we haven't broken any rules until someone sees us doing it. She calls it Schrödinger's Law. Mom says that if you use common sense and respect as your guide, and you don't leave any clues of your crime, then you don't have to memorize all of the rules because you'll already know how to keep everyone safe. That's called "responsibility."

For example, we live in a place that's great for hiking, but it's also covered in human preserve land. Dogs aren't allowed in human preserves because they might frighten the humans away from their habitat[1]. A world without humans is supposed to be a bad thing, but Mom and I are always searching for the places where humans are rare. If I run in the preserves early enough, before the humans are active, then I'm Schrödinger's Dog and no one can prove that it ever happened. That's why we wake up very early, so that we can run when the world is only for us.

---

[1] If the humans are too scared to visit their habitats because a dog might come up and say hello, then many humans would stay home watching Netflix instead. That's bad because Netflix has all the seasons of *Law & Order*, and they might forget to stop watching and die of old age on their couches, and eventually humans might go extinct and there would be no one to open the package of cheese.

When we're not being outlaws, Mom and I run on a road for not-cars called My Trail, or on the flat dirt trails in The Wetlands that Smell Like a Fart. We patrol these trails so much that they started to feel as much like home as my house. Because I know every bush and tree and flattened McDonald's cup, and because we often run in the dark, I don't even need to look around on our runs, and the only interesting thing to pay attention to are the other trail users. So I appointed myself Mayor of the Trail and greet the good citizens, protecting them by barking at the rule breakers who take unauthorized walking breaks or just generally look fishy. Every time I meet someone who is breaking a new rule, like standing still and looking at their phone, or rollerblading, or limping, or being another handsome dog, I needed to add another thing to my list of things to look for, and the responsibility of all of those rules was starting to pile up and crush out all of the fun of running.

To make everything even a little bit more stressful still, there were other trail users who also thought that *they* were the mayor. They made up their own dumb rules, like "dogs should be seen and not heard," or "everyone should stay on their own side of the line on the trail," or that "false mayors have right of way." Sometimes I wanted to fight about these rules, but Mom said that false mayors aren't safe for hunky dogs, and the better thing to do is to walk away. Then she would drag me away from the debate by the leash, which I hated because I dislike having disagreements with Mom almost as much as I hate to lose.

The most dangerous threat came one morning while Mom and I were running a long run to her work. I didn't get to be a busy-ness dog very often, so this morning was special and we were enjoying running as outlaws along the rare few miles of trail that connected My Trail with The Wetlands that Smell Like a Fart. Slowly, a big truck rolled down the trail toward us. Mom pulled me into the weeds by the side of the trail and stopped to wait for the truck to go by. Since this wasn't part of my jurisdiction, I didn't have Mayor's right of way, and sat next to her patiently waiting for the truck to pass. She would have whistled not-guiltily, but Mom doesn't know how to whistle, so instead she put her paw on her hip and tried to look like she had a complaint on the tip of her tongue. Humans hate whining, so she hoped that the truck would drive by without looking at us.

Instead, the truck stopped and a man's head popped out of the window. "You know you can't have dogs on this part of the trail," the man said.

"You can't have trucks on this road either!" I barked when I saw his big, dumb face.

"...You're going to have to go back," the man continued.

"I can't go back," Mom said. "My car is this way." That was a lie. We were running because we weren't using the car at all, but the man didn't know that, and if he knew that Mom was using her feet rather than a car, then he would assume that she was a crazy person. Anyway, it was too much work to explain that if we went backward, then we would be at home and not at work.

"Well then you'll have to go back and go along the road," the man said.

"But the road is a mile behind me, and the place where dogs are allowed is a mile in front of me," Mom explained. Because humans are better at math than dogs, this told the man that we would be outlaws for just as long if advanced or if we retreated. "How about I run this mile as fast as I can, I don't let him stop, and we never come back here again?" Mom asked.

"Okay," the Outlaw Mayor said. "But don't let the rangers catch you. The fine for having a dog in the nesting habitat is $25,000."

"That's absurd!" Mom said. "That's like the take-home pay of a minimum wage worker for an entire year."

"OH NO!" I barked once the truck had left. "Now that we've been ub-served, are they going to put us to death like Schrödinger's cat?"

"Not 'observed,' 'absurd,'" Mom explained. "It means that it's a rule that doesn't make any sense. You can't dig up a nesting owl if you're on a leash, and that's enough money to buy a whole house in somewhere like Oklahoma. Anyway, they plow under this section of dirt every summer. You know how I told you how Schrödinger's cat might die if she gets caught inside the box? Well if Schrödinger's dog gets caught, then you need to buy a house for nesting owls."

But humans do *so many* things that are ub-served. They run past the house over and over at the end of their run, because they promised to run ten miles, not 9.67 miles. They leave their dogs at home to go to jobs that make them tired and cranky, and then they spend the money that their jobs give them on silly things like shampoo, and new cars to replace the cars that aren't broken yet, and more than one pair of shoes. That's why Mom needs a life coach so badly.

Oscar the Birthday Boy

I was supposed to have a really fun adventure on my fourth birthday. One of my Second Favorite People was going to join Mom and me for a hike on a very pretty mountain that stands between the ocean and the Bay. But we got so lost in the car trying to find my friend that Mom cried. You see, Mom's sense of direction comes from mapps that live in the sky. The sky mapps watch her drive around and then call her phone and tell her where to go, but for some reason the sky couldn't see us that day. I sat in the back seat, staring at the sky and wondering why it didn't see me back. I had many hours to think about it, and eventually figured out that the sky must have been distracted by the suspense of the huge, lumpy mountain sneaking up on the unsuspecting bay. The sky was so distracted that it didn't notice the smaller drama of the narrow little road having a hysterical fit over the mountain's ruffles, and the even smaller drama of Mom having a fit on that road, too. As little as we were, and as far away as the sky is, it still had to be deaf to not hear Mom shouting at the phone to tell us where smell to go.

We never did find my friend, and I never even got out to run or hike. It wasn't a very fun birthday...

After my birthday was ruined, I had to have a tough conversation with Mom. Mom speaks Human, and I bark, but just like anyone who is in love, we don't need words to understand each other. All you have to do to understand someone is to pay attention, and if you love them then paying attention isn't hard. I can tell what Mom is saying just by the groan of her voice, a look on her face, how she moves, the sound of her pawsteps, and how she smells. It's like her thought bubbles pop, and I can smell them in the air. That's why I call it extra-scent-sory paw-ception, but Mom says that's too much of a mouthful. Because we can't agree on what to call it, we'll just call it "doggie telepathy." But like I said, even though we use different words for the same thing, we can still understand each other.

When I came home with Mom for the first time, I was making an promise that I was going to give her as much love as her heart could hold. Sometimes she might not need so much to keep her heart full, but sometimes life drains all of the love out of a heart, and I need to work extra to fill it back up again. Lately Mom's heart was on empty all the time, and no matter how much love I poured into her, her heart was like a bowl with a hole in the bottom.

"All we do lately is work," I told her when we were back home and Mom had stopped crying and slamming things. "We wake up early, go on patrol, then I have to guard the house and you have to guard your desk all day. Even when you come home at night we don't have time for fun because we have to hurry up and go to bed so that we can wake up for our patrol tomorrow. That's no life for a human."

"I'm sorry for ruining your birthday," Mom said. "You're right. I can't remember the last time we saw something new and fun." For her part, Mom had committed to giving me the best dog life. For a man-dog like me, that means adventuring. An "adventure" is when you experience new things while moving quickly and boisterously[2]. But lately we hadn't done much advenuring *or* exploring, just patrolling and searching for things to be upset at.

"Tell you what," Mom said, as a thought took hold of her, lifting her chin and straightening her spine. "For your birthday present, I'll take you on a road trip. I'll make the year that you're four the best year that a dog has ever had."

"Don't forget to make it a great human year too..." I reminded her. "You yell at me for having fun when you're grouchy, and it spoils it."

Because I was four, Mom said that she was going to take me to visit all four states in this country: California, Nevada, Arizona and Utah. California is where I live, but the rest of the states had never seen an Oscar before. It would take a long time for us to see all of these new states, so Mom had to quit her job so that we could spend a few weeks driving to new places, running, hiking, and letting adventure find us.

---

[2] If you move more slowly, it's called "exploring." Mom used to do lots of exploring with me too, but the good thing about adventuring is that you can even do it in places where you've been before.

"But Mom, what if you get lost again? You couldn't even find a mountain on my birthday and you were driving all over it the whole time. What if you can't find Utah?" When I imagined what it would be like to lose not a mountain but a whole state, I got a little scared. "I don't want you to cry again."

"If we don't find Utah, then we'll just stay in Nevada and have fun there."

"What if we go so deep into Nevada and Utah and Arizona that we can't find California again?" I asked. "Then we can never go home and you will definitely cry..."

"Oscar, there's been too much worrying lately. We're not going to worry about things on this trip. Whatever happens and wherever we go will be just where we're meant to be, so it will be perfect."

Even though Mom had quit her job, it would be a working vacation for us. My job was to be a life coach and help Mom remember what makes her happy, so she

could figure out what she wants to do with her life. Mom would have to work hard on this trip too. She would be my stenographer, taking down all of my stories and finding just the right spots in the wilder-ness to blow my words through the sky to where they could reach the internet and all of my fans.

Planning and Dog-gistics

Mom and I agree that runs are not for lollygagging, but we disagree about walks. Mom thinks that a walk is about steady, constant movement. If she had her way, we would walk out the door, and then just keep walking in straight lines until we arrived back at the door again. That's not what a walk is all about! A walk is for curiosity, and sniffing all of the things that are happening in the neighborhood, leaving bulletins of your own, and barking at the neighbors. If she didn't have me to remind her of all that, Mom would miss out on the good stuff.

When Mom and I go for a walk she walks along all relaxed and lost in thought, staring at the sidewalk a few feet in front of her. Me on the other hand, I have to be **ON!** I keep my head up and down at the same time so that I can smell the future on the air from down the street, but also smell the past and who walked on this ground before I got here. If I never stopped, then I would miss the excitement, like when someone drops fast food wrappers, or when a squirrel runs by on the wires in the sky. If I smell something important, I have to be tense and make myself an anchor, or else Mom will pull me away before I even find out what I'm missing. But if I'm prepared for something interesting to happen and can root myself to the spot before Mom notices, then *she's* the one that goes *boing,* and spins around at the end of the leash.

You know how some dogs get a little screwy if they don't have a job to do? Mom is that sort of dog, and ever since she'd decided that she was going to stop working, she'd been acting screwy by finding ways to turn our everyday routines into work. She had quit her job with her words, but it took awhile before the quitting caught up to how she spent her days. She still went to work every day, and then she came home and spent the evening planning the places that we would visit on my birthday trip. "Mom... are you going to get nervous taking this vacation like a dog rather than a human? Are you going to be okay without rules and schedules?"

"I don't honestly know," she said.

"...Cuz I don't want you to just trade your laptop for a steering wheel. You always ignore me when you're on your laptop. I don't want to go through all the states like we do on a run. It's not a race to get back home again. I want to see the nice things, not just the freeway rest stops."

"Okay, Oscar. We'll take the back roads and the scenic routes."

"Yeah but Mom, you also can't just drive past everything like you do on our walks. I want to stop and sniff stuff too."

"Okay. I promise. We won't ever drive for more than three hours without getting out and exploring..."

"Nuh-uh," I stopped her. "That's a human way of adventuring. What if something interesting happens after just one hour and it's not time to stop yet? We'll miss it! I never want to go longer than three *dog* hours without stopping."

"I know what a dog year is, but what's a dog hour?" asked Mom.

"I don't know. It's something that I just made up, so it can be as long as I want," I explained. "It means that we're not going to be on a schedule. We'll just stop whenever something good happens, but we won't go so slow that we miss the good stuff in front of us."

"Okay. Deal. Instead of the interstate, we'll drive through the forests. And when we have to go to the bathroom we'll stop at trailheads and go to the bathroom behind trees. And when we're done, we'll explore for a dog hour or two before getting back in the car."

"And I want to spend just as much of this trip on paws as we do in the car," I told her.

"Okay, I promise. We'll make sure we never hike and run less than a minimum of ten miles a day and..." Then she looked at me. "...I mean, we'll try to do a run and a hike every day."

"Unless we don't feel like it."

"Unless we don't feel like it," Mom agreed. "Luckily I'll be traveling with the best life coach in the world," she reminded me. "And I don't think the transition will be too tough for me because I'm going to have a job to do transcribing the field notes from your observations as a life coach... Unless I don't feel like it."

"Nope," I told her. "That's one job that you can't skip. Who knows when we're going to get to take another trip like this again. You're going to transcribe your lessons every day so that you can remember our adventure forever."

Oscar the Naturalist

On the first day of our adventure, Mom and I started at our normal house, in our normal bed. We wanted to get a little bit of home stuck in our soles before our paws touched nothing but new dirt for the next few weeks. So we got up early like we usually do and went to one of our favorite trails to run on the same dirt that we've tracked into the car dozens of times before.

We started running in the dark in order to get to the top of the mountain right when the sun got to the top of the next mountain, so that we could all be in the sky together. When we got up there, Mom and I stopped for a minute to look across the bay. "Look, Mom! That's where we're going!" I said, pointing my nose toward the sun and Utah behind it.

"We'll go that way eventually, but today we're going that way." Mom pointed to the left.

"What's up there?" I asked.

"Well, the hotel where you almost got us kicked out because you were barking so much that our neighbors checked out early, for one… But lots of other stuff too."

"Oh." I had forgotten that sometimes travel is scary, like when Mom leaves you alone in an empty motel room and you don't know if she's ever coming back.

If we'd had more time, we could have gone another mile all the way to the tippy top of the mountain, where you can see the Pacific Ocean and the end of the world. But today we had to hurry back home so that both

Mom and I could take a bath to start our adventure smelling fresh like Head and Shoulders for Men. We would see the ocean later anyway...

It took us awhile to sign all the borrowing papers and move all of our stuff into the car-house we'd be living in for the next two weeks. Mom was getting stressed out because she was eager to get going, but I was keeping busy collecting butt scratches from strangers and trying to learn about the funny squirrel in the cage in the back of the room. It made a noise like a turkey gobbling underwater. Mom said the turkey-squirrel was called a guinea pig, but since it's a hard word to spell, it was okay to call it a turkey-squirrel from now on.

I didn't know if I liked the car-house so much. It was different from My Car and didn't have any of my favorite places to sit, like my copilot's seat next to Mom's driving chair, or my fainting couch in the back. I tried sitting on my butt like a human in the seat next to Mom where the empty bottles and cans usually live, but it was too hard to nap there with all the twisting and turning going around. When I got scared of all the swooshing back and forth, I sat down on the floor between Mom's seat and mine. Even though it wasn't a good place to drive from, it was the perfect height for me to put my head in Mom's lap so she could scratch my ears while she drove. That made it a little less scary.

Our first hiking stop wasn't much fun because we just hiked around the block that Starbucks was on, and a crazy man made me kiss him on the face. We were supposed to be hiking and running and relaxing, but so far we had just gotten lost and stressed and walked around on sidewalks just like we do at home. I was beginning to think this whole road trip thing was one of those things that is supposed to be fun, but isn't; Like chasing balls, or swimming.

But then we stopped for our second potty break in a place called Tamales Bay. I thought that the ocean was always a place that you had to hike to, but in Tamales Bay we stopped in a place where cars turn into boats and then boats turn back into cars. We parked just a few steps from the water and watched some men pulling big wire boxes out of the bay.

I sniffed the air wafting from the trays. "What's that?" I asked.

"They're oyster beds."

"They don't look very comfortable…"

"Well they're comfortable for the oysters. But oysters are strange creatures…" Then Mom explained how oysters are fish that fancy people love, even though they look like crumpled up wads of wet newspaper. The fancy people like to eat the oysters right out of their wadded-up shells, even though Mom says that they look like snot and probably taste that way too. Oysters are also special because they make their own booger-rocks that old ladies like to stick to their heads and call it "elegant." So already I'd learned about turkey-squirrels, that fancy people like to stick boogers on their face, and that cars turn into boats when they touch the water. Road trips are great ways to learn about the kooky stuff that people do when their homes are different from mine.

Then Mom and I explored the beach and climbed over some big rocks together, and stuck our paws in the water. I couldn't believe how many fun things there were to smell and look at, but also that Mom let me do it all off leash! Usually I am real careful to never smile for too long so that Mom can't get good pictures, but I was so wrapped up in my adventures that I forgot to look tough for the camera, and Mom got pictures of me grinning like a dufus.

The ocean had gotten bigger at our next bathroom break. This time we had to walk a long way from the road, and then down a big box filled with stairs that went round and round until they had drilled all the way down the cliff to the beach. Mom dropped my leash on the floor and went down the stairs real slow with her hands on both railings. Her face looked like someone was trying to feed her medicine she didn't want to eat. "What's wrong with you?" I asked.

"I'm not good at heights, Oscar."

"What's to be good at? You don't even have to try, see? The heights come right to you in these holes between the stairs." I stuck my face in the hole and sniffed at the sand way, way below us so that Mom would see where the sky was coming in. She whimpered like a puppy, closed her eyes, and stretched the corners of her mouth down her neck.

"Please don't do that, Oscar! You might be sucked through!"

But I wasn't.

Finally we got down to the beach and Mom was able to walk like a normal human again. This beach was totally different from the last one, and I got to run around even more, sniffing stuff and seeing how the beach looked and smelled different depending on where I was standing. I ran around and around trying to stand in all the places at once because I knew that I didn't have much time, and I wanted to make sure I got it all. I was supposed to be on leash, but Mom said that it was okay because there wasn't a single person there to see us. *Not one!* Except in my own bathroom, I'd never been totally alone outside in the daytime before. Where we lived, you were bound to run into someone to bark at, even hours before sunrise.

I ran around and around in circles sniffing things and barking at all the nobody until my face hurt. It took me awhile to figure out that it was from smiling. I didn't know that smiles were something that could make you tired because I'd never tried doing so much of it. "Mom, where was this stuff before we got here?" I asked.

"This place has always been here, Oscar."

"Then why haven't we been here before? This is way better than The Fart."

"Because we have to work."

"Why? Why can't exploring be our jobs?"

"Because I need to pay for things like our house, and your food, and your friend that takes you on adventures while I'm at work. You work too, remember? You have to patrol Your Trail every day."

"Yeah, but now that we're here, I can't really remember why it's so important to serve and protect My Trail anymore." Then I had a thought, "Mom, are there houses in places like this too?"

"There are, but there isn't a lot of work to do for the people that live in them."

"But you still haven't explained why it's so important to work to live in houses rather than going on adventures."

"I'm really not sure, Oscar. I'll have to get back to you on that."

Doggie Telepaphone

The next morning Mom woke up early like she always does, but this time was different because we were sleeping in a car-house and had nowhere we had to be. Since it was kind of cold in the car-house, Mom wanted to turn on the car part so that the heater could make the house part cozy, but instead of making car noises the car-house just made clicking noises.

This apparently meant that we were marooned and there would be no morning run.

Since we lived here now, we decided to explore our new home. We were shipwrecked on a beach in a little cove with big rocks on both sides, just like old explorers in pirate times. Only, instead of looking for buried treasure, we were looking for cell phone bars. We patrolled all around our beach and looked on top of all the highest rocks, but we didn't find a our lost cell signal on any of them. We did find a stick that I thought was pretty great, but Mom said it wasn't the same thing.

Finally, the world woke up and a nice man came to rescue us. I barked at him, but he wasn't scared, so I knew he was a friend and I let him fix our car-house. He attached metal alligators to the car-house's heart, and then he didn't say "CLEAR!" and zapped the car-house back to life. When we finally got out of there, it was late and Mom promised we would just find a trail along the way. But we drove for hours and hours through the mountains and didn't do any running. "Mom, why don't you stop?!?!"

"Because apparently there are no trailheads in this whole darned forest! Everything says not to stop." Now that we were living in a car-house, we needed to be careful of rules. Just like some people don't like dogs and so don't let me in their buildings and on their trails, Mom said that other people don't like people who don't have houses, so we needed to be respectful.

Finally, after we had gone so far that I was sure we were going to fall off the edge of the world, we came to a city. That's where Mom finally spotted a sign for a trail. If we turned left then we could run along the waterfront, and if we turned right we could run in the forest. "Forest, please!" I said.

The forest was way far away behind the city, on a road that didn't like car-houses and kept kicking us in the butts. A sign near where we parked the car-house said, "Dogs must be on leash or under voice control."

"What's voice control?" I asked Mom. "Is that like when I want to bark, but I just growl instead?"

"No, it means that you have to come to me when I call you, no matter what."

"Okay," I said. "Promise." Now that I'm four, I can handle more responsibility, which is another word for running off leash. When I wear responsibility instead of a leash, I can stop to smell something interesting, or drink from a puddle, or run in the bushes instead of the trail, and Mom doesn't need to wait for me. While I have responsibility, Mom can keep moving in straight lines as fast as she can and miss all the good stuff, just like she likes to do. If she gets ahead, responsibility tells me that

I've gotten too far away and pulls me back into range as fast as I can sprint.

I don't really know why humans like to tie themselves to their dogs with leashes. I think it's a human behavior that means, 'Our lives are tied together, and wherever you adventure, I will adventure too.' I thought the leash was kind of annoying when I was a puppy because it meant that I couldn't adventure more than a few feet away from Mom on her boring, straight path. She would always use the leash to pull me off from eating a delicious pile of poo, or chasing an interesting critter. But as I became a man-dog, I realized that the leash helped me understand Mom a lot better. I didn't have to watch her closely to see if she was slowing or speeding up, if she was turning or stopping. I could just feel it in the leash. And if she needed me, she didn't have to say my name like I was in trouble, she just had to tap on the leash and I knew to pay attention. I think that the leash is exactly what love is, turning a dog and his human into one meat-beast with two parts, and each part can feel what the other part is doing without barking a word.

But a leash is just a training tool for true love. When Mom let me off the leash, I learned that I could still feel where she was and what she was doing, as long as I didn't go out of range. Mom and I don't need to have voice control out loud, because we have extra-sensory paw-ception... or... fine, doggie telepathy. I can tell what Mom is doing without even looking at her, just by listening to her steps and her breathing. I can tell by the way her foot hits the ground when she is about to walk, when she's about to run, and when she's speeding up or slowing down. If I hear a walking step, then I stop and wait for her to come back into range again before I spin around and haul butt through the bushes again. I can also tell when she's out of shape because her feet stay on the ground longer and I can hear her breathing from farther away. On this trip, Mom's feet were hitting the ground like an elephant's paws and her breathing was so loud I could hear it from Utah, so I could run very far away indeed without losing touch with her.

"Look! I have responsibility!" I beamed at a couple of ladies that were walking in the other direction. I bounded closer to them so they could see me better, and then I did a little jig.

"That is one happy dog," the lady said to Mom. Another terrific thing about responsibility is that it gets you attention.

When I turned to Mom, she was running just where I thought she would be, and she had the same grin on her face that I could feel on mine. "Mom, do you ever think that we're the same person?" I asked. Mom didn't answer, but I think I know the answer...

...it's NO, duh! That's impossible! Humans don't have the exciting inner life that dogs have. That's why they need dogs to show them that it's okay to be marooned on a desert beach... or to scrap the plan and let adventure find you on the highways... or fly the flag of an outlaw, ignore the rules, and invade a trail where you're not supposed to be.

Dognapped!

Mom promised me that this trip would be all about us, but so far it had been all about the car-house that we had borrowed. Instead of spending our second night in the woods, we stayed in the sort of place where Mom said that people live who aren't allowed within a thousand feet of a school or playground. I'm not quite sure what that means, but the lady at the car-house welcome house told Mom not to go outside of the park alone, because people get peoplenapped on that road. A few years ago a lady was peoplenapped just a few miles from where we were standing, "...And they had her for six months," the lady explained, like she actually meant something else.

"What was she doing for those six months?" I asked.

"You know what it's like when you take a bath? How you don't like it, but you stop fighting and just wait for it to be over?" Mom said. "For six months she had to take baths over and over with people who didn't even love her." The thought of something like that made me so scared that I didn't even want to think about it. I wished that we could leave this horrible peoplenapper habitat, but Mom said we needed to be in a city with phone reception and big stores, just in case the car-house didn't start again and we needed to call for help, or to go to the car vet.

Which we did.

We got up at sunrise, and instead of finding a run, Mom used her phone to call for help getting the house started. She was on the phone a lot, and every time she sat down to eat breakfast or something, her phone would shout again and she would have to stop and climb around the car-house for a little while searching for things. So far, our road trip had been just as un-relaxing as our regular life at home. Finally, after two hours, a helper man came with the car-saving alligators, and he zapped our house back into a car-house. Now, instead of driving right to the mountains, we had to drive to a car vet to get a battery transplant.

While we were at the vet shop, Mom made me stay in the car-house while she went inside and talked to the people. Then she walked away to make another phone call. While she was gone, a strange man opened the door to the car-house, climbed inside with me, and drove me away.

It was happening!

I was getting dognapped!

I was going to have to spend the next six months (which is *years* to a dog) getting baths over and over from people who didn't love me. Worst of all, Mom wouldn't even know where I was, and she would have to go on without a life coach! She needs so much help, I wasn't sure if she would make it on her own. I was bugging out, but I sat real still in the back so that maybe the man wouldn't get mad and make me take a bath right away.

The dognapper took me and the car-house into a room with lots of loud and scary noises, and left it there with me inside. I didn't know whether this was a Scary Thing or a Normal Thing, so I just sat on the bed inside the car-house and waited to hear the water running. Then I heard someone opening the door. *This was it!* My life passed before my nose. Now I would know what it was like to have a rough and loveless bath! The door opened and it was...

MOM!!!!!!!

She had come to rescue me! I was so happy to see her that I jumped and squealed (in a manly way, of course). She took me to sit on the grass outside the vet shop and I was so happy that we were reunited that I wasn't even scared by the crazy man across the street screaming at the sky. He sounded more upset than anyone I have ever heard in my entire life, and his anger was so strong that it made his hair stand out from his head in squiggles, and blew out from inside him with such ferocity that it had torn holes in his clothes and singed them almost black. "What's he so upset about, Mom?" I asked.

"He's seeing imaginary nightmares because he's on meth," she explained, like it was a sad thing and not really a scary thing.

"What's math? Is that like when you can't remember how far we have to run to get back to the car?"

"Meth is like kidnapping, but for your mind. It takes people's brains and it makes them feel horrible things that are too scary to keep inside. It takes people's whole lives, and sometimes they never get them back."

"Is our car-house math?"

"No. Sometimes there are real things to be upset about that aren't meth. And this car-house may take our vacation, but it won't take our whole lives away."

Finally, half a day after Mom had picked up the phone to call for help, we got to leave the Scary Place and go do the run that we wanted to do early this morning. "We don't have time to do the long run all the way up to the dam anymore," said Mom, "but maybe we can still have a nice time doing a shorter run."

We had planned to run on a path next to a river, but Mom was having trouble finding the path in the car-house. According to Mom, it's hard to search for bike paths on the internet "because a GPS can only look for points, and a path is a line." Like that explained anything. That's what she told me anyway when she stopped in a dirt parking lot high up on a hill and explained that we would need to run down a steep, mile-long dirt road to get to the path. But we were running again, we were in a beautiful place, we were together. Things were looking up!

…then it started to rain.

Neither Mom nor I like the rain. It's messy and it's cold and it ruins all the good sights and washes away all the good smells.

"No, Oscar, we will *NOT* let this ruin our run,"
Mom said in that voice that I could tell the run was
already ruined. She went on, "I had hoped that we could
get out before the rain started, but now it's here... And so
are we. And so is the river, and all of these pretty
mountains. And you and I are together. And that's all we
need." She said all this through her teeth like she was
growling at a mailman that was trying to decide whether
to open the gate, or just throw the boxes over the fence
and move on.

We ran about six and a half miles, and I explored a
little river and waterfall. But I could tell that Mom was
forcing herself through it.

I didn't really want to go back to work so soon
after the trauma of being dognapped, but Mom needed
my services. "What's wrong?" I asked, booting up life
coach mode. "The rain isn't so bad. See? We're not even
that soaked, and it's kind of warm out. And there are all
those colors that I can't see... The grey river, and the grey
trees, and the dark grey and white mountains..."

"I don't know, Oscar. I'm just so frustrated. I
haven't really had a day off for over two years. I had to
quit my job to even get a chance to go out into the
wilderness where no one could reach me. But now
instead of a boss it's the stupid rental van that won't let
me go off the grid. This is just like when we were home:
there is always some reason why I can't relax, or why I
can't do the things I planned for us to do. I spend so
much time taking care of the things that are breaking that

I have to rush through the good things. I'm having a hard time keeping a positive attitude."

"But isn't it enough that we're together?"

"But don't we deserve more than just being together? Is it too much to ask to be together someplace other than a parking lot on the automile in some rotten meth city?"

After we climbed the steep dirt road back to the car-house, we had a picnic in the rain before we started driving again. We got really lost, but Mom didn't care because we were so deep in the beautiful mountains that her phone didn't work for hours and hours, which she insists is why we got so lost. Eventually, Mom just couldn't wait for nature any longer and pulled over next to a gate that said "CLOSED." This decision was the best thing that happened all day, because all we had to do to be free was walk around the gate and into the trees.

What we found was a museum-trail that showed us all about volcanoes. Usually museum-trails are for old people who can't handle much excitement without having a heart attack, so the little signs just point out boring things like bushes and flowers. But volcanoes are exciting, like action movies... even if the movie happened in such slow motion that no one lived long enough to see the whole thing. The spots had names like, "Sunken Pit," "Bat Cave" and "Splatter Cone." Sometimes things with good names are lame and disappointing, but not on our Good Luck Trail. The Sunken Pit was so big you could fit a house in it. The Bat Cave went so deep that Mom froze and refused to move when she got close to it. I had responsibility so I could get closer to the mouth of the cave, even though Mom had turned to stone. When I ducked under the wire that was in the way of exploring, Mom actually screamed — out loud. The hole went down and down and down and I couldn't even see the bottom.

"Oscar, get away from there."

"But, Mom! Batman might be down there!"

"Cujo was too curious around a bat cave and it didn't work out so well for him..." Mom warned. *Cujo* is a fable about a dog that gets bitten by a bat and then math gets him. It's a tragedy because he dies at the end. I didn't want to die, so I came back to Mom.

The whole time we could see lots of big, pointy mountains all around us. The biggest and pointiest of all had snow on its hat, and the snow was still coming down from the clouds, so the sky went from mountain, to snow, to clouds in one smudge like the mountain was blending into the sky. Mom said that the smudge was called Mt. Shasta, which is a good name for a rapper but a funny name for a mountain.

Even though I was doing this hike with responsibility, I was real careful to stay close to Mom so that we could look at all of the interesting museum things together. Interesting things are more fun when you learn them with someone else. "See, Mom. We're together, and we're having fun, and it's beautiful. Isn't that enough?"

"Wouldn't you rather have been doing this than spending those four hours in the scary place with the kidnappers? Don't we deserve this?" she asked back.

I wasn't sure if a good life was supposed to mean that nothing bad or scary ever happens. I'm a good life coach, but that question gave me a lot to think about; more than a dog could think on in one walk, anyway.

Oscar the Time Traveler

When I was only three, I won Second Dog in a half marathong. The word "marathong" comes from the Greek *mara* meaning something really, really long and *thong*, meaning something that is uncomfortable, but only if you think about it too much. We ran with other two- and four-legged runners around a giant valley with mountains on the outside, and cows in the middle. It was one of the favorite things that Mom and I have done together, and we were glad we practiced running every day so that we could be ready to do fun things like half marathongs.

Mom wanted to revisit Second Dog Valley, since it was a beautiful place where we had happy memories. You need to travel back in time to revisit a good memory, and because time travel is hard some things always turn out a little cattywampus in the second copy. On our way to the past, we went back a little too far to ancient times when people didn't travel with phones to tell them where to go. I was worried that we would be lost in the past forever, so Mom explained that when ancient people got lost, they went into a gas station and asked for directions. If the directions were really complicated, they wrote them down on a piece of paper. The piece of paper didn't talk or anything, and if you missed a turn, the paper didn't change to tell you how to get back to where you went wrong. I know it sounds incredible, but people really lived like that. Some of them are probably still out there today, wandering the country roads like ghosts, trying to find their way home or to the mall.

Since we're not from The Past, it took us four times driving past the same gas station to remember that we could ask other humans for help. Mom went into the building and came out a little while later with a piece of paper with directions on it. I sure hoped she knew what she was doing.

Mom and I had been to Second Dog Valley a bunch of times and never run in the woods because we were too busy winning Second Dog in a half marathong (me), or riding bikes (Mom). Sometimes a place really doesn't want you to see it. The piece of paper took us to the right place, but the woods and mountains of Second Dog Valley were hidden behind a wall of rain.

Even though Mom and I both hate the rain, we had traveled so far and so long ago to get here that Mom suggested we run anyway. We got ready to run listening to the pitter patter of the falling water with the same feeling of doom that I get when Mom takes off my collar while the shower is running. Before leaving, I went on a potty break and I noticed that the ground was more puddles than dirt. If it kept raining then we would be sitting in a lake.

"Does it actually sound like fun to you to run in this?" I asked in my coach voice.

"Well no, not really," she admitted.

"Isn't this trip supposed to be all about having fun?"

"I guess you're right. Let's go out to breakfast instead."

So we did.

Mom left me in the car-house and came back a few minutes later with two boxes of the most delicious smelling food I had ever smelled. I smelled chicken butt, and pig butt, and potato, and lots and lots of grease. I sure hoped that she would share with me. Mom put one of the boxes right under my nose, and I could smell the eggs and bacon and potatoes yearning for my mouth. "This... is for you!" she said, opening the box with a TA-DAAAAAAAA flourish.

"Oh! Oh! Start eating quick so that I can have some!!!" I hyperventilated.

"No, Oscar, the whole thing is for you." I couldn't believe it! A whole plate of food just for me! I had only ever smelled bacon with my nose and never my mouth because Mom's a vegetarian... Could dreams possibly still come true on such a rotten day?

"Oh no, I couldn't possibly..." I said, sniffing the bacon more closely.

"Seriously, Oscar! Eat it! It's your reward for being so brave when you were dognapped." So I gave the bacon an experimental lick. Bacon is even better when you chew and swallow it than when you just sniff it! Now bacon is my favorite thing. I ate the bacon in three big bites, and then I got to work on the eggs and potatoes.

It rained and rained all the way through the mountains, past dozens and dozens of exciting trails. It was still raining when we got to the desert in Nevada, where it's not supposed to rain. We drove for almost an hour down a nearly abandoned road past a bunch of dirt tracks that could have been trails, or maybe they were some kind of road without pavement. Finally, Mom pulled over at one of them. "Let's just find out where they go," she said.

It turned out to be a trail after all! Not a great trail, but a trail nonetheless. There were critters that lived in the ground, and funny bushes and rocks. The trail didn't go very far -- only about half a mile – and at the end there was a flat spot with a bunch of of smooshed things that smelled like rust.

"Is this a museum trail? Did history happen here?" I asked

"I don't think so," said Mom. "Unless it's a beer-drinking-in-the-middle-of-nowhere museum. Let's keep going." Mom had a glint in her eye. "Let's hike like we're wild. We can just walk on the regular ground where there's no trail. I bet we can at least get to those rocks up there." I thought that maybe once we got too far from the trail we'd run into an invisible wall or fall into the ground or something, but our paws worked on this ground just like they worked on the trail! So we hiked wild.

"Mom, how do you know we're not going to get lost in the wild?" I asked, thinking about how yesterday we spent the whole day lost, and how there were no gas stations out here to help us.

"Oscar, we can see everything for miles around. We'll be able to see the van wherever we go. We're not going to get lost." She had a point. There wasn't so much as a bump for miles on the valley floor, and the only thing on all that blank land was the road, and the only thing on the road was the car-house. We'd walked a mile and a half, and could still see the car-house waiting patiently for us in the middle of the empty desert.

It would have been fun to keep walking up and up the mountain to where the ground disappeared into the clouds, and see how far we could explore. We could go until we couldn't see the van anymore, and then we would really be adventuring. But it could start raining again at any second, and we weren't *that* adventurous. And Mom thought that we could find something better.

We got back in the car-house and kept driving down the road, but not long after that, the pavement disappeared and turned into trail. We tried driving on the mud for a minute or two, but the car-house is not wild like us and it sounded like it was going to rattle to bits. So we had to turn back, and Mom decided that today would be an "administrative day," which meant we would find a really nice campground and she would take a shower and do laundry and we could relax all evening.

But when we got to the campground, it was all full up. Mom came back to the car-house fuming. "They wouldn't even let me pay to take shower. They treated me like a homeless person. Who the heck do they think they are? They're just a parking lot with a lousy water feature out front, they're not the dog-gone Ritz."

I had never thought about it that way before. We have a home, but right now we were strays because we were on vacation. Are all strays just regular people who wanted to work less and spend more time with their dogs?

"It's probably because you're dressed like a stray and don't smell very nice," I said. Mom had put my lobster bandana on me because she said it makes me easier to spot when I have responsibility, and I kind of liked what it did for my look. "If I had gone in there with my snappy tie, they probably would have treated me with respect. You have to think about presentation, Mom..."

"Well maybe if I could take a freaking shower I wouldn't look like a hobo..." Mom grumbled.

We drove another half hour to another park that reminded me of the scary park where people steal other people. But they were full too. This time Mom came back to the car perplexed. "They're full with people who live here and work at Tesla. God, this place is just so run-down. What must living in a place like this do to your self-esteem?" So there *are* people who live in car-houses all the time... but they still have to work and can't spend time with their dogs. What's the point? "I guess we'll have to stay at Wal*Mart. Wal*Mart is the Ritz of parking lots!" she said.

I was excited to see the Ritz of Parking Lots and how big its water feature must be, but it wasn't as grand as I hoped. There were no trees, and a big truck came and made really loud noises that made me jump. Mom was thrilled though. She disappeared for like an hour and came back with a whole cart of stuff that barely fit in the car-house. "And they're open all night, in case I have to go to the bathroom!" she gushed. "I had planned to take the interstate to Salt Lake, but you know what? We're not getting on the interstate again for the rest of this trip!" Mom swore. "No more truck stops and Wal*Marts for us! We're not homeless, we're camping."

"But I thought that Wal*Mart was the Ritz of Parking Lots," I said.

"Well sure... Bathrooms and fresh vegetables and clean underwear are great, but we have those at home.

This is supposed to be an adventure. I'll just use the dog bathroom, and who needs clean underwear?"

Some people save up for months and months to sit still in a place with humungous people bathrooms and tons of places to lie down. They call that being "pampered." But I was starting to pick up on something. If you didn't care if anyone thought you were a stray, then you could go on vacation a lot easier than all that. You can always find a place that cooks bacon in tons of grease, and a nice patch of dirt to go potty in, and a peaceful place to lie down without saving up any money at all. Watching Mom's shoulders slowly climb out of her ears the further away from people we got, I thought that being campered was more relaxing for humans than being pampered anyway. I wonder if I was the first life coach to ever notice how relaxing nature is. "Hey, Mom," I said. "I've got something mindblowing that you've got to tell all my fans!"

Oscar the Tracker

When we woke up in the Wal*Mart car kennel, it was still raining cats and squirrels. Mom said that the car-house may take our time away, that we may have to live like a couple of strays, but "Dognabbit, this trip was supposed to be for running and hiking and that's what we are going to do, rain or shine!" She said it through her teeth, which usually means that life coaches should butt out and play along.

We weren't staying in the National Park part of the desert, but Mom found a place where we could run three miles around a little lake. We parked the house and ran up a short trail to the ugly little lake. The ground was

 made of sand and puddles, which made it hard running because the sand swallowed our steps when we pushed into it. The lake was really just an enormous puddle in the middle of all that sand and scruffy bushes. There were underwear and food wrappers growing on the bushes instead of leaves, and it was pouring the kind of rain that has little wasps in it. Mom said that she needed a shower anyway, with her fangs still clenched, and I

remembered how much she had said she liked clean underwear. So maybe it would be a nice run after all. At least the trail was short and we would be back in the dry car-house soon, driving to somewhere more fun.

After a couple of miles, the rain started to let up and we could sort of see mountains in the distance where only a grey smudge had been before. But we had a problem: now that the rain had stopped and we could see, everything looked different and we didn't know what direction we'd be facing when we got to the end. There wasn't just one way to get to the lake. There were lots of trails that came from different directions to meet the trail that circled the lake. If we looked from above, the trails would have looked like the sun, with the trail we were running drawing a circle around the lake, and other trails heading straight into the desert like the sun's rays. From the ground, we could see that it wasn't just one trail going around the lake either, but a bunch of trails that braided together and went in the same direction but never took exactly the same route. If we chose the wrong arm of the braid, we might miss the sunbeam that led back to the car-house entirely. At this rate, we could run round and round the lake forever and never know which exit to take. Or we might leave at the wrong spot and run into the desert forever. To make matters worse, Mom had left her phone in the car-house to protect it from the rain, so we had no way for the sky to call and tell us which way to go, or maps, or even a compass. After a few miles mom looked around and said, "I think this is the right exit," and started running away from the lake. We made one turn and then another, always going in a direction that we thought might lead to the road.

Once we had run away from the lake for nearly a mile she said, "I don't remember making this many turns when we left the van..." *Uh oh...* Then I saw a river. We definitely hadn't run past a river before.

"Mom, how are we going to find the lake again?" I asked. "And how are we going to get back to the car-house?"

"Yesterday when we got lost, we traveled back in time for help. This time, we'll go even further back in time... to when people could track animals and each other by their footprints." Why would you track something using its pawprints when you could just sniff its trail, I wondered. Only the rain had washed all the scent trails away. "If we follow our footprints in this soft, wet sand, then we can tell where we've been and find our way back to the lake," she explained.

Mom was living in make-believe again. This plan would never work... We would lose our way and start following lost paw prints, and then we would be like the pathetic ghosts who missed a turn on MapQuest and were doomed to wander the back roads forever... Hadn't she ever heard the ghost story about how Winnie the Pooh and Piglet followed a heffalump's pawprints, and it turned out that they were following their own pawprints, and then they were eaten alive by the heffalump?

But it *did* work! We followed the small human prints next to the elegant dog prints backwards the way we had come. Sometimes we had to look around a bit to find our old feet, but we always found them, and they eventually brought us back to the lake so we could continue around the circle. But now that we were back at the lake, we still had to figure out the right exit to take us back to the car-house.

Finally, just when I thought we might have to run around the whole lake again to find the way out, Mom recognized a signpost, and soon after that we found the car-house, right where we'd left it.

I didn't want to tell Mom at the time, but I can tell you guys now that it's over: I was a little scared we were going to be at that ugly lake forever!

We drove for several more dog hours. When we pulled over to go potty, Mom noticed a tiny sign like a road sign for a chihuahua that said TRAIL. "Let's see where it goes!" she said.

Almost as soon as we got on the TRAIL I saw a pile of droppings shaped like little baby gumdrops. I sniffed them and they smelled like something I could almost place. It was... "Bunnies!!!!!!!" I whined and whined for Mom to give me responsibility.

As soon as Mom set me free, I ran responsibly into the desert panting, "goody goody bunny droppings!" Humans may track footprints with their eyeballs, but dogs track pawprints with their noses, and I could smell that this place was positively hopping with bunnies. I ran all around that place like my favorite action hero, Dwayne

"The Rock" Johnson, smell-ell-ell-elling the air, leaping over bushes and snorting into holes.

This TRAIL was a part of adventuring history. Back in the olden times, the internet was made of people and ponies that used to ride this trail for hundreds and hundreds and hundreds of miles to bring emails across the desert. They didn't do it for very long, because the next year the real internet was invented and dial-up was faster than ponies, but imagine the adventures those ponies must have had! Mom only hiked on the pony trail for three miles, and I think I ran more like 742 miles chasing bunnies and stuff. But those ponies used to go even further! I wished that I had been a Pony Express dog. I can't imagine a better existence than chasing bunnies across the desert every day, barking at the hostile people who tried to stop me, and being a hero for it.

After awhile we found a pile of rocks. Mom said that it was a house for the Pony Express people to eat and rest and change to new ponies. I know a load of baloney when I hear it! I have eyes, and I know it was a pile of rocks. Mom insisted that there used to be people who lived in that pile of rocks in the desert, miles and miles from anyone, just so they could help the Ponies. I thought that might be a pretty great way to live too, if I couldn't be a pony. But if I were the architect, I would probably build a house with walls higher than an Oscar so that humans could come in too. And I'd also build a roof.

We had another miracle at the next bathroom, which turned out to be another museum-trail. This museum-trail had funny rocks that were shaped like cheese. There were old scratches in the rocks that were important enough for somebody to build a sign in front of them, but I didn't care about those. I just wanted to climb on the rocks to stand on top of the cliffs and sniff into the sky.

When I stood on top of the big cliff and looked out at the desert so far below, and all the mountains in the distance, and no towns anywhere, I felt like the last dog in the world. What were the chances of anyone finding these old rock scratchings in all that empty space? You could have a million dogs following bunny trails their whole lives and maybe no one would ever find this spot again. It wasn't just the earth that was open and empty, I had never seen so much empty air either, without trees or hills, or even tall rocks in between. "Hey, Mom, look at this!" I barked over my shoulder as I stood on the edge and looked out over the desert so far below that it looked like part of a different scene. But Mom was frozen in horror again because this was a high place.

"Come back from there! The wind will blow you off the edge of the world!" she choked. Then, a gust of wind came and blew her hat off her head, and she screamed. But her hat didn't blow away into the empty sky, it just got caught in her head tail.

I rolled my eyes at her. "Now don't you feel silly?" I said. "Sometimes you get so freaked out when there's no danger. Do you think that maybe strangers, and jobs, and talking on the phone, and doing the dishes might not be as scary as you think either?"

"You just don't understand, Oscar. Talking to a stranger on the phone is the one thing in the whole world scarier than standing on top of a cliff."

Oscar the Speedster

That night we stayed on top of a mountain and it got very cold in the car-house while we slept. Luckily, we had lots of blankets and Mom and I could huddle together for warmth, but the cold made it really hard to get out of our cozy blanket nest in the morning. So instead we snuggled and cuddled and Mom put her face on my face so that kisses would happen. I don't know why it was so important to get up early and hurry to the next place, but when you've had places to go and too many things to do for a long time, it feels like you will be in trouble if you don't hurry, even if you don't know where you're going and no one's waiting for you when you get there.

But that morning, for once, we did know where we were going. We had found lots of great adventures so far, but we hadn't actually been on many nature trails yet. So Mom had done some research and found a place where we could run for six or seven miles on real hiking trails, not just dirt tracks we found at the side of the road. For once, all the roads to get to the trail existed just where the mapps said they were, and they were paved, and there was a place to park the house and everything. Mom had no idea what the trail would look like, or even exactly how long it was, but she promised me that we wouldn't get lost. Probably.

The trail turned out to climb a mountain and loop around a big rock that stuck up out of the forest like a 1970s office building. The forest that we ran through was made of dry old pine trees that weren't trying very hard to be a forest, but that was fine because it meant that we could see the mountains, and the big squat rock, and a lake, and the valley. Mom kept stopping to take my picture, which I think was in part because I looked handsome with the nature behind me, but also because the air wasn't working right and she wanted to rest. I am unstoppable, but Mom is a little more sensitive to stuff like not having enough air, and apparently being seven thousand feet in the sky is hard on a human.

Because we were in some special park, I had to stay on leash even though I'm a responsible dog and we didn't see another living soul the whole time we were there. The leash was hard on both of us because the trail was really narrow and had lots of rocks and stuff on it. I'm an expert at leash running, but even I was having trouble matching Mom's twitchy pace as she worked her way around the trail. Sometimes she could run medium-fast, but sometimes she had to be super careful with her paws, and she went real slow. For her part, Mom needed to pay attention to me too, and be extra careful not to trip on the leash and fall off a cliff or break her face.

We didn't have breakfast until after we'd run the seven and a half miles. That was partly because we had to sit outside to make and eat breakfast, and it had been too cold earlier in the morning, but also because my appetite is different now that I'm a drifter dog. When I'm home I eat on a routine, and I also get lots of treats. If I don't get my first breakfast, second breakfast, or dinner on time – or if Mom forgets the treats on our walk – I feel **starving** and need to follow Mom around until she feeds me. When we're living like tramps, on the other paw, we have to stop what we're doing and prepare a meal. And then eat it in the cold. And then wait while Mom washes all the dishes in the silly sink-like thing that's up high on the back of the car-house. It really makes you think about whether you are hungry or not. When our noses and eyes and feet have so many things to feast on, we don't need our mouths and bellies to keep things interesting. Sometimes when Mom put my kibble out on the floor of the car-house, I would sniff it and say, "Nah, I'm good." I wonder if it's traveling that fills me up so that there isn't room for food inside, or if maybe I'm just a greedy dog when I'm at home.

Our next stop was in Utah, but Utah wouldn't load. You know how when Google Maps (what? You think a dog can't read a map??) won't load right you can see the road you're on, but everything else is just a grey blankness? Where we stopped was like that: road that cut through blankness until the next section of the map where you could see mountains again. On the map section behind us, all of the mountains were grey-brown and dry. On the section in front of us all the mountains were pointy and white. And in the middle was us, sitting in miles and miles and miles of flat, grey nothing.

Mom and I got out of the car-house and walked right off of the sidewalk onto the blank space. At first I wasn't so sure about it. The ground was sandy and smelled a bit like the ocean. Then I decided that it was *AWESOME!* This was definitely something that I wanted to bring back to the car-house in my fur to make sure that it was in our bed for the rest of the trip. So I did a somersault and rolled around kicking my legs in the air like crazy. Then I got up, ran around in a circle, and did another cartwheel and rolled around some more. Then I barked at the blankness and did another gymnastics floor routine. In the car kennel there had been a sign that said that this was a place where land speed records were set, so once I had done enough gymnastics, I sprinted around a bit and set a new land speed record.

I didn't think that Mom was fast like me, but I forgot to tell you that she also got her own speed certificate as we were leaving our morning run. We pulled the house over and then suddenly a strange man stuck his big, fat face in my window. He had a fur stripe under his nose, and big, shiny mirrors over his eyes. I barked at him, so he went to Mom's window instead where it would be less scary for him. Mom talked to him and handed him some stuff, and I barked at him not to try any funny business. He must have been real scared, because he took the stuff that Mom gave him and hid in his flashing car for a really long time. Then he came back with Mom's stuff and awarded her her own speed certificate. So I guess we're a pretty speedy family!

Outlaw Lands

You know what's the hardest thing about the tramp lifestyle? Planning. There are so many things to see in The West that if we don't plan our route, then we might wander around The West forever and pass by the best things because they're hidden just over the horizon. Every day Mom spent hours in the back of the car-house looking at mapps. She needed to figure out where we were going to hike and run, how far she thought we could drive in a day, where we were going to stay each night, and the best way to get there avoiding the interstates where campers are treated like trampers. All the information she needed was on different mapps, and she had to flip back and forth between three mapps to figure everything out. Even letting luck be our guide (what Mom calls "the duck it method") had its challenges: you may find something cool like the Pony Express, or you may wind up sleeping in The Ritz of Parking Lots.

Our first night in Utah we accidentally landed too close to a big city when it was time to stop for the night. Cities are bad places for campers because all the car-house kennels are filled with people's homes, and there are rules in cities against sleeping in a car-houses or humans using the dog bathroom. We didn't want to spend our first night in Utah at a Wal*Mart, so we just kept driving through the city and into the unknown. All three of the mapps showed nothing but open space in the heart of Utah, know why? Because all that's out there is big, empty space called "public lands."

Where we come from, people are crazy about their land. They pay huge amounts of money for it, or give it a name and train people to follow lots of rules on it, or build a road to it and then put up signs along that road telling visitors go away. So the idea of so much stray land that no one wanted to adopt was new to us. If they're public lands, Mom figured we could probably sleep on them and run on them, so she pulled the car-house into a dirt parking spot next to a dirt road through the nowhere so that we could sleep there for the night and then run there in the morning.

It was even colder when we woke up than it had been on top of the mountain in Nevada the day before. We're California runners and have a very high freezing point, but just like when she made us run in the rain, Mom said that we couldn't spend the whole day in the car-house being scared of the weather. We needed to toughen up so that we could have plenty of time for adventure. Once we had toughened up, we started running down the frosty dirt road into the emptiness.

One good thing about public lands is that they follow the kinds of rules that people who don't like rules make, and I was free to exercise my first doggie amendment right: freedom of leash! Then again, people who don't like rules also tend to enjoy hunting. There were all these plastic things on the ground that Mom said were hunter droppings. She must have learned about hunters from TV, because we come from a place where all the rules forced hunters into extinction long ago. Since hunters were unfamiliar beasts that we only knew about

from Netflix, we weren't sure how to spot them, or what would make them attack. Mom hoped that her red hat and my red lobster bandana would keep us safe, but she's a suburban vegetarian liberal who isn't any more of an expert on hunter behavior than she is at spotting them. She was afraid that maybe hunters were hiding in the bushes right at that very moment, waiting to shoot at us. It was seven on a Monday morning, and we were ten miles outside of a town of two hundred people, so maybe it was unlikely that a hunter would be close to us in all that wilder-ness. Then again, are busy-ness hours important to a wilder-ness hunter?

I thought that hunters were made from humans, and in my experience humans generally didn't want to shoot other people, so I reckoned that maybe they would do things to avoid it. But Mom thought that maybe hunters are like T-rexes and attack anything that moves. She thought that maybe they were also like bears and her voice would scare them away if she talked real loud. So she narrated everything we were doing out loud the whole time we were running, just in case the hunters were listening.

Another part of Mom's hunter security plan was that I had to stay close to her. I saw a bunny and I took off after it. But then Mom made that "eh, eh, eh!" noise she makes when I have a naughty thought, and I froze, even though it meant that the bunny got away. Then she told me to "c'mere," and I did c'mere after just a few minutes' sniffing and staring longingly after the bunny.

We ran just under five miles without getting shot, and then we got back in the car-house and hit the road. We drove higher and higher and higher all morning until finally we were so high up that there were hardly any trees, and a bit of mountaintop whiteness stuck out of the ground. Mom had picked out a hike further along the route, but hiking up here on the roof of the world seemed so much more exotic. So she pulled over in a spot that had one of those information boards with maps that they put at the bottom of hiking trails. But the map showed the whole state of Utah, and didn't give any clues about where this trail went. We drove further up the trail behind the map and found nothing but a Private Property sign. We are experts in private property signs, because they are native to where we come from, so we knew they meant that we had to leave. When I jumped out of the car for a drink and pee break, my paws sunk up to the ankles in mud. "What the heck is this?" I asked, shaking out my paw. To get back into the car-house without my paws getting dirty again, Mom had to lift me into the driver's seat. "Now don't you feel silly for ignoring the plan?" I asked.

"This is what adventure is like, Oscar," Mom explained. "It's just that this is the part that usually gets edited out." Well I'm a dog of many words, so now you know that real-life adventure gets stuck between your toes and stains the inside of your car-house.

"No. This is what comes when you don't earn the thing you want," I corrected her. "You can't just expect the best things in life to find you, you have to plan for them. Otherwise, you wind up surrounded by all the things you want but can't have."

"I don't know why there would be a sign with a map of all the forest land in Utah if there weren't hiking trails nearby. It was a good guess. Give me a break."

"You're going to ruin it! We're going to run out of time. Let's just go straight to the place you picked out and no more Duck It Method, okay?"

"Okay, promise," Mom said.

But then, only a few miles later she saw a brown sign for a state park. "It's only ten miles out of our way, and they're sure to have hiking there!" Mom said. "Why wouldn't you have hiking at a state park on top of a mountain? Let's go!"

"What about the plan?! You spent hours finding a trail that was along the route. Let's just keep driving." But she already had the turn clicker on. So we drove the ten miles to the park.

When we got there the "park" was just a car kennel where cars turn into fishing boats. There were no trails at all.

"See what happens when you don't follow the plan?" I asked, trying to make this a teachable moment. "If you throw out your plan for something that MIGHT be a shortcut, you could wind up trying to hike in a park for fish. Now we're behind schedule. This is exactly what happened to the Donner Party..."

"Okay. No more stops. Pinky swear." she said. But dogs don't have pinkies.

We drove several more dog hours until we weren't in the roof of the world anymore, we were now in Breaking Bad[3]. When we pulled into the car kennel, something was wrong. "This is... not what I was expecting..." Mom said.

"What the heck is this?!" I asked. There were picnic tables and the little hydrant that eats envelopes of money, just like in all the best parks, but there were also a LOT of trucks – really big trucks that look like trains because they pull many boxes of rocks. Every couple of minutes a truck would pull into the picnic area, turn around, and then leave again. We could not figure out what the heck they were doing. They never stopped, just drove in and out, kicking up a cloud of dust and ugly

---

[3] I know about Breaking Bad because Mom watched it twice. It is a story about how a chemistry teacher uses math to pay his medical bills and take care of his family. I like it because it teaches about loyalty and hard work. I fell asleep before the end.

noises that ruined our picnic. Even when there were no trucks in the picnic ground, a big truck Mom called a caterpillar sat growling twenty-five yards away in a very un-caterpillar-like way, occasionally chirping backup beeps. "Mom, I don't like it here," I said.

"What do you always tell me, Oscar? If you don't like a place, all you have to do is look up. Sometimes it's dirty on the ground, but when you look up into the distance it's always beautiful." So we looked up. It looked like someone had poured a bunch of sand on some overturned boxes. It looked like we were in a Road Runner cartoon. It was hard to find the beauty. "Maybe it will be better when we're hiking?" she suggested.

We tried to find the trail, but this place was covered in dozens of unmarked trails that all crisscrossed each other. What if we got really lost? This was a country where outlaws like Geronimo and Billy the Kid could hide out on no-dogs-allowed trails for years and no one ever found them, even if they looked really hard. We were leash outlaws sometimes, and we frequently trespassed on trails that aren't dog friendly, but I didn't think that we needed to live in the canyons like Billy the Kid over all that. On top of that, Mom's phone battery was dangerously low. So instead we just walked up a dry riverbed and pretended like it was a trail.

Part of the reason that we couldn't find anything to like about the picnic tables where the trucks danced was because we were looking in the wrong place. The desert is prettier close up than it is from far away. Close up the sand had clumped and flaked and dried in a bunch of cool ways that I had never seen before. When I looked up, all of the big piles of sand looked different from one step to the next. I ran ahead of Mom like the Road Runner, stopping every now and then to watch her stumble haplessly up the trail.

We were starting to have fun, but it was getting hot. Eventually, I found a spot in the shade of a rock and flopped down. "That's it! I can't go any further!" I panted. Mom gave me some water, and then we turned around and headed back to the trucks. I followed Mom, but every time I found a large patch of shade, I sagged down again. "You go on without me!" I gasped. "Save yourself! I'll just sit here and wait for death."

"We only went like a mile. I think you can make it."

"No, no... I think the desert has gotten me. Tell my fans I love them. Maybe start a foundation in my honor that gives eggs to dogs with a B12 deficiency."

"It's only like seventy degrees out here. You can't be suffering that badly. You didn't even finish the bowl of water I gave you five minutes ago."

"Fine, I'll try to go on. But don't be surprised when I collapse and you have to carry me out..." I warned.

I dug deep and crawled on out of love for Mom. Okay, sometimes I forgot that I was dying and ran up to explore an interesting thing. But I made sure to let my tongue loll out real far and heave for dramatic effect when Mom looked at me. When we finally got back to the house, I flopped down in the shade, panting in relief. Sometimes danger finds you on an adventure, even when you did all the planning right.

Oscar the Desert Hound

That night we made it to a place called Moab.
Moab is like an enchanted neverland for outdoor families
like mine – except that Mom is afraid of cliffs and I'm not
fond of the heat, so maybe not... There are lots of other
tramps living in car-houses in Moab, so the townspeople
were used to dirty humans like Mom in their shops and
restaurants, and doggy people like me on their trails, and
we didn't get kicked out of anywhere the whole time we
were there. There was so much dog-friendly hiking that
we could have spent our whole trip here and hiked a
different trail every day. We were planning to hike on a
trail that Mom said is one of the most famous mountain
biking trails in the world, but then she read that all the
rough sandstone could wear a dog's paws into bloody
stumps. Mom's no better with blood than she is with
heights, so she looked for a different trail instead.

Moab is filled with cliffs, and if we got too close to
one and I tried to pull on the leash, then Mom would have
to lie belly-down on the ground and cry so she wouldn't
slip off. You can't hike back to the car-house if you're
lying whimpering on a rock like a lichen. Moab was lovely,
but I didn't want to be a lichen there, so it was very
important that we find a trail that would let me hike off
leash.

We started on a trail that they call "The
Stairmaster" because it climbs a thousand feet in a mile,
and if you climbed it every day you would have a butt that
would be as tight and irresistible as mine. The

Stairmaster was like climbing a basketball, and it would have been easy to get lost if they hadn't painted a line on the rock to tell us where to go. Even still, we got a little lost sometimes and had to go around in circles a bit to find a path to the top that wasn't interrupted by a cliff.

Once we were on top of the basketball, we ran whenever we could. It was hard to run for too long because we had to climb over a lot of rocks, and sometimes it was really sandy or steep. There were so many things to see that I think Mom spent more time taking pictures than running anyway.

At the end of the trail, the world stopped abruptly. The red-grey sandstone earth was there, and then it just wasn't. Way, way, way, way, way down below was a green town, and then a couple of miles away, off in the distance, the red-grey world started again. It was like someone had spliced in a section of the wrong mapp; like there was a square of high desert, then a slice of sea-level Ohio, and then more Utah again. Mom wanted to get a picture of me right up near the edge so you could see how scary the fall was, but just like the last time we got close to a cliff, she screamed bloody murder when I got close enough for the camera to see Ohio behind me. So I came away from the edge a bit so that Mom could stop screaming long enough take my picture.

On the way down from the edge of the world we ran more than we had on the way up. We even ran down the stairmaster, which I thought would scare Mom what with her fear of heights and all, but I guess she's okay with falling off of a cliff as long as it happens at running speed.

I hadn't had much breakfast, and when we got back to the car-house Mom tried to give me the kibble I'd left behind from before our hike. But now that I've had bacon, I would have to be pretty desperate to eat a bowl of dog food. Mom said that I was being a "spoiled brat" and she ought to make me eat it, but she still felt bad for ruining my birthday, so instead we went to a very fancy restaurant called a "diner." I got scrambled eggs, hashbrowns and bacon, and Mom ordered the same thing, only with no bacon. I felt really lucky to have a Mom who knew that dogs were people too, and that we deserve deliciousness just like humans.

I thought that all I had to do for the rest of the afternoon was to nap and make sure that Mom's fingers had a soft head to scratch, but Mom had another surprise in store. We got in our traveling positions and drove across town to *another* trail! I was pretty pooped, but Mom said that she didn't know when we would be back here again and she wanted to explore more. Luckily, this trail was mostly shady and stayed tucked next to a river. The trail crossed the river over and over, so I had lots to drink, and the water on my paws kept me cool.

This time Mom had me wear the GoPro. The harness is annoying, but people always give me lots of attention when I'm wearing it, so I guess I like being an action photographer. Anyway, when I was working with the GoPro no one cared that I wasn't wearing a leash, which is good because it's hard for me and Mom to balance when we're tied together climbing over big rocks or jumping over cracks. At one point we had to squeeze through narrow spot to climb through some rocks. I watched Mom slither through, using her front paws to hold on and scooting on her butt like she had a dingleberry, until she could reach the ground with her back paws. "I see how you're doing that..." I said, fascinated. This was the first time I ever understood why Mom only walks on her back paws. It was harder for me to get through the spot, because I have to go face-first and needed a little bit of runway at the bottom to get all my feet under me, or else I would have landed with my face under me.

Only a few minutes into our hike, the GoPro memory card was already full. "Oh bother," said Mom. "I thought this would be a great day for video."

"It's okay, Mom. You and I have more memory in our heads than the camera anyway. We can just pay really close attention to all the details and save it in our own memories. That will be better because we won't need to look it up on some screen machine to enjoy it."

I thought that was pretty good life coach advice, but despite her best intentions I don't think that Mom got it. I knew she wasn't paying attention to her surroundings, because after the trail ended in a big rock wall that curved over our heads like the inside of a cathedral, we were supposed to walk back out of the canyon the way we'd come. But when Mom stopped to take my picture, she stood up and started walking the wrong way. I thought for sure she would notice that we were walking uphill again, but she didn't.

Then we passed a poo bag that someone had left on the trail. Wouldn't she notice that we'd passed it just a few minutes before? "Gorsh, I can't believe how many people just leave their trash in the middle of the trail like that," she said. "That's the second poop bag we've seen in just a few minutes. What pigs!" And we kept going.

Then we saw some of the people that we'd seen before. "Coming back for more?" they asked. But Mom thought they said, "Coming back for more!" She smiled at them, then hiked on.

Finally we met another group that we'd already passed, and I greeted their dog. "Heading back in, are you?" said the man while I was sniffing the dog's butt.

"What?" said Mom.

"You're headed back up the trail."

"I am?" Mom was surprised.

Then I smelled that this dog was a real snob. "No, *your* family's clueless!" I shouted, and then I kept shouting comebacks to all the judgy things I could tell he was thinking about Mom. So Mom took away my responsibility and made me run for a little while to put some space between us and the other family. Running after such a spirited debate got me really excited, and when we saw some people puppies playing in the river, I tried to yank Mom into the river after them. This made Mom grouchy because now her socks were wet. Nothing makes Mom grumpier than wet socks, and so she stopped having fun. Since fun makes Mom want to take pictures, she stopped paying attention to her surroundings and started looking where she was going again. Now that Mom was paying attention, we found our way out of the canyon after all.

By the time we got back to the car-house, we had run and hiked over fifteen miles, and I was bushed. As Mom drove us out of Moab to a new sleeping place, I sacked out in the back and let her take me wherever destiny wanted us to go. There is such a thing as a planning overdose after all.

Mitten Gods and Freedom

After all of our hard hiking in Moab, Mom decided that we were close enough to push on to our next stop before bed time. So even though I was too tired to help, Mom drove toward Arizona while I got the bed warmed up for an epic night's rest. We got to a place called

Monument Valley just in time for sunset and stopped on the side of the highway to watch the sun disappear behind the desert. Mom had trouble deciding when the sunset was done being splendid and it was safe to turn our backs and find a sleeping place.

Mom said that Monument Valley was a very special place, and even though we'd just watched the sun disappear, she wanted to watch it come back too. So even though serious runners need their rest, we got up real early so that we could be on the road before first light. The problem was that apparently the sun rises at a different time depending on whether you're in Utah or Arizona, and we were sitting right on the border. None of our clocks could agree on whether we were in Utah or Arizona, so we left an hour darker than we needed to. Luckily, Mom spent our extra hour getting lost in the blackness. What was strange was that whenever we crossed the border (which we did many, many times as the car-house roamed through the dark), the sun and moon and sky were always in the same spot in both states. I didn't understand how we could travel back and forth in time and have everything still look exactly the same at 5:07am as it did at 6:07am, but it did. When the first stripes of sun burst out of the distance, we sat right on the border and watched the sun rise an hour apart in two states.

If you have ever seen an old western movie, then you know that Monument Valley is a place with big rocks that look like buildings, surrounded by a lot of flat desert. The people who lived there used think that the big rocks were the gods, which makes sense. There was something about them that reminded me of Mom when she stands over me looking stern and tells me to "sit" even though I don't want to. If a god were made out of the earth rather than sky, I bet that's what he or she would look like. Mom got out a camp chair and made me sit in the dirt at the side of the road while we watched the sunrise.

Watching the sunrise in Monument Valley is not as fun as it looks in the cowboy movies. All the plants have prickles, there is lots of beer litter everywhere, and it is real cold in the morning. But like I always say: if a place looks crappy, then all you have to do is look up. When I looked up I could still see the moon behind one of the gods on one side, and on the other I could see the sunbeams striping through the clouds. Finally, when the light had soaked into the desert and spread evenly over all the places, Mom let me back in the car-house and we left to find a place to run.

When we parked at the trailhead Mom pointed to two of the gods and said, "Look, Oscar, they're mittens! You see the thumbs?"

"Dogs don't have thumbs," I grumbled. I was cranky because I was still tired from so much sun, and so little sleep.

"Well mittens do have thumbs. Stop being an old fuddy-duddy," Mom said.

"Who worships a mitten?" I asked.

"Never, ever make fun of other people's beliefs," Mom said sternly as a mitten. "Let's go."

The run was about four miles around the base of one of the mittens. Even though the god was made of rock, the ground was mostly sand like in the cartoon desert, so it was slow running. There is something kind of spooky about being next to something that big. It looks like something that should be really far away, even if you're running right below it. Maybe it was because I was spooked, and maybe I was just cranky because Mom wouldn't give me responsibility, but I was annoyed and barked whenever we saw other people exploring around the mitten-god.

I was still barking at the crummy people when I saw something that annoyed me even more. It was a dog that was off leash, but I could tell that he had no responsibility. Something about the idea of somedog having all that freedom and no accountability to the rules really freaked me out. "HEY! Where are your people?!" I shouted at him. He ignored me. "You need a bath, pal!" I bellowed. "You've got dingleberries in your butt fur!" He ignored us and went to the other people to beg for treats. "Don't you speak barking?!" I shouted after him.

"What's up with him?" I asked Mom when he was out of telepathy range.

"You know how we're just pretending to be homeless?" Mom said. "Well he actually is homeless."

"You must be confused. People can be homeless, but dogs are never homeless. If they ever lose their homes, nice people pick them up and find them families to love them and give them belly scratches and post it on The Dodo."

"We're in a different nation right now, Oscar. They have different rules about the services that they provide. They don't have the resources to put their homeless dogs in shelters because they need to take care of the people first. So the dogs take care of themselves."

"But how does he open the dog food fortress to get to his kibble?" I wondered. "He must be dying for a bed and some toys to rip up on it. Why don't we take him home? We have enough to share."

"Oscar, that dog has never lived in a house or with a person. A dog that hasn't grown up with all the privilege you have might be more uncomfortable living in a house than he is living off the land. Remember how embarrassed Jack felt when he went to the fancy dinner on the Titanic and didn't know what fork to use? That dog wouldn't know all the rules and would get yelled at all the time. He would spend his time wishing for responsibility in a place where the kind of freedom he's used to is dangerous, and then everyone would be unhappy."

As we drove around that day, we saw lots of wild dogs and even a horse grazing at the gas station. I thought it might actually be a nice life living in nature without rules or schedules. We could buy a car-house of our own and just be stray drifters forever. But then I saw a dead dog lying by the side of the road. No one had taught him how to be safe, and no one came to hug him and kiss him and make him feel better while he died. That made me feel very, very sad and lonely. If you're an outlaw, you don't have rules, but you don't have anyone to protect you either. I thought about all of the rules I knew, and realized that Mom had taught me almost all of them. All that time I thought that I was playing for treats, but Mom must have known what she was doing the whole time. How empty must a life be without a Mom following you around!

We were supposed to do a second hike that day, but after we drove three dog hours to the next place, we couldn't find any trails. The first one we tried was many miles down a dirt road that was too difficult for the car-house to climb. The second one was on private property. At the third one we got out and tried to walk, but I flopped down under the nearest tree and refused to move. It was hot and I was thirsty and cranky. Then Mom checked the mapp. We had driven so far looking for a trail that we had overshot our next stop - the Grand Canyon.

Dogs were only allowed on the south side of the Canyon, and here we were north of it. That meant that there was a giant hole in the ground blocking the way to tomorrow's trail, and we would have to drive halfway across Arizona to go around and get to the dog-friendly side of the hole. So instead of hiking, we spent the afternoon in the air conditioned car-house driving the long way around the Grand Canyon. Mom was upset, but I was happy to spend the afternoon catching up on sleep. I snoozed right through Mom's fits of growling and sighing like they were the relaxing rumble of a rain storm.

We stopped for a short walk at the Glen Canyon Dam. Unlike most of the cliffs along the river, the Dam is not a natural cliff. Instead, ancient people decided to separate the river so that most of it would live in a lake at the top of the dam, and only some of it would continue through the canyon hundreds of feet below. Before they built the dam and stopped the river, people had lived in towns in the valley that became the lake. Those towns still live at the bottom of Lake Powell somewhere, but now the only people that live in them are fishes.

"Did you know that this dam is an engineering disaster?" Mom asked, as we cowered far enough away from the bridge so that the cliff couldn't suck us off.

"What's an engineering disaster?" I asked.

"You know Pinterest fails? Well an engineering disaster is like a Pinterest fail, but with arts and crafts projects big enough to kill lots of people when they go wrong." Mom pointed down the empty side of the dam, where the tiny river flowed at the bottom of a deep-deep canyon. "Do you know what dug that canyon?" Mom asked.

I thought about our picnic with the dancing trucks. "Was it caterpillars?"

"No, it was water. Lots, and lots, and lots of water." Then she pointed toward the lake side of the dam. "What's that?" She asked.

"It's lots, and lots, and lots of water, of course. That's what a lake is, Mom."

Then she pointed at the canyon rock that hugged both sides of the dam. "So if all it takes to make a canyon is lots, and lots, and lots of water flowing over this kind of rock, and this rock is all that's holding that concrete dam in place, then what do you think is going to happen after a few decades of storms and lake currents with all that pressure of the lake pushing up against that dam?"

I thought about it. I thought about how the water would make the rocks on each side of the dam just a few grains farther apart every year. And then I pictured what would happen when just a couple of drops of water could squeeze through. Suddenly all of the water in the lake would rush to push through that tiny crack. In no time the sea monster that lived at the bottom of the lake would want to check out what the commotion was about. When he saw that his house was leaking, he would get so excited to escape that he'd kick over the dam and trample it on his way to wherever the river went.

"Mom, what else is down that river?" I asked.

"Las Vegas, Yuma, Needles, Mexico... Millions and millions of people, and millions and millions square miles of things that need to be dry to live."

Mom and I had just listened to a book[4] about some real-life guys who maybe planned to blow up the dam because some made-up guys blew up the dam in a different book[5]. But the real-life guys got in a shootout instead and hid in the same canyons we'd been hiking and driving through for the past few days. One of them lived for years in the desert, sleeping in caves and canyons like a wolf. Except for the murder and terrorism part, it sounded like a great adventure to live like an

---

[4] Translator's note: Dan Schultz's *Dead Run: The Murder of a Lawman and the Greatest Manhunt of the Modern American West* (2013)

[5] Translator's note: Edward Abbey's *The Monkey Wrench Gang* (1975)

outlaw, hiking and camping for the rest of our lives. Then I remembered the homeless dog and realized that it was probably a lot tougher than it sounded, and might include dingleberries. Not only are dingleberry's nature's greatest betrayal, they can also ruin a good picture.

Living in our car-house was fun because I'd seen a lot of new stuff and been with Mom all day, but I was starting to miss naps and predictability, and not being covered in itchy dust all the time. Mom wanted to keep going, but she did miss washing her hands more than once or twice a day. Maybe it was better to be a part-time outlaw, but still have a stuck house to come back to when adventuring got old. Maybe it wasn't the wildest outlaw in The West that had the most fun.

Great Heights

The next day Mom and I got to see the Grand Canyon, which is the second really famous place I've ever visited (the Golden Gate Bridge near my house being the other). So I'm Level Two Famous now. Mom and I didn't agree at first about whether to include a stop at the Grand Canyon because the one and only trail where dogs can run in the whole entire park is the sidewalk that follows the shuttle route from bus stop to bus stop. In the end I convinced Mom that a famous dog must visit famous places, and reminded her that if we had to pass by the Grand Canyon anyway then it would be silly to not be famous.

I will spare you the details about our troubles finding the trail, but know that there were lots of duck-bombs and some crocodile tears, and our run got off to a later start than expected. Mom would have liked to fall at running pace down one of the trails into the canyon because she had never climbed into a canyon before. But dogs aren't allowed into the canyon, probably because the rangers think we'll dig it up and ruin it. Instead we ran on the Rim Trail. Do you know what a "rim" is? It is the seam of a cliff where the ground turns into open air. And you know Mom and cliffs…

The Grand Canyon must have been out of breath, because the hardest thing about our day following the shuttle bus was that it was really, really windy. Mom said that the sustained winds were going to be neighborhood driving speed, with gusts up to highway driving speed.

"That's an exaggeration!" I said. "It's never as windy as a car window. You just think it's that windy because you want people to know you were miserable." But then she showed me the weather report, and now I owe her a freeze-dried liver treat because the lady in her phone said Mom was telling the truth!

The wind had rocked our car-house like a cradle while we were sleeping. If it could move our great, big car-house, what would it do to a medium-sized dog and his little human? I wondered if Mom would misbehave when we ran along the world's most famous cliffs in winds strong enough to pick us up like a couple of kites?

When Mom stopped our run to take my picture for the first time, a stranger lady offered to take our picture together, but Mom refused. "Are you kidding me?!" Mom said, pointing at the nothing a few feet away, where the ground wasn't. "There's no way I'm turning my back to that thing!"

As Mom explained to me in our pre-run safety briefing, the reason that she's scared of heights is because you can't count on sticking to the ground when you stand in a high place. That's because there's a monster that lives just over the edge of drop-offs like cliffs, and high buildings, and stairs that have open space between the steps. The monster waits for its victim to stand too close to the open air, and then when they're not paying attention, it sucks them off the edge where they fall until they splat into a million pieces. That's why you need to be very, very vigilant and take measures to protect yourself. The best way to protect yourself is to get low to the ground, face-down with as much of your body touching the ground as possible and with your eyes squeezed shut. Then you're supposed to whimper. But you can't run from that position, and instead you have to spend the rest of the day barking at everyone around you that you're *fine* and they should just leave you alone and go around you, dammit, because you're not moving from this spot right here where it's safe. I thought people might think I was crazy if I acted like that, but this was a non-optional rule...

Wind can be scary, but the other thing about wind is that it is stressful. Everything you do in the wind takes more effort, and things fly into your eyes and nose and mouth. For someone like Mom who has long fur next to her eyes and nose and mouth, it can be a real problem. But just like the cold, the wind turned out to be more scary from inside the car-house than when we were out in it. Surprisingly, it actually takes a stronger wind than neighborhood driving speed to suck even a very small human like Mom off a cliff.

We didn't look at the scenery much in the nine miles we ran because Mom said that looking off in the distance might trick us into running right into thin air like Wile E Coyote. We had to concentrate very hard on the trail directly in front of us and not look away for even a nanosecond, and never, ever, ever look down into the canyon. Instead of thinking about the beautiful scenery, we had to be constantly planning where we would lie down like lichens if The Monster tried to suck us over the edge.

When we did finally stop and look at the canyon (standing very still, and crouched to flee if we needed to), I wasn't as excited by it as I am whenever I cross the Golden Gate Bridge to visit Bodie. When I'm on The Bridge I like to think about how people come from all over the world to visit a place that is just part of the way to my sister's house. I like to look up as we drive under the proud towers and think about how strong they have to be to stand so high over the sucking ocean, and hold that mountain on the other side in place close enough that The City can reach it. The Grand Canyon didn't have a job to do, so it just sat there looking self-conscious. "It looks like it's painted there," I told Mom.

"That's because it's so enormous. All of that stuff you see, it's much further away than it seems. Everything here is bigger than it looks, including the distance to the bottom."

"No, it's definitely fake. See? The cliffs in the close by are real because I can see them in high definition. But when you look in the distance it's all low def and smudgy like an old TV. That's an old movie trick they used before CGI."

"Your brain doesn't know how to handle the scale, so it searches for an interpretation of what it doesn't understand and tells you that it's fake. Lots of things that are fake look real, but this is a real thing that looks like an illusion, and that's why it's one of the natural wonders of the world." Maybe *Mom's* brain couldn't understand the canyon, but I wasn't fooled. The day before, the mitten-god had looked far away even though it was close. Today the canyon was supposed to look close even though it's far away? Baloni.

Most of the time we ran like normal, but sometimes Mom needed to shuffle along like a very old person without taking any feet off the ground, for safety. I was a very good boy and didn't pull, mostly because I was tired and pulling takes a lot of effort, even with the cliff monster helping you. When I did pull a little bit, Mom froze in place and said my name with so much stress that her voice broke.

After our run, we got in the car-house and drove all day without getting out except a few potty breaks. Even though we had stopped running to drink water every few minutes, I didn't have to go potty any more than normal, which is good for car trips. I was glad to take the afternoon off. I didn't know that there was such a thing as too much adventure, but there is. Mom is one of those people that when she finds something good, she wants more and more of it every day until she's had too much and the thing makes her unhappy again. I'm different. I need to take naps and let each adventure soak in and then dry out of me like a sponge. If I don't get time to rest, I can't absorb the next adventure, and it runs right off of me and I forget. That's why I don't like the idea of "vacation." Why should you save up all of your fun and have it in one big blow-out? I think it would be much better to spread your fun out in tiny doses throughout the year so that you can soak all of the fun out of each adventure and not waste a drop.

A Desert Execution

I was beginning to suspect that Mom was trying to kill me. Did she resent all of my high-quality life coach advice? (Some people just don't want to change...) She said we needed to "seize the day" and "take advantage of this once-in-a-lifetime trip..." and also that we can't be inside the parked car-house in the heat of the day. But I suspected these were all excuses, and she had murder in her heart.

But I'm getting ahead of myself... We started our day with a hike-run on top of a nine-thousand-foot mountain. Most days nine thousand feet wouldn't be so high, since we have been sleeping at six or seven thousand feet, but that night we had slept on shorter ground and the car-house had a long way to climb. As the car-house put-put-putted up the hill at half the speed limit, I looked down the side of the mountain that dropped like a wall to the valley floor. "How high have we climbed anyway?" I asked.

Mom didn't know, so she asked the Lady in Her Phone, "What is the altitude of Las Vegas?"

"Las Vegas is at 2001 feet above sea level," said The Lady in Mom's Phone, who is a real know-it-all and kind of judgy too. If we had slept at two thousand feet, and were climbing to nine thousand feet, then that meant that the car-house had to climb eleven thousand feet to get to the trail! Or, I think that's how it works anyway. Dogs aren't so good at word problems.

"I think I can, I think I can..." said the car-house. Mom was afraid that the car-house would run out of food, even though it started the morning with a half-full belly. If it did, it would be a worse fate than MapQuest because there was nothing on this mountainside for us to eat but rocks and dirt.

The wind had been gusting at Wizard of Oz speeds at the bottom of the world where we'd slept. When Mom got out to feed the car-house, it had blown so strong against the door that the door booped her hard on the head, and she said a bad word. But the air was peaceful and calm up here on top of the world. We were so high up that we were in the mountain's white hat, and I got to smell the air conditioner smell of white dirt up close for the first time. The white dirt lay there like other dirt, so I ignored it and sniffed the pine and sky smells that flowed gently toward me from the gaps between the mountains' hats.

Even though we were already on the roof of the world, the trail kept going up and up and up. It wasn't very steep, but the air was really broken up here and we kept having to slow down and hike to catch our breaths. Every time we turned a corner Mom said, "This one *must* be the top!" But it wasn't. According to Mom, if a trail goes up a certain amount, then it has to go down by the same amount. But I know better. I've learned from experience that trails always go up much more than they go down, and this trail was really showing off.

Finally, just when I thought that Mom was going to give up running altogether, the trail gave in instead and started going down. Usually it's my downhill job to follow right behind Mom so that her heels kick me in the chin for safety and sympathy, but since I was tired, I had followed Mom all the way up the hill and now it was my turn at the front. Suddenly a love for running whooshed back into me, and I got a serious case of the zoomies. I started bounding down the trail as fast as joy, like the wind from the desert bottom was in my feet. The times I looked back at Mom, she looked weightless too. Usually she's stiff and ungainly as a water buffalo with bad self esteem when she runs, but now she looked a little less plodding – not graceful, but kind of like a shopping cart with a wonky wheel rolling down a hill – which meant that she was having fun too.

When we were done on the mountain, Mom turned the car-house into a kind of sled and we let gravity take us down the mountain. Mom and the car-house must share a soul, because the car-house wobbled like a shopping cart with a wonky wheel too as it rolled down the steep hill. Once we were off the mountain, we turned the engine back on and kept going down gradually until we were even lower than the ocean sits. We have been in a lot of deserts on this trip, and this was one of the uglier ones. It looked like it wasn't done being made yet. Someone had built the mountains and valleys, but forgot to decorate them with trees and bushes and different colored rocks, and then they'd abandoned the whole project to be covered in dust.

Mom pulled over and parked the car-house at the bottom of a dirt track. "This is our next hike?!" I asked, incredulous. "We can't! It's too hot!"

"It's only like seventy degrees. And look, I have plenty of water. And I'll soak your bandana so that it keeps you cool."

"But… it's so ugly!" This place was even uglier than the Wile E. Coyote wilderness where we'd hiked in the dump-picnicground. It was nothing but whitish sand, whitish rocks, mangey, boney mountains, and nothing else. It wasn't even a real trail, just a dirt road wide enough for two cars to pass each other.

"AllTrails says that there's a waterfall at the top!" Mom said.

"Oh it did, did it? And you didn't think it might be a hoax?" I said. "Really! A waterfall in the dry desert at the bottom of the world…"

"But there were pictures!" Mom insisted.

"And every picture on the internet is real? Come on! I look for the toy every time you fake throw it, and even *I* know you can't believe everything you see on the internet." Mom was definitely walking me into the desert to kill me. *Breaking Bad, True Detective*… I knew that this is how people do murders in the desert. She was going to walk me up this trail, then she was going to tell me to dig, and at sunset she was going to tell me to "sit-stay" at the edge of the hole… And then only one of us was going to hike back out of the desert into the sunset.

As we hiked up the road, one car after another passed us coming down the hill. "Where do you supposed they're all coming from?" Mom asked. I couldn't imagine why anyone would visit anything in this dung-hole, so they must be other murderers coming back from executions of their own.

After more than two miles we came to where all of the cars were coming from: a car kennel. *Ooh-la-la!* So many interesting places to see in The West, and we'd found a car kennel in the middle of the desert. But... I'll be darned if there wasn't a sign with a picture of a waterfall where the trail left the car kennel. These pranksters had really gone the extra mile with their waterfall hoax.

Beyond the car kennel, the desert was just as deserted. But I had to admit it did kind of look like a dry riverbed, and where there was a riverbed there must have once been water. Then, suddenly the ground was wet, and there were a few trees that smelled green. We followed the water about half a mile up into a little canyon. All the while more and more trees popped out of the sand, and the little brook was getting wider and wider. We had to climb some pretty tough spots where I thought for sure either Mom or I were going to slip and fall off the slippery rocks with our wet feet and splash into the brook. But we didn't because one of us is a nimble tough person, and the other one is lucky.

Much to my surprise, after almost three and a half miles of hiking through the ugliest, deadest desert I'd ever seen, we found a beautiful waterfall pouring into a clear pool in a cool little glade of trees. It was like something that you would have seen in the center of the kind of fancy shopping mall where dogs shop while riding in purses.

Mom didn't end up murdering me either, because there were witnesses. As we hiked back down to the car-house, people driving down from the car kennel stopped and asked if we were okay. "No! She's going to murder me execution style!" I shouted with telepathy.

"Yup, we're fine. My van just can't make it up this road so we parked at the bottom," Mom said.

"Do you have water for the pooch?" the Good Samaritan asked.

"No! This is a forced march! She wants to hike me to death!" I screamed.

"Oh, be quiet, Oscar. You just peed like ten minutes ago. You're not in danger, you're just uncomfortable," said Mom. Out loud to the man she said, "Yup. I have a backpack full of it!" But she DIDN'T have a backpack full of it, because I'd already drunk most of it. So that was a lie too.

To be honest, I was feeling better now that I'd been in the shade. I had so much energy that instead of hanging out depressed behind Mom, I ran ahead to convince her to hurry up. When I pulled so far ahead that I was out of range, Mom would run until she counted to 100, and then she would walk until I had trotted too far ahead again. That way we got to the car-house before I croaked, and so I'm able to tell you guys this story.

White Dirt

For the first time in the whole trip Mom and I slept in the same place for two nights in a row! We were in a place called Lone Pine, which is famous because it's part of the Badwater Ultramarathong route. It is also right at the bottom of a really big mountain with spikes on top.

If we looked in one direction we could see the ugly brown mountains that go to what I'm calling Death Valley (because Mom tried to kill me there). On the other side were the pretty grey and white Sierras with their spikey rock crowns and white capes. Instead of doing two small hikes like we usually do, Mom and I planned to spend the day doing one long hike on the grey-and-white Sierra side of town.

We drove the car-house up and up and up a road that had such sharp turns next to such steep drops that Mom drove with two wheels on each side of the line in the middle of the road, for safety. We climbed until we were on the mountain's white hat. Now that we were close, I could see that the white dirt didn't cover the whole ground, only parts of it. But in the places where the dirt was white, it didn't only stay on the ground but covered *everything*, including the rocks and bushes and the trail. I'd already seen white dirt on the other mountain the day before, so I was already an expert, but this was the first time I'd tried stepping on it. It was...

... AWESOME!!!

The white dirt was kind of hard but kind of soft too, and it was a little bit slippery and very cold, and felt delightful on my fur. Just like when we were in the place where the earth wouldn't load, running on white dirt was love at first step, and I knew that this stuff was something that I wanted to keep in my coat for the rest of the trip. I rolled onto my back and kicked my feet in the air while I wriggled and basked. Then I felt a severe case of the zoomies coming on and tried to run on it. Running in the white dirt wasn't like running in regular dirt or sand. It was more like running in the ocean, where your foot sinks in and you have to pick it all the way back out to take your next step. There was no way to move in the stuff other than to leap and dance like I was jumping for joy. "Have you ever seen anything so wonderful in your entire life?!" I asked Mom.

"I have, actually. I grew up with snow..." she said, doing her best Squidward impression.

"Is that what this stuff is called? Snow? And you *left*?! What's the matter with you?"

"It's different when it's sitting on your car and blocking your driveway and you're late for work..." Mom grumbled, like there was some history there.

Despite growing up in it, Mom did not know how to move in the white dirt as easily as I did, and she picked her way carefully through it like it was full of mouse traps. A few times both of us slipped and slid sideways down the slope and off the trail, but only a little bit.

The white dirt wasn't covering everything, though, and the hiking was great in the spots where the regular ground stuck out. Unfortunately, though, the higher we climbed, the deeper and more troublesome the white dirt got. The other humans on the trail weren't dressed like Mom. They wore big, scary masks that turned the whole top half of their faces into mirrors, held poking sticks like an extra set of legs, and carried long planks and tennis racket shoes strapped to their packpacks. Mom just had on running shorts, a long sleeved shirt, and the little packpack with my water in it.

When I was up to my knees in white dirt after little more than a mile, Mom pointed out that the trail was going to be harder to find the higher we climbed. Instead, she suggested we try another trail that we had passed on the sunny and more colorful side of the mountain. This trail faced a waterfall that we tried to climb to. The trouble was that the trail kept disappearing into the bushes, or under a bunch of rocks someone had spilled there, and we had to fight our way through like trailblazers. Finally we reached a point where every time we stepped up the mountain, an equal part of the mountain fell down under us so that we stayed in one place like a dreadmill. Mom said that it was time to call it a day.

Even though we hadn't gone very far, both of us had gotten a great workout. Climbing mountains is good for your butt, and balancing on slippery white dirt and falling rocks is good for your balance. Balance isn't so important if you walk sensibly on all four paws, but for stubborn hikers that want to stand tall on their back paws, it is essential.

"There have got to be other trails a little further down the mountain that aren't covered with snow!" Mom said, pulling out her phone.

The nearest trail is an hour away, The Lady that Lives in her Phone told Mom.

"Lies! That can't be!" Mom said, poking and pinching the screen to look for hidden trails you could only see if you looked at the mapps closely. She looked and looked through the mountains but The Witch just said *Nanny-nanny-boo-boo*. So we wobbled the car-house back down the center of the scary road and Mom explored other mountain roads while I took a nap and dreamed about chasing bunnies through the white dirt.

I was jolted awake by the car-house rattling so violently that everything inside was being knocked over and thrown around, including handsome dogs. Carquakes like this usually meant that Mom was turning the car-house around because the trail she was looking for was hidden behind a long dirt road. But this time the violence continued. I climbed into the front seat to check on Mom, who obviously couldn't be trusted with the responsibility of unsupervised navigation. "What are you doing?!" I asked as she pulled through a concrete passageway that was only a couple of inches wider than the car-house, and was decorated with lots of dangerous-looking signs. She was driving like a slow motion version of the opening scene in *Breaking Bad*... and I was the dead guy in the back.

"I'm so sick of driving for hours just to find that the trail is only accessible to four wheel drive vehicles!" Mom said through her fangs.

"But..."

"...But this road seems somewhat well maintained and I'm going for it."

"But how far up is the trailhead?!" I asked.

"Just five miles."

I looked at how fast we were going. (I'm an expert on speed and often help Mom drive, so I know how to read the speedometer.) "But you're going less than five miles an hour! That's even slower than we run!" The car-house rolled over rocks, throwing us first left, then right. "At this rate it will take us hours to get there. We could go faster on foot!"

"I had noticed that..." Mom admitted sheepishly. "But this track isn't wide enough for me to turn around so... we're kind of committed."

"What if we break the car-house or we get stuck in some deep sand and then we're *really* committed?!" I asked, alarmed.

"Where's your sense of adventure, Oscar?!"

The further we went, the rougher the ground got and the more violent it was riding in the car-house. Finally, we got to a slightly wider spot in the trail and Mom parked the house. "That's it. From here we're proceeding on foot!" she announced, then she opened the side hatch and made me dismount into a prickle bush.

To my dismay, the day had gotten warm and there was very little shade out here. "It's hot out here. Can we go home?" I asked, flopping down in the shade under the car-house.

"It's not so hot." She pulled out her phone. "What's the temperature?" she asked the Lady That Lives in Her Phone.

It's 61 degrees outside, lied the Lady that Lives in the Phone, and I could tell by her voice that she was sticking her tongue out at me. That suck-up witch always takes Mom's side.

The Witch Inside the Phone had promised that the trailhead was only a mile from where we'd left the house, but when we had walked a mile, Mom looked at the trail mapp and we didn't seem any closer to the trailhead. Luckily, there was a little shady glade and a stream, and I headed into it to cool off while Mom figured things out with the Lady in the Phone.

But once I got to the cool, wet spot I was surrounded by awful, buzzing flies trying to get into my ears and nose and eyeballs. I snapped my teeth to scare them away, but that only attracted more of them to find out what all the excitement was about. Mom crouched down and pointed the the phone's eye to take a picture of me acting all crazy, and the flies attacked her too.

"Let's get the heck out of here!" she said, standing tall and waving her paws around her face like a fire dance.

We continued up the track-trail thing for another half mile, but our blue dot never got any closer to the trailhead on the map. Every time we tried to cool off, we were tormented by a plague of flies. I was hot and walking as slow as I could to discourage Mom from going too far. Finally, after consulting the mapp for the millionth time, Mom said, "This isn't even the right dirt road! The lady in the GPS lied to us!" The Lady in the GPS must be part cat, because that seemed like the kind of dirty trick a cat would play. But for once the cat in the phone was on my side, because finally we turned around and headed back to the car-house.

When we got back to civilization Mom bought me Chicken McRotguts to apologize. They were exquisite! And healthy, because they're all white meat chicken. A healthy diet is very important for runners.

Out of the Desert

Since we couldn't find any more trails to visit, the next day we left the mountain-desert campground and came down to where the air was thicker and smelled like green. I could tell that we were getting closer to home because when we parked the car-house at the bottom of the trail, the other people in the car kennel talked like home. I call these guys "dude-bruhs" because that's what they call each other. As in, "Wanna go shopping for flip flops and board shorts, dude?" "Nah, let's go surfing, bruh." They are common where I live, but not so common in the desert because dude-bruhs are amphibious beasts and there's no surfing in the desert.

Now that we were out of the wilder-ness and back among humans, Mom dug through the bottom of the car-house for the leash. We hadn't needed it in thousands of miles, so she had buried under stinky shorts, towels, and empty cooking grenades for safe keeping. Even though we were out of the lawless hunting country, there was still one handsome and furry hunter in this parking lot who didn't plan to stop roaming wild. The second Mom opened the door to the car-house, I streaked right past her, hot on the heels of a critter. Mom was left standing by the car-house screaming, with the dogless leash in her paw.

We started jogging with the leash between us, but we had been running wild and free for too long for Mom to take my responsibility away for long. The non-desert was Critter City, and I needed to stop and sniff about each one. Mom must have had the zoomies, because she got impatient waiting for me, and set herself free. I meant to run with Mom, but every time I finished with one critter and thought about coming back to her, I would catch the scent of another beastie and couldn't go back yet. Mom was apoplectic because she hardly saw me for the first couple of miles, but now that I was a Wild Westerner, I needed elbow room. Anyhow, there was no way I was going to lose her with her screaming like that, and this was great country for long-distance sprints to tell her about what I'd discovered. With open grass meadows instead of sand I could build blurry speed, and I didn't get scraped up by the soft leafy bushes as I zoomed past them and around the big boulders which bubbled out of the ground.

Eventually, Mom led me high enough that there were fewer critters to chase, so I came back to walk with her on the trail. This trail wasn't flat like a sidewalk. It had a tiny little canyon running down the middle of it where the rain had dug it into a V, so we had to go slow to find places wide enough to hold all of our feet. Now that I didn't have the sprint wind running through my ears, I noticed that it was getting warm. "I'm hooooooooooooot!" I panted as Mom marched resolutely up the mountain.

"I've got plenty of water for you, Oscar. And look! Something we haven't seen in days: there's shade on this trail!"

"How far are we running today?" I asked.

"Like nine miles. But only half of it's uphill."

"That's a myth!" I huffed, flopping down in a shady spot and stretching out like Rose Dewitt Bukater posing for her sexy portrait. I tried to flop sensually in the dirt, but the crack in the middle of the trail was really steep in that spot, and when I relaxed my hunky muscles, my butt slipped down toward the crack. "Aah, this is more comfortable!" I lied, shifting my shoulders to settle in the spot where I'd slipped to a stop. Then my shoulders slipped down into the crack, too. "I meant to do that..." I said, adjusting myself again... until my butt slipped yet again. Soon I had slipped right into the crotch of deep V-shaped crack and had cool dirt hugging me on both sides. "Aaah. Perfect!" I said, flopping my head down on the dirt and letting my tongue loll to the ground.

"I would find this more believable if you hadn't just chased a squirrel for a quarter mile," Mom said, pouring me some water.

I drank what I wanted, and then reached out my paw and knocked the rest into the dirt. "Ugh! Room temperature!"

"Oscar! Look what you've done!" Mom said with grief in her voice, like I'd drunk her goldfish or something. "I've been saving my water for you. When you throw it on the ground, that's like throwing away my water." Mom can be so dramatic sometimes. Humans don't need water, obviously. They carry so much water inside of them already that it sloshes out of their skin whenever they run, like squeezing a sponge. All that trapped water inside is why Mom is all soft and snuggly like a waterbed where I'm solid and muscular.

We climbed on and on until we'd run half of nine miles and arrived at... nowhere. The trail kept going up and up the hill to the peak in front of us, and then behind that we could see it climbing to the even higher peak beyond that. Mom looked at the mapp... we were still probably a couple of miles from the end of the trail. "See!" I grumbled. "I told you it was more than half up..."

I was spared from having to go all the way to the summit by the fact that more than half of the water was gone. Even though it was much cooler up here, we still had to get Mom all the way back down without drinking the water I'd poured in the dirt. So we "shifted into neutral" as Mom put it, and let the mountain carry us back down. I pranced gracefully in my spot right behind

Mom. Rather than the grace of a shopping cart, Mom was back to running like a water buffalo trying to tap dance. "Ow, ow, ow, ow," she grunted as she ran. Apparently it was hard on her hooves running in the V that the crack in the trail made. Sometimes she tried hopping from one side of the crack to the other every few steps to find flat places to put her feet. Sometimes she ran with one paw on each side of the crack like an angry gorilla. Sometimes her foot landed in the canyon and twisted at her ankle viciously, and then she bellowed.

We hadn't seen a single person on the trail. When we got back to the car-house, Mom sat eating her lunch and watched everyone get out of their cars and walk the opposite direction from where we had run. So after lunch, she took away my responsibility again and we followed the trail of dude-bruhs to explore where they were all going. At the bottom we found a river, and turned away from shouting and splashing dude-bruhs to find a little solitude. Mom threw a stick into the water for me. Usually I'm not a fetch dog, but sticks are terrific so I remembered that I knew how to swim and fetched the stick as many times as she would throw it. I could feel all the dust from almost two weeks in the desert washing out of my dustrous coat. From now on, that dust would only live on in my memory, and in our bedclothes. Once I had cooled off, Mom went back and found where all the dude-bruhs were hanging out. They were floating in bunch of little pools that smelled like eggs. We found an empty one, and Mom stuck her feet in up to the knees. I didn't want to touch the stuff. "Um... are you sure you want to track that into the car-house?" I asked. "It's kind of stinky."

"You're right," she admitted. "I never did like hot springs all that much. They always reminded me of dirty dishwater. They're kind of slimy." So we left to find our next home for the night.

Bingo!

The next morning Mom really nailed the planning, and we were up early so that we could hit the trail right when the sun got there to meet us. The trail was nearby, so we would have plenty of time to do a long run and be done long before the dog-roasting part of the day. The Lady Who Lives in the Phone suggested that the trail that we were going to hike/run would be eight miles, but Mom and I were prepared for ten just in case. We were finally figuring this road trip thing out: If you try to make all the things look like the plan, then you're going to miss a lot and spend the whole adventure being frustrated. Frustration can ruin even the best run, so you need to be ready to change the plan to match the trail.

The trail went up, of course, but in a way where Mom could run a lot of the time, and we covered the distance quickly. When she couldn't run we just hiked instead and that was okay too. If you only visit the trails that you can run without slowing down and hiking, you will miss white dirt, and climbing on rocks, and secret desert waterfalls. Just like you will never catch all the jackalopes in the desert, you can never run all the trails. Some of them you can't reach because your car-house gives up too far away. Some of them you can't get to because they are too long, and if you try to do the whole thing *you* are the one who will be too far away from the car-house. Some trails that you think exist simply don't, but there are others that you find where you weren't expecting one. It's a great, big world out there, and a dog could spend his whole life exploring it and never get to see the whole thing. That makes Mom anxious because she wants to see all the things, but it makes me relax because it means that I never have to finish, and no matter how long I keep exploring there will always be more adventures to have and more jackalopes to chase.

This trail went up a mountain that had almost no trees on it, and hardly any boulders even, so we could see the other mountains shrugging up across the valley. These were calmer mountains than the ones further up in the sky, and as the sun came up behind the clouds it put stripes on the mountains' sides in a way that looked more like something out of a movie than real life.

When mom let me have responsibility, there was too much exploring to do to wait for her. I just had to run ahead and sniff things, or stand proud like a statue at a windy spot on the edge of the mountain and smell the air fly by. Every once in awhile I went out of range, and Mom would tell me to "c'mere." Every time she said it, I was obedient and froze in place until she came close enough to watch me turn my butt toward her and sprint away again. That always made her squawk and point her finger emphatically at the ground, which I think is a human way of saying "good job."

When we got to where the mapp said our route ended, there was supposed to be some sort of monument, but Mom and I couldn't find it. We looked in all the bushes and behind all the rocks, but we didn't find anything more special than regular nature. The trail went on up to a higher peak, and another higher peak after that, so maybe the sign was up on one of those? But a cloud was stuck on the mountain with us. It was icy and dark inside the cloud and little rain droplets were getting in my fur. Water kills the Lady in Mom's phone, just like a witch, and Mom said that now that she doesn't have a job to replace the Phone Witch anymore, that we had to protect her. Usually we turn back because we don't have enough water, but this time we would turn back because there might be too much of it. So we turned our tails on the tippity top of the trail and raced the rain back down to the car-house.

It didn't take long before it was clear that we were going to win our race with the rain. The sun came back out, and the chill left the air. But with two miles still to run back to the car-house, the wet made a surprise comeback. Suddenly, out of nowhere, Mom's bladder started leaking all over her shorts and down her leg.

[Oscar, that's not fair. You're being deceptive. Tell them what really happened...]

That was Mom, helping me write this story. It wasn't the bladder inside of her body that failed, it was the bladder in her packpack that let go and dumped drinking water down her back, butt and legs. We stopped and adjusted everything in the pack-pack, and she squeezed her shirt and flapped her shorts to try to dry out, but there was nothing she could do about her socks and shoes, and she had to finish the run squish-squishing like a jellyfish.

After our run we consulted the Phone Witch and looked at the weather report for the spot where we planned to stop next. The forecast said it was going to snow high enough to bury me up to my belly. "Goody!!!" I said. "Fresh white dirt!"

"I don't think the van can handle driving those mountain roads in the snow…" Mom said, crushing my dreams. "And we don't have chains."

"Who needs chains?!" I said. "We're free now, remember?"

"Sorry, Oscar. I think we should head to the coast instead."

So we drove a long way without adventuring. We left the mountains and drove through orchards and fields and into hills that looked like a puppy playing under a blanket. We stopped for a potty break at a Public Bathroom & Museum dedicated a guy named James Dean who was a rebel like me. We read the museum signs outside the bathroom that taught us about how James Dean loved speed, was very handsome, and popular with the ladies. After he rode his motorcycle through the intersection that we could see from the bathrooms, he learned about the dangers of being a rebel and went on to live a long and cautious life of responsibility and always following the rules. At least that's what I think it said… I'm not good at reading without Mom's help, and she was in the bathroom.

Soon we were driving on curly roads through curly trees that reminded me of the car trips that we take within a few hours of home. We drove down one very long, very twisty road that threw me back and forth in my seat, and then suddenly we came over the top of a mountain that I didn't even realize that we were climbing, and I could see and smell the ocean stuck at the bottom of a steep, steep mountainside. We hadn't seen the ocean since the first morning of our trip, when the car-house wouldn't start and Mom and I were marooned the pirate's beach. So much had happened since then, and I was a different dog; I wondered if the ocean would notice the difference in me.

Mom and I parked the car-house at what would be our last home of the trip and took a short hike down to the beach. The last time I was on the beach, I had thought it would be pretty cool to be a pirate and live the life of an outlaw on the open seas, but after this afternoon's drive I decided that with all that swaying back and forth, a pirate's life wasn't for me. If I was going to live the life of an outlaw, I'd rather run along the canyons of the desert where ponies ran thousands of miles to deliver emails, where the bunnies are famous for their sprinting, where people worship mittens, and where the mountains are so high that their dirt turns white like the clouds.

When I looked back at Mom, she looked real sad. "What's the matter?" I asked.

"I'm sad that it's almost over," she said. "We haven't had all of the adventures yet. There's still so much left to see and do."

"But don't you want those people-things that you enjoy? Like dishwashers, showers, tea kettles, hand-washing with soap and water, and reliable cell service?"

"True, I do love those things…"

"And guess what? I'm not done having birthdays. I plan to turn four-and-a-half, and five, and six, and seven… and 84, and 85… We'll still have plenty of adventures left for those birthdays too."

"I guess you're right…" Mom said. "It'll be hard, but maybe I can find a job that will let me have more dog adventure time, even if it's for less money. Now that I know it's not scary to live like homeless people."

"And Bingo was his name-o!" said the future Nobel Prize winner of Life Coachery. I think that Mom finally understood the lesson that we'd left home to learn.

The End of the World

It was our last day in the car-house and so the last day of my birthday. We had reached the end of the world, where the mountains blink out as suddenly as when the power goes down when you're watching Mom watch Netflix. Beyond this place there was only ocean forever and ever, so there was nowhere to go from here but home. As a final challenge, Mom planned our longest hike-run of the trip for the last day. She picked the tallest mountain at the end of the world. It was eleven miles to the top, and the packpack couldn't hold enough water for us both to get all the way there and back, so we would run like a tennis ball thrown by Mom: not very high, and probably really far from where we intended to go. Then we would have to fall back down to the ocean and return the car-house to the turkey-squirrel. I think that Mom would have liked to keep climbing until she cleared the top of the mountain, and then continue running east and into the mountains and desert forever. But our Stuck House was sucking us back, and we weren't running fast enough to hit escape velocity yet.

For the first couple of miles the trail ran in the same shape as the coast along the side of the mountain, so that to our right there was a wall of mountain, and to our left there was salty air. This was one of those places that was beautiful from both close under my nose, and also if I lifted my head and smelled it from a distance. It smelled like ocean and mountain, like woods and grass, and not like city at all. The colors were so bright that I could almost see them and Mom could almost smell them. The ocean was bright like the sky, with edges the color of a 1970's bathroom, and waves exploding and fluffing against the rocks. The mountain smelled like the brightest green, with tiny little wild flowers the color of red skittles and purple skittles and an orange creamsicle. Mom said that this place is usually foggy in the morning, so she was glad that the weather had cooperated for our special day.

After about three miles on the edge of the world, the trail turned away from the ocean and into the forest. The trees went up and down like normal, but they also went sideways and diagonal in places, and Mom had to use them and rocks to cross a river back and forth. I tried to show her how it was easier for her to just walk through the water, like me, but she refused to try and said that I would understand if I wore socks.

Instead, she teetered and wobbled across, and because we were hiking with a leash I had to guess when she was going to jump or when she was going to stop. When I guessed wrong, the leash would pull on her and she'd wobble even more, make embarrassing noises, and wave her arms like those wind socks outside a car dealership that always need a lot of barking at. I encouraged her to set me free, but she said that now that we were back home people were a lot more uptight about doggie rights, and we needed to follow rules about leashes and showers and tooth brushing again if we were going to re-enter civilization.

Mom was trotting at her "forever pace," or the pace that she can maintain all day. She would run as long as it was easy, and then hike when she started breathing hard. But now that we were back at the ocean, breathing was easier and we could run a lot of the way up the mountain, so it wasn't too boring. I thought that we were probably just running on a flat trail, but every time I checked how far we were above the ocean, it was further and further below us. That meant that all of our time in running in the high mountains made running in our home mountains feel like flatland. Most mountains are longer on the way up than the way down, so this must have been a magic mountain because it felt short the whole way up.

After running in the shade of the mountain and then the shade of the trees for a few dog hours, we popped out of the trees onto a saddle with just the hats of the mountains higher than us. Mom and I stopped for a snack and a drink in the sun. Now that we were so strong from mountain experience, we probably could have handled going the last couple of miles all the way to the mountaintop, but Mom said that there was no reason to beat ourselves up.

We were about to turn back down when The Witch in Mom's Phone interrupted us with a buzz. There was cell reception up here! This was a magic mountain indeed! But it was just the Witch playing a trick on us again with one of those pretend cell signals that you get in the wilder-ness. When Mom tried to check what civilization wanted to say to us, nothing but empty Utah would load. We ran another half mile around the side of the peak with Mom holding her phone out in front of her like a baby that had just overflowed its diaper, trying to catch a hidden signal. But mountains must not need to check their updates very often, because we couldn't find any more bars to tell us how far we were from the nearest Starbucks.

That meant that it was time to finally come back to earth. We dropped back through the forest and popped out of the trees a few miles later to run back down the open mountainside. The trail was in no hurry to dive back into the water. Instead, it tried to hang on to its height by swinging from one pleat of the mountain to the next. That was poetic and symbolic and all, and maybe Mom wanted to keep running forever, but it was getting warm in the sun and I was one pooped pooch. Just like a feather, the trail did eventually settle down to the road... and just unlike a feather, I plopped down in the car-house to rest.

Mom told me that we could have a special lunch on the way home, but we would have to drive a little way first. I was starving after my long run up the magic mountain and wanted my giant quesadilla right away, but it seemed like Mom was desperate to add extra time to the adventure before it ended. Every couple of minutes Mom stopped the car-house and sat in a car conga line for long minutes waiting for a man with a sign to wave us through. "Moooom! What's going on?!" I manly-whined. "Why can't we drive to quesadillas?"

"The Big Sur Marathon comes through here next week," she said. "I think that they're trying to make sure that everything is cleaned up and the road work is done before that."

"What's the Big Sir Marathong?" I asked. "Is it something that I should be doing?"

"Heck no!" Mom spat. "The Big Sur Marathon was my first marathon, and ever since then I have an annual tradition of *not* running it. This will be the thirteenth year in a row that I observe I'm Never Doing That Again Day."

"But it's so beautiful here!" I said. "I want to do my first marathong somewhere beautiful!"

"It was cloudy and grey and not very beautiful at all when I ran it, to be honest..." she said. "And you only see the toenail of Big Sur when you run on the road. You and I ran right to the heart of it today. Isn't that nicer?"

"I suppose so..." I admitted.

"Plus, you're seeing the course right now from the comfort of your car-house! So you don't need to spend all that energy to run it!" It was true, I was beat, which is why I was curled up in my bed next to the driver's seat with my head in Mom's lap. The idea of running ten more miles sounded exhausting. "And do you want to know something extra special?" Mom went on. "...The finish line is in the same spot where you finished your New Year's 10K this year! ...*And* there's a Starbucks there!"

Now that really was something! I thought long and hard about it while we waited for the conga line to move.

I had run a long run in Big Sir. I had seen the whole course end-to-end. I had crossed the finish line. *Ergo*, I had run the Big Sir Marathong, just like Mom! What's more, since everyone else wouldn't run it till this weekend, and I was here now, well... I was in first place!

After dog-hours of quesadilla starvation, I started to smell the human smells of houses, and the car-house eased into the stop-motion of driving in civilization. Then Mom made a turn off the highway and I looked out the window and recognized where I was. This was the Starbucks at the finish line of my New Year's 10K! Which means that it was also the Official Finish Line Starbucks of the Big Sir Marathong. Which means that I got to finish my birthday vacation by winning the Big Sir Marathong before celebrating with a quesadilla the size of a frisbee, which seemed like a great end to the story.

Oscar the Cattle Dog

Just because we were home, that didn't mean that the adventures had to stop. Or, that's what Mom said when she woke me up early one morning to go to a trail we rarely visit about a week after we got back to our stuck house. When we got there, I couldn't tear my nose from the ground. There was cow poo absolutely everywhere! Mom was impatient and tried to pull on the leash, but I asked her to heel. "There are cows here!!!" I told her, urgently.

This hill is really steep. Not as steep as some of the trails that we climbed on my birthday adventure, but too steep for Mom to run the whole thing. For the first time in a long time I put my running coach collar back on. "Tell you what," I told Mom. "When you're tired and want to walk, I want you to count down from fifty before you stop running. If it's really steep, count down from thirty. If you're walking too much, I'll impose a penalty by stopping to sniff cow poo. Because it's too steep for you to pull me off of it, you'll be pinned to the spot like you're tied up outside of Starbucks until I'm done."

"Deal," Mom didn't say. Instead she whined and pulled on the leash like Bodie's squirrel sprints each time I anchored Mom for her laziness penalty.

That's how we made our way up the mountain, with Mom running as much as she could and me sniffing as much cow poo as I could. It was still dark, so I was relying on my nose to tell me what was going on.

Suddenly I could smell some very, very fresh cow poo. I looked up and there were two big eyes shining back in my spotlight. That big black blob in the darkness was a cow!!! Then, a few yards away, a bunny ran by. Oh, difficult choices! I searched deep in my heart and remembered that I am part cattle dog, so I let the bunny go and barked at the cow until I thought my heart would explode from joy.

When we got to the final scramble up to the summit, the sun was just starting to rise behind the cows on the hilltop and it was a beautiful morning. But Mom really had her hackles up about a dozen hikers who were blocking the trail. They were yowling and squawking at each other, and one was talking in the teakettle voice that I find as exciting as a dog whistle. Usually people use that voice only for dogs, but this lady was using it to talk to other people. The Tea Kettle Lady's voice made Mom bristle even more.

"Even when we run on a trail at 5:30am on a Thursday we can't get away from crowds..." Mom grumbled.

"Oh stop being such a grouch," I said. "This is lovely. It's sunrise, it's not too cold, and these people are singing flamenco!"

"Um, I think they're just speaking Cantonese, Oscar."

"Are you sure it's not flamenco?" I asked. Then I took off my running coach collar and put on the one I use for life coaching. "I have another challenge for you."

"Ooh! I love challenges! They make it fun for me to work on the problem behaviors that I find difficult!" Mom didn't say.

"You have to smile and greet every person that we meet on the way down the hill. You don't have to sniff

their butt or anything, just open yourself up to eye contact and wish them a good morning." So she did. She even had to greet the people that she thought were using our trail wrong. Some people smiled and waved back, others kept their eyes on the ground, and we even stopped to have a conversation with two nice ladies who cheered for me. I did the same hello challenge with all the cows, with even more enthusiasm but less friendliness in return.

By the time we got to the bottom we were both feeling much better about things: Mom because she had connected with other humans rather than being annoyed by and judging them; me, because I'd done what I was born to do — run around and bark at cows!

Unbirthday Present

Now that I had explored all four states in the country, the adventures near our stuck house just didn't seem as exciting as before. The trails were the same every time we visited them, and my responsibility was so strong now that it wasn't even hard to behave anymore. So one day Mom woke me up and told me that today our run wasn't just for fun, it was actually a very important assignment.

For my unbirthday, Mom bought us a big car so that we could make it into a car-house of our very own. The car still thought that it was a mailman van, and didn't know it was going to be a car-house yet, and so we had lots of things to do to train it for our next running trip. First we needed to teach it not to look like a mailman-van, so people wouldn't see it coming and think that the mailman was coming to murder them and their families. We taught it to look cool by putting black glass in its windows so that Mom and I could have privacy when we were inside, no matter where we parked.

The car-house also needed to get into shape to run thousands and thousands of miles. Even though the car-house was almost a dog century old, it hadn't spent its life running many miles a day, and we didn't know if it could keep up with the adventurous lifestyle Mom and I lead. We didn't want to get marooned again like on the last trip, so Mom paid a car-vet to do a checkup to make sure that this car-house was healthy enough for our adventure. Our new car-vet was very nice, and scratched my butt and said my name a lot, only he said it like "Oh-scar." He didn't try to dognap me at all, and let me sniff all of the filthy and fascinating things in his shop so I knew I could trust him.

Now that the mailman-van was healthy on the inside and looking sharp on the outside, my very important assignment was to ride in it all the way to the dog beach to make sure that it was healthy enough to take us to runs. It wasn't a very nice day for swimming or sunbathing because where we live there is a thing called "June gloom" which means that summer is more like winter. But that's okay because we were there to run, and the June gloom is perfect running weather!

When we got there, Mom let the car-house rest in the car kennel and took off her shoes and socks so that we could run for miles along the beach, letting the waves come up to our ankles. I love the beach so much and I couldn't decide whether I wanted to be in the waves, or digging in the sand, or chasing the birds, or barking at friends, or just exploring. So I cycled through each of those fun things for about two seconds at a time. Mom is really jealous and insecure, so every time she thought that I was in danger of making a new friend, she shouted my name and I stopped what I was doing and come closer to her so that she wouldn't feel threatened.

When Mom turned back toward the Covered Wagon, I wanted to keep going. But running without shoes is hard on a tenderpaw like Mom, and we needed to keep her healthy for our trip. "Oscar, I'm glad that you come the first or second time I call you now. Your responsibility makes me feel so much less embarrassed."

"You don't need to be embarrassed, Mom. Lots of people are jealous of their life partners. But I do think that maybe you should get some therapy about it..."

"Oh, I'm not jealous of you," Mom said. "I'm very proud that you're not such a jerk anymore and you can make friends. I'm just embarrassed because my Boston accent comes out when I shout. Why the heck did I name you Oscar?"

I had never noticed it before, but when Mom says my name it sounds more like "Aw-skuh." Now it's driving me nuts.

"So what would my name be if it wasn't Oscar?!" I asked. She calls me "Stupid" and "Poop" so much that I thought she would say one of those.

"I always kind of thought I should have named you Hector..." Mom said. Only, she said it "Hektuh."

"Oh yeah. That's way better," I said. Not because it's true, but because I love her.

Since the car-house passed the fitness test by driving to the dog beach and back, we packed all of our new things inside. We put in a sleeping pad with pillows and blankets, a string of extra lights to go around the roof, a big cooler of food, a special stove for cooking without a kitchen, and some clothes. Then we were ready to go north.

Six Star Adventure

Our first day was an adventure, and not the kind we were looking for. After all the work we did to make the car into a house, we slept our first night in a fancy hotel called the Motel Six Stars. It's not because we're not tough and resourceful campers that we spent the night in a hotel, but because we needed air conditioning and a shower for safety. You may not believe me now that we had to check into a luxury hotel for safety, but you will after you hear the story...

Mom wanted to do our first run at Lake Berryessa, which is not very far from our stay-at-home house. But Mom thinks it is very beautiful there, so we planned to stop along the way to more exotic adventures. I know Lake Berryessa is dangerous because Mom played a book in the car about a real-life mailman who killed a bunch of people there, then he acted all mysterious and puzzling like a TV murderer. But you know he was a real murderer because he killed unattractive people, and they never found out who he was, neither of which ever happens on TV. "Mom, do you think that it's such a good idea for us to be running where a murderer is on the loose?!" I asked.

"I wouldn't worry about it, Oscar. That was like fifty years ago, so he's probably too old to hike a trail that Alltrails rates as HARD. Anyway, the guy they think did it died a few years ago. We should be safe."

... "We should be safe," she said. ::eye roll emoji::

We woke up very early in the morning and arrived at the trail when there was still dew on the grass. "Mom, they forgot to mow the trail!" I said, stretching my head up so that I could see her over the grass.

"That just means that we can let you off leash because no one uses this trail much. Let's go mow it ourselves with our feet!" Mom said.

"Okay, cool. I'm going to go chase this deer then," I said.

There was no risk of losing Mom because the "squelch, squelch, squelch" noise that her shoes made from all the water that jumped from the grass to her socks let me know where she was at all times, so I ran ahead. If I couldn't hear her shoes anymore I stopped and ate salad until she came back into view. "OSCAR! NO!" she screamed when she came around the corner and saw me eating some superfoods.

"But Mom, salads are good for you. Athletes like me need the fiber and phytonutrients to be healthy."

"That's foxtail," she said. "Its fibers have little microscopic hooks on them. They burrow into your skin and never come out until you go to the vet and have very expensive, scary surgery." I thought that cliffs and stripey stink-cats were dangerous, but I didn't know that you could get hurt from eating enough fiber.

As we hiked, I kept thinking I could hear a tiny little voice saying, "Hang on boys, here he comes!" And then more little voices screaming, "Bomb's awaaaaay!" When we stopped for water halfway to the top, I scratched my ear hard with my paw and said, "Mom, I have itches."

Mom took a closer look. "Holy dung, Oscar. You're covered in ticks! I can see them from here!"

"Ow! What are ticks?" I asked as she picked at me with her pinchers.

"They're awful little bugs that hide in your fur and suck your blood for days until they blow up like nasty balloons. Sometimes you don't even notice they're there and then they give you horrible diseases. I think that we should go back…"

"But back that way is where all the ticks came from," I pointed out. "Now that I've got a thousand ticks on me, it's not like another thousand is going to make a difference. Let's keep exploring."

"I don't know, Oscar. I had a friend that got lyme disease. She went a little daffy and no one could figure out what was wrong with her for years. Even her doctor and her psychiatrist thought she was crazy."

"Don't worry, Mom. They can't hurt me. Anyway, I take medicine that makes me like poison to ticks, and I'm too handsome for something so nasty…" Then Mom screamed. She often screams when we're running because she trips or rolls her ankle, but those screams sound more like roars. This sounded like a cartoon haunted house scream. "What is it?" I asked, running back to her. She had frozen very, very still, but once I was behind her, she slowly stepped in my way to block me from the trail.

"What... the duck... kind of snake... is that?!" she asked slowly and quietly, but like her voice was about to explode. Not an inch from where I'd just run by was a coiled-up spaghetti monster the size of a big pile of cow poop. We don't know much about spaghetti monsters, but this one was as big around as a banana, and rather than those dopey eyes that you see on some boring spaghetti muppets, this one was scowling at us villainously. There was something about its big, flat head that looked like something you might see on TV. It's not the dopey snakes that get the TV contracts... it's the murderer-snakes. "See?!" I said. "I told you that Berryessa is full of murderers!"

But Mom was already pushing me back down the hill saying, "Nope, nope, nope, nope, nope. I'm not doing this..."

When we got back to the car-house, Mom set about picking all the ticks off of me. There were so many of them! Mom says that sometimes I exaggerate a little bit, but she is sure that she pulled off between fifty and a hundred of them. She even stuck her fingers in the private places where only vets usually touch, and everywhere she pinched her fingers, she come away with more ticks. I'm surprised I'm not bald from all the fur she pulled away with them.

After pulling out one hundred ticks, she looked around and realized that we were still standing in grass. While she had been pulling all the ticks off of one leg, more ticks were climbing up the other three. So she took me to stand in the middle of the street while she kept picking. But she still kept finding more and more and more ticks. We looked down at the ground, and there were the dozens of ticks that she had pulled off and thrown on the ground, marching toward me and back up my legs. So we ran about ten yards down the road and then Mom went back to picking. Once she'd pulled off another dozen or so, she marched me down the street a little further so the ticks we'd already pulled off couldn't hop back on. When she was satisfied that she'd found most of them, we still needed to figure out how to escape. Mom didn't want to let me and the ticks into the car-house, but we had to get out of here somehow.

Before we could drive away to safety, Mom had to check my belly for ticks. Despite all the attention she was giving me, I didn't like the look in her eye so I didn't want to roll on my back to let her give me belly scratches. Mom wrestled me so furiously anyway that we ripped down the curtains that we had just hung the day before. Mom was being such a maniac that I had to finally submit and lay still while she picked over the lush white hair on my belly.

When Mom left the car-house to get in the driving chair, I got confused and started to jump back outside with her. "NO!" she screamed, so I pulled my front paws back inside. They hadn't been touching the ground for even a full second, and already there were four ticks on my legs. When Mom was finally satisfied that she had de-ticked the best she could, she pulled the door shut, and in that moment a tick fell from her hat. There were also ticks in Mom's fur, and her clothes, and her socks.

We drove a short way to the lake, where she threw a stick far into the water for me. I had to swim out a long way to get it, and when I brought it back she threw it back in over and over. I thought that was marvelous, and could feel all the ticks flying off of me when I shook off the water. But the know-it-all Witch that Lives in Mom's Phone said that ticks can live underwater for days, and that we would have to take even more drastic steps to be safe.

The Witch claimed that the only thing that gets rid of ticks and their eggs is a special shampoo and a very long and vigorous bath. I think she made that part up just to make me suffer, and also to keep Mom out of nature and in places where The Witch has lots of bars and wifi. But Mom is real gullible and believes everything that The Witch tells her, so she started thinking about where we could find a bath.

The Witch was probably grouchy because *she* was having problems of her own. See, The Witch needs to be fed many times a day in order for her to tell us where we are at all times, and answer our questions about ticks. But today The Witch's feeding tube wasn't working for some reason. In fact, none of the stuff that we were plugging into the car-house was working, including the box that kept my cheese safe, the kettle that makes Mom's poop juice, or the portable Witch food we could carry with us in case The Witch needed life support.

So we went where all desperate travelers go when they're in trouble and need help: Wal*Mart. We had to drive an hour to get there, and when we arrived, the car-house started screaming. Mom finally tore her eyes away from The Witch, and found that the car-house was crying for help with a warning light on the dashboard. *Oh bother and tarnation!* Now everyone was having an emergency.

Mom was facing a decision. She had to decide whether to save her brave and handsome dog, The Witch that Lives in Her Phone, our cheese and eggs, the car-house, or herself. She bought the shampoo first, but decided to keep the ticks along for the adventure until the car-house was fixed. We found a car-vet, who said that he would need to take the car-house for a long time so he could check it out, so Mom, and the ticks, and The Witch, and I were turned out on the street for a few hours.

While we were waiting, Mom asked for The Witch's help again, and searched for a groomer nearby. She found one, but The Witch had pulled another dirty trick because this place was *a vet's office!!!* I had never been there before, but I could smell the fear and hear the misery coming from the back room, and I was not fooled. I clamped my tail over my tick-hole and tried to make myself an anchor so I didn't have to go inside. Luckily, the vet said that just like the car-house, they couldn't fix me without first giving me an exam. Since I already have a vet, Mom said that that wasn't necessary. They told us that a tick couldn't spread disease until it had been sucking on a handsome dog's blood for a day or two, so we were still safe. And since I am a responsible dog who takes my medication on time, I am poisonous to all things filthy and disgusting. Their advice was that Mom should just continue picking the ticks off of me, and that they would probably all be dead before they could make me sick.

"And what about humans," Mom asked, pulling another wriggling tick from her own fur as she said it.

Mom picked ticks off of me outside the vet's office for a very long time, trying to think of where we could find a shower. We learned on our last trip that staying in car-house parks and campgrounds when you're in a city is kind of scary because some of the people that live there are so bad at responsibility that they aren't allowed to live anywhere else. Also, they often have rules about handsome dogs using the human showers, or pouring tick-shampoo suds onto the grass. And who knew if the car-house would even be healthy enough to continue on our trip, or if it would have to stay in the hospital overnight.

Eventually we went back to the car-vet and waited and picked and scratched some more. When the vet was finally finished, he came to show us what was wrong. "Your car is fine," he said. "You just blew a fuse by plugging in something too powerful." He was talking about the box that keeps my cheese and eggs cold. "The brake sensor runs off the same fuse, so that's why it turned on. I replaced the fuse, and so you can drive it away right now!"

Mom couldn't believe her luck. "That's wonderful! So how much does that cost?"

"Two dollars and twenty-two cents," the man said.

I thought that must be a lot of money, and I think Mom did too because she said, "You're kidding!"

"Well…" said the car-vet, "Plus the $130 diagnostic fee…" They don't teach math classes in puppy school, but I know that a one is smaller than a two, so I guessed that maybe that wasn't a lot of money after all. Good news all around! "And I'll give you a spare fuse for free, in case it happens again," said the car-vet. So not only was the car-house okay and we got a bargain on repairs, but we also got a free fuzz in case we need to fix the car-house ourselves. Our luck was starting to turn!

Mom didn't want either of us spending much time in the car-house until we could wash the ticks off. It was too hot to sit in a parked car-house anyway. So that's how we wound up at the Motel Six Stars. Mom said that at the same price as a car-house exam, a night at the Six Stars is outrageously priced, and that this has been the most expensive trail run she has ever done in her life. But I reminded her that free places like The Ritz are only five stars, and you have to pay for luxury.

We took a long shower in the spa-like shower tardis, and Mom used the tick shampoo on both of our fur, even though it said all over the bottle that it's only supposed to be for dogs. Then we each got two more washings with the special shampoo, just to make sure. Then we spent the rest of the evening sitting in air conditioning. The car-house stayed downstairs in the car kennel taking its own tick medication, my cheese stayed safe in a refrigerator, and The Witch sat happily sucking power from a wall. To apologize for giving me such a vigorous bath, Mom served me a very special dinner of hard boiled eggs and a new treat called Spam, which is like hard boiled bacon.

Sometimes adventure needs to test you to make sure that you wouldn't rather just spend the time relaxing at home. But we had definitely earned six star adventures from then on. We would try again tomorrow.

Ready Doggo One

The next day was much better. Mom and I left the Motel Six Stars when it was still the middle of the night so that we could catch up with our adventure. Mom wanted to be on the trail early because she thought it might get hot if we started too late, but she needn't have worried because we did start late and it didn't get hot. After about five dog hours in the car-house, several get-losts and some trail driving, we found the trailhead. There were some guys sleeping in a tent in the spot where we parked, and they were just waking up when we got there. I wished that Mom had thought of that.

Mom read the information sign to me; it said, "You are entering a special place.." Then it said nothing at all about leashes! So Mom and I set each other free to explore the Special Place in our own ways, which for me was a mix of sprinting and waiting, and for Mom it was a mix of hiking and something that looked a little bit like running.

Mom was still on edge about all the dangers the day before, and spent most of the adventure picking her fingers through her head fur looking for ticks, but eventually even she settled in and started enjoying The Special Place. Instead of tall tick grass, the ground was covered in soft pine needles, and prickly pine cones, and lots and lots of rocks of all sizes for us to run over.

If there were a beauty contest for trails, this one wouldn't even make it to the semifinal round, but the thing about nature is that there isn't only eye beauty, there's also leg beauty. Some of the trails with epic views and incredible colors and fascinating smells are so boring and monotonous for your legs. The Special Trail trail was like a video game for our legs, and a puzzle game for our feet. There were so many bends and rocks and pine cones and roots on the trail that I had to pick my path strategically, and then my legs had to land in just the right place and bounce in just the right way or it was Game Over. Sometimes I leapt over a rock like a horse, and other times I used a rock to vault myself even faster down the trail. Sometimes it made sense to cross a stream by jumping from rock to rock, and sometimes it made more sense to kick my paws up high and splash straight through. Unlike the boring paths we run at home that use the same muscles over and over like a backbeat, this trail used every muscle in my hunky body in neverending combinations like an orchestra. Mom's running wasn't as nice to look at, but her footwork got frisky in her own plodding and deliberate way. She ran less like an orchestra and more like marching band of people puppies playing recorders and kazoos.

We were planning to run a loop path, but just when we got to the furthest point where running forward was supposed to start curving back toward the car-house, the trail disappeared under some of that magnificent white dirt. Since we weren't planning on going any higher, and white dirt only lives at the tops of mountains, Mom thought maybe we could hike through the white dirt for awhile and soon we would go down in elevation a little bit and the trail would poke out from underneath. We were right at the border of the white dirt, so it couldn't be far, she explained like she knew what she was talking about.

So we wandered around in circles, looking for something in the blankness that looked like it might be leading somewhere. Suddenly, my legs disappeared into the white dirt up to my leg pits and I was left standing in the snow on my belly like a baked potato. I climbed out and Mom and I would have laughed about it, except at that very moment Mom disappeared to halfway up her thighs. The white dirt was blissfully cold and she was wearing shorts, so she had less of a sense of humor about it. She said that we should probably go back down the way we'd come because of safety.

When we got back to the car-house, Mom had hiked-run almost nine miles, and I'd hiked closer to eighty-two, and our legs were sore. So after a lunch Mom and I went to a river to stand in the cold water, which is supposed to help our legs recover, but also makes some of us less stinky.

Instead of camping out in a six star motel that night, we were going to learn from the two guys we'd seen that morning and sleep at the bottom of tomorrow's trail. When we pulled off the main highway and onto a dirt road, Mom looked at the map to see how far we had to go to the trailhead. "That can't be right," she said as she zoomed out and out and out to get all of the dirt road in the picture. It looked like we were going to have to drive for years on this car trail to get to the trailhead. A human hour and a half later, we were still driving (although to be fair, Mom did have to stop the car-house and get out a bunch of times to throw big rocks off the road and over the side of the mountain so that it would be safe for driving). We drove up so high that we could see the mountains all around us, and it was very beautiful. But Mom was getting sick of driving the car-house so slow, and I wasn't entirely sure if it was a good idea to be driving our ex-mailman-van on such a rough road without proper training. So when we were maybe close to the end (but maybe not really, there was no way to tell), Mom stopped the car-house and said, "Right! That's good enough! We're sleeping here. We'll see how we feel in the morning and decide whether we drive the rest of the way, or just run from here."

The Covered Wagon

Now that we were in the woods and miles away from a paved road, we were real western explorers like the Oregon trail adventurers and the Donner Party... only the Donner Party had a little more success than we did, because some of them got to their destination. Mom decided to drive the car-house a little further up the mountain from where we'd slept to see if we could find the trailhead. The problem was that The Witch in Mom's Phone was ignoring us, so we had to try to figure things out for ourselves. When we came to a place where four trails crossed, we left the car-house and continued exploring on foot.

Since we're good explorers, we know that most car trails go toward the spot where the mountains are the lowest, and most running trails tend to go toward where the mountain is highest. Therefore, the trail would meet the road at a spot right before the road went downhill. Or so Mom figured. If we chose the car trails that went toward the nearest peak, and stayed away from the ones that went downhill, then eventually we would find the spot where the road and trail parted ways. So when we came to a place where four roads met, we decided to run up the road that went uphill in the direction of the peak. But after about two miles, the trail disappeared under the most giant tree I'd ever seen, lolling on its side and blocking the whole road from the cliff side to the mountain side. So we turned around a tried a different way.

When we got back to the intersection, we followed a road that went uphill but seemed to be moving away from the peak. This one ended in a big, round dirt area less than a mile from the intersection, so again we turned around and went back.

We knew that the trail we were looking for wasn't in the direction that we'd come from, so that only left the trail that went downhill and away from the peak. It couldn't be down there, because that would mean that Mom's Made-up Rules of Wilder-ness Navigation were wrong, and Mom told me that she had never been wrong in her life. It was okay that the trail didn't exist though, because Mom was feeling the joy she gets when she is the victim of someone doing something stupid and she gets to complain about it. I didn't want to point out that Mom had invented the rules herself, so it was no good to get mad that the world wasn't following them. I was enjoying exploring and didn't want to make her grumpy by suggesting she might be wrong. So we ran blissfully down the road where we were *sure* to never find the trailhead.

After going down the "it's definitely not here" road for just over a mile, much to our surprise we found a sign nailed to a pole in the middle of the wilder-ness. It was the trail that we were looking for! It had been less than two miles away from where we'd given up and spent the night! The problem was that the trail was an eleven-mile loop, and we'd already run more than six, and Mom had drunk most of our water. So we couldn't see the whole thing without death overtaking us, and would have to turn around at some point.

The trail was messy like no one had cleaned up in a really long time, with sticks and pine cones covering the path so thoroughly that our feet could barely find it. The trail climbed steep like a ladder, not shallow like a staircase. I bet if we just got to the top we would get really high and there would be some great views for Mom to sniff. But Mom said that she was getting icked out by all the spiderwebs getting caught in her sweat, and she was hungry and wanted to go back to the car-house now.

"Mom, do you think we're safe ten miles up on the mountain with The Witch ignoring us?" I asked. Then I remembered how our last car-house had been scared of steep downhills and shuddered when we were driving on them. "Do you think the car-house can get back safely???"

"Gosh, I sure hope so. Otherwise we're in some serious doo-doo..." Mom said, like she wasn't really convinced herself. "I don't know how those covered wagons made it through this terrain in the Old West days."

"What's a covered wagon?"

"When the Oregon Trail explorers traveled this way, they put everything they needed in these old-fashioned wagons that were white and round on top and didn't move very fast."

"Our mailman-van has all our stuff in it, and is old fashioned and white and rounded, and doesn't move very fast! Is it a covered wagon? Are we Oregon Trailers?"

"Not exactly, but close enough..."

Just like the Donner Party, we all made it safely off the mountain with no stories to tell. Our next stop was almost five hours away and the Old Us never would have been able to find it without The Witch's cooperation, but Mom is getting better at exploring. She'd taken a picture of the list of all the turns we needed to take, just in case. It was like a modern version of the prehistoric gas station paper, or MapQuest. "Let's just hope that we don't have to take a detour," Mom said. "If we have to deviate from the instructions, then we're in trouble."

It was getting pretty hot in the Covered Wagon once it got to be afternoon, so we stopped for a river swim to cool off and so that Mom could wash the sweat and cobwebs off of her. I like swimming in lakes and ponds to rescue sticks, but I don't trust water that moves on its own, like rivers and the ocean. Mom kept throwing sticks into the water, and I kept running out to a big underwater rock that I could stand on to wait for the sticks to drift by. The sticks kept coming close, some of them within an inch or two of my nose, but they never came close enough for me to pluck them out of the water.

I watched stick after stick drift by, and barked after them once they had flowed out of reach. "Hey! Stick! Stick, come back!"

"Why don't you swim after it, stupid?" Mom laughed, not unkindly.

"Because I'm a runner, not a swimmer. Duh! Why don't you throw better? You're worse at pitching than you are at running."

"Oscar, when you want something great you can't just wait for the current to bring it right to you. Sometimes you've got to put in effort to help luck along. You've got to swim after it!"

"Who's the life coach here?!" I asked. "If you chase the wrong stick, then you wind up up to your neck in cold water and drifting away from your rock where you were warm and dry and had a good view. Then you have to paddle like crazy just to get back to where you were in the first place. You wind up spending all your energy on paddling rather than chewing up the stick. There will always be more sticks. Success is about waiting for the right opportunity."

"But look at us this morning. We drove up that whole mountain and then stopped searching just before we found the trail, and as a result we didn't get to explore it."

She did have a point there... "Well that's because The Witch is out to get us. Usually if you don't succeed it's someone else's fault," I explained.

"I'm pretty sure that's not good advice," Mom said. But she's not the expert.

We continued driving toward the next day's trail for many more hours, using a very zoomed-out map that showed practically the whole Oregon Trail for guidance. We were supposed to be less than a human hour from the end when we pulled up short in front of a sign blocking the road. "ROAD CLOSED AHEAD" the sign shouted.

This was very, very bad. Mom looked at the zoomed-out map and saw that we would have to go halfway across Oregon to find another route. "Unless..." she said, zooming in. "...it looks like there's a road here!" So we backtracked for about an hour and a half until we found the road. By now we were both cranky and ready for dinner, but we also needed to find a good place to stop.

After ten miles, the new road turned into a dirt road too. "I think this road must be forty or fifty miles long, Oscar..." Mom said, poking at the map again. "I'm not driving fifty miles on a dirt road in a minivan. I think that we're going to need to take the long way around to get out of here."

"Sometimes you just need to go a little bit further to get the prize," I reminded her. "Remember the stick? According to your life coaching advice we should keep going on the dirt road and just try a little harder."

"Okay, fine, you're right," Mom said, like she wanted to start a fight, not end it. "Sometimes you just have to give up and wait for another opportunity... Let's go find the nearest campground."

Devil's Punchbowl

Do you ever have one of those days that doesn't work out the way you had planned, and then everything goes wrong, and it still turns out okay in the end? That was what our last day California was like. After having to backtrack for some hours the day before to find a paved road, we were going to have to drive another many more hours, cross half of Oregon, and then come back into California to get to the trail that we wanted to run. Don't think we didn't think about just skipping it and moving on with our trip, but Mom and I agreed that "The Devil's Punchbowl" is a really cool name for a trail, and since The Witch wasn't talking to us, we didn't know where there were other dog-friendly and Covered-Wagon-friendly trails with cool names. Plus, AllTrails said that there was a people potty at the trailhead. How hard could it be to get there if there was a perma-potty there? It's not like they build toilet tardises on the tops of mountains in the middle of the wilder-ness, right?

So we got up very, very early in order to get to the trail when it was still a little bit early. I visited Oregon for the first time and traveled over a hundred miles without ever leaving the Covered Wagon, and then we came back to California. In California there was a man who must have been very hungry for salad, because he was making all the cars stop so that he could check them for plants. "Do you know if the Forest Route is open?" Mom asked him when she rolled down the window. "We're trying to hike the Devil's P—" but she didn't finish because she was flinching from my powerful lungs screeching into her ear.

"...Because we've been on a seven-hour detour, and I haven't pooped yet, and we really want to hike this trail...!" I explained from my spot in the front seat.

"The Devil's Punchbowl?" he asked. So he *did* know it! It must be famous and very easy to get to. The Hungry Man said that he wasn't an expert on how to get there, but he knew that the road we were looking for was open, and it was even paved! Today was going to be a good day.

But when we got to the open, paved road, there was a sign that said, "ROAD CLOSED AHEAD."

"Maybe our parking lot is before the road closure..." Mom said hopefully.

"That's what you said yesterday," I said. "Before the seven-hour overnight detour."

The road was very beautiful, but steeper than any car road that I'd ever seen before. When we drove up it, the Covered Wagon's nose was so much higher than its butt that everything inside the car-house slipped downhill as we drove. Then suddenly, out of nowhere, our way was blocked by a big gate, and behind that a concrete barrier, and behind that a pile of rocks. Someone *really* didn't want us to hike this trail.

Mom had to drive backwards down the steep, narrow road for what felt like forever until she found a place to park the Covered Wagon so that we could sit and think about what to do next. Once we had pulled in, we could see that there was another car parked in the flat spot next to the steep road.

"Good morning!" said the man who came out of the other car.

"Grrr! I am so frustrated right now!" growled Mom, who is poorly socialized and never meets friendly people with the right attitude.

"What's that fluffy thing stuck to your face, you big weirdo!" I barked at him. "I don't like it!"

"It just means that we'll have a longer hike today than expected," said the smiling, wooly monster.

"That's it!" Mom said to me, "We're doing the nine-mile trail, **plus** the five miles each way to and from the trailhead." The one thing that will guarantee that Mom will commit to doing something hard is if someone nicer and more cheerful than her says that they are going to do it too. It's okay to be outperformed by a jerk, but if Mom gives up before someone with the personality of a marshmallow, she couldn't look herself in the rear view mirror in the morning. So while the Wooly Marshmallow climbed over the barrier, and the barrier behind the barrier, and the barrier behind that, Mom packed extra snacks and put lots of water into our biggest packpack.

Once we got to the wild side of the barrier, I could see that we had another thrilling problem: the white dirt was everywhere! It was piled higher than Mom in places, and sometimes it covered the whole trail for fifty or more yards at a time. I had never seen anything so wonderful in my life, and did gymnastics, and sprints, and digging, and biting and each one was fantastic. Mom, who was wearing shorts and low socks and doesn't appreciate the white dirt because she had many traumatic windshield ice scrapings as a puppy, wasn't as enthusiastic about it, and wanted to turn back. But soon we caught up to The Marshmallow again.

"What's with your giant packpack and those stupid sticks you're carrying?" I shouted at him. "You look like a turtle walking with chopsticks!"

"Do you think there's this much snow on the whole trail?" Mom asked him.

"I don't know," he said. "But I have the GPS to guide me, so if it's covered in snow then I will just go slower." The Witch had GPS too, but it wasn't very good since she was still giving us the cold shoulder. "I have my stuff to camp on the mountain overnight if it takes too long," he said, tapping his turtle shell. This guy really wasn't giving Mom a way out, since Mom is always out to prove that preparation is a waste of time. "But you're really going to have to hustle if you plan to make it back to your car before dark," he warned. Oh brother, if Mom could ever find it within herself be outdone by a marshmallow, she could *never* give up if someone suggests she *can't* do it.

...So we were doing this.

It turned out that even if the road hadn't been closed, we still would have had to park the Covered Wagon many miles from the mythical trailhead potty, because soon the road turned into what Mom calls a "fire road," which is one of those trails that is easy for running, but very hard for mail-man vans. Plus there were the heaps of white dirt. Of the five miles we had to go to the trailhead, only about one mile of it was covered in the white dirt, and much of that Mom could pick her way around without getting her socks wet by walking very, very carefully on the edge of the mountain. The rest of the time we ran, and put distance between ourselves and the Marshmallow and his dumb tent, and his useless extra layers, and his stupid GPS, and that darned friendly smile.

Finally we found the toilet at the trailhead. Someone really had traveled miles and miles into the wilder-ness to install a tardis so that they could poop in privacy, and then open the door to the view of mountains above and sky below. Wonders never cease...! But whatever industrious nature-loving and well-hydrated human had built the potty hadn't bothered to bring a shovel up here to dig it out from under several feet of white dirt. And so it sat alone in the car kennel, sealed shut by white dirt piled an Oscar high outside its door.

Now that we were on the real trail, we could follow the route without much trouble, even though it meant prancing and stomping through the jacket of white dirt that covered the ground. We saw little streams trying to become waterfalls, and we heard a deep noise coming from redwoods that sounded like someone tooting on a didgeridoo.

Then we reached a clearing that looked like a great, blank field of white dirt but sounded like a troop of mailmen unrolling packing tape. "What's that noise?" I asked, looking for a hint in all of that emptiness. I ran into the middle of the clearing to look for a clue, and the snoring of the packing tape stopped abruptly.

"Be careful, Oscar," Mom called after me. There's a swamp or a pond or something under that snow, and I doubt the ice will hold."

There were no other footprints to follow anywhere, and no sign about where the trail might be buried, so while Mom looked carefully for clues around the outside of the clearing, I ran over every inch of that meadow like a fearless alpine explorer. I left hundreds of loops of pawprints to confuse the Marshmallow when he came through. I also kept half-disappearing into the drifts of white dirt and so left plenty of bellyprints too.

It was even worse for Mom, who is bigger and fatter and less snow-resistant. She kept falling through up to her waist, and then when she tried to get out, she would fall back in again with her next step. If you ever go up there yourself to see the millions of pawprints I left behind, there probably won't be much white dirt left for you to see because it all went into Mom's socks. We eventually found the way out of the meadow, but soon we lost the trail again. Mom could see on the map that her blue dot was only a few yards from the line of the trail, but every time we thought we were getting close, we would just find ourselves standing in a bush, or a fallen-down tree, or a giant white dirt pile. The more we explored, the more the snow ate our legs and the more confused Mom became.

We knew from the trail description that there would be some "very challenging" switchbacks later on, and we weren't sure what made them "challenging." Maybe they were the fall-off-a-cliff kind of challenging, which didn't seem like a great idea with the trail hidden under white dirt, even for a brave dog like me.

"That one guy on AllTrails said that he carried his wife on his back for two miles when she got tired," I cautioned Mom.

"Yeah, I call BS on that review..." Mom said. "First of all, what grown woman consents to ride piggyback for two miles. Secondly, how could it possibly be so technical that she couldn't go on, but the reviewer was still able to navigate it with an adult human on his back?" That's the problem with reviews: Most of the people leaving them are either marshmallows, liars, dumb, or so out of shape that they need to ride half the trail on their hiking partner's backs. "You can't trust a word anyone says in a review..." Mom explained.

Even though Mom had no intention of riding on my back if she got tired, she still thought that it might be dangerous for us to keep looking for the Devil's Punchbowl in case there were cliffs. So even though we were going to be outperformed by a friendly marshmallow, we turned around and went back to the Covered Wagon. It was hard to be too disappointed, though, because we had seen mountains and trees and streams, and by the time we were done we would have run and hiked fourteen tough miles of adventure.

When we were so close to the Covered Wagon that we could practically see it, we had to pass a spot where something had taken a big bite out of the road.

This bite was why they had built the barrier to keep people out. I thought that something had happened with the weather, and part of the road had just fallen off the side of the mountain, but as I passed by, I saw something moving just over the edge.

"Holy dog doo!" I screamed, backing up. "Dog doo! Dog doo! Dog doo! There's a thing!" I barked, hiding my panic behind a macho screech.

"It's just some plastic, Oscar," Mom laughed. "The road workers must have left it there to protect the pavement from water damage and keep the ground from crumbling more." She had survived walking past The Thing and was on the downhill side of it. The Thing must be really mad now that it had missed Mom, and it would be even more bloodthirsty for a ripe, juicy victim.

I turned on my heels and started running back up the mountain, barking "Nope, nope, nope, nope, nope" the whole time, just like when Mom saw the battlesnake.

"Come back!" Mom said. "You can walk on the far side of the road, see? You don't have to get close to it."

"Heavens no! I always thought that you were exaggerating when you said that there's a monster that pulls you off of cliffs if you get too close to the edge. But it's real! *I JUST SAW IT!*" I kept running up the mountain and back toward the Devil's Punchbowl. My plan was to run back up to the world's most beautiful and remote potty and live there forever, eating sticks for food and white dirt for water.

But when I turned around, I saw that Mom hadn't followed me. My choices were to either run past The

Monster to rejoin Mom on the civilization side, or abandon Mom forever. Then Mom started running downhill and away from me. I had to make the hardest decision of my life, and I had to make it quickly.

I cautiously approached the spot where The Thing had taken a bite out of the road, and when I got close, I quietly and quickly ran past The Thing as lightly as I could. Once I was safely on the other side I didn't even slow down to greet Mom, I just kept right on running away from The Monster, checking over my shoulder the whole time to make sure that it wasn't following me.

Luckily, it didn't chase us and we lived to drive the Covered Wagon down off the mountain. The Covered Wagon was working so hard not to fall down the hill that it smelled like stinky burning by the time we got back to the highway, but we were safe from The Monster now because there was nothing to fall off of anymore.

There's no way of knowing what happened to The Marshmallow, but he let me lick his legs when we met him on our return, so I sure hope that he wasn't ripped off the side of the mountain by The Thing. Meanwhile, Mom

and I decided to sleep by the beach, where there's no white dirt to block the roads, and everything is flat, flat, flat all the way to Japan, and there is nothing to fall off of.

Humbug

After the white dirt stole so many of our roads the day before, Mom decided that we should leave the mountains and travel through Oregon along the coast instead. Since we'd abandoned the plan, we needed to find a new trail to explore. If I let Mom pick the trail, we would spend the whole day inside the car-house looking at mapps, so I needed to trick her into making a quick decision. Humans love to judge things with stars and likes and swipes, so I gave Mom a judging assignment; I told her to pick the trail with the coolest name, and then I reminded her check the reviews.

"I always check the reviews," Mom protested. "Okay, I *sometimes* check the reviews," she added after a moment.

"So why did we hike the one with the reviews that said, 'The road is closed?'" I asked.

"I thought that was just a temporary thing."

"What about the one that said, 'It's covered in white dirt?'"

"Well two winters ago was very snowy. I thought it might be an old review."

"What about the lady that said, 'I'm giving this five stars even though I haven't hiked it yet'?"

"Well that one *could* have turned out alright..."

Anyway, my trick worked because coolest trail name we could find was Humbug Mountain, whose trailhead actually touched the highway so we didn't have to do any extra driving. Things sure are easier when you don't complicate them with human thoughts.

After hiking in so many deserts and exotic mountaintops, Humbug Mountain smelled a lot like our trails at home in the wintertime: like wet dirt, and ocean, and shade, and the breath of millions of leaves. It was a dirt path just wide enough for one hiker at a time to twist and wind their way through redwoods and ferns and moss and things, so it even *looked* familiar.

Ever since Mom stopped running fast a few years ago, the amount of discomfort that she's willing to put up with has gotten less and less, and our pace has gotten slower and slower until lately what she's doing can barely be called running at all. When I run it feels like there should be exciting trumpets playing in the background, but these days Mom runs like a tuba sounds. But not today. Maybe it was because the trail felt so familiar that Mom ran almost the whole way to the top of the Humbug without needing to walk and rest. It was like the old days when we used to do "training" rather than just running at whatever pace falls most comfortably out of Mom's legs.

"What's gotten into you?" I asked.

"Oscar, I've discovered what my butt is for again!" she said.

"Mom... I don't want to hurt your feelings, but there's only one member of this family with the assets to be a butt model. And it's not you..."

"No! I mean I just rediscovered the muscles in my butt and how they help me run strong! It's like I've been stuck in a low gear, and just found my big ring. I was sitting on it the whole time!"

"Your what?" I immediately regretted getting her started. When Mom winds herself up about movement mechanics, she forgets that it's not polite to talk when you're boring.

"Look! As I've gotten lazier I've gotten into the habit of running like this because it's less springy and takes less effort..." she leaned over like she was trying to push an upright piano into the wind. "But the reason it takes less effort is because it switches off your glutes and you're just using your hamstrings to pull your body forward, and your calves..." Then my brain turned off and I thought about interesting things for a while like cats and cold eggs while she droned on about too much sitting at a desk and tight hip flexors and stuff. "...But now that I'm not sitting at a desk all day, and we're moving over so many different surfaces, all of the muscles in my legs are waking up again! I'm remembering how to move, and that my butt isn't just a cushion for sitting on...!" Cheese and rice! She really could go on and on... I'm telling you guys, her butt really isn't anything special.

"...I just stand up straight like this, see?" she said, pulling herself high like she was trying to look taller. "And then I can drive my knee a little higher, see?" and her leg swung a millimeter further in front of her before landing on the ground. *Whoop-dee-doo.* "And then that weird hitch in my right hip and the hunch in my back go away, plus it gives me the lift to spring off using my glutes rather than..." I stopped listening again. She really is a snooze sometimes.

But as I watched her run, I had to admit that she did look a lot better. She wasn't running like heralding trumpets or anything, but more like a people puppy trying to play the recorder; it wasn't pretty, but at least you could recognize the tune.

After the Humbug, Mom remembered that driving the coast involves a lot of stop lights and is actually kind of boring. Once you've seen one big rock climbing out of the waves like a Wild Thing, you've seen 'em all. So we went back inland toward a trail with a waterfall that looked on the mapp like it was next to the highway. It was true that it was only about twenty miles off of the highway, but one thing that we're learning about The West is that most of it is so empty that it turns into wilder-ness in a shorter distance than a Tuesday morning run. I'm surprised that the roads don't go out of business with so few cars driving on them. Humans don't chew on things when they're bored, so building roads in the wilder-ness is a good way to keep busy if your teeth aren't sharp enough to chew through a flip flop, I guess. We traveled for half a dog hour along a narrow mountain road before the road gave up and turned back to dirt. This place was so remote, and we were tucked in so tight to the mountain, that The Witch couldn't even find us to move our blue dot. We decided to just park the car-house and see what we could find. We looked out over the side of the mountain at waves of hills as far as the eye could see. On each hilltop we could see several miniature dirt roads ending together in a clearing just big enough to turn your covered wagon around in. Just think of all the places you could get lost if you used MapQuest in here!

In our clearing was a deep and vibrant grey lake with a very steep wall behind it. It looked like a giant tostada bowl. Mom said that this is what a "rock quarry" looks like, which is a place where people mine rocks.

"What's in the rocks?" I asked.

"I don't think anything's in them. They're just for people who need rocks, I suppose."

"Why would you need rocks?"

"I don't know… for construction, maybe? Or gravel paths? Maybe they just grind up the mountain so that they can build gravel roads for people to get lost on all the other mountains." …The things that humans dream up keep busy when they could just be tearing a slipper to ribbons!

We tried to hike around the quarry, but the trail didn't go very far at all. All over the place there were empty soda bottles, and beer cans, and old food wrappers, and a pile of burnt wood, and signs that yelled "NO CAMPFIRES." We stopped in a few more places, and everywhere we went it seemed like the spot was so remote that no one would ever find it, and yet there was so much trash that you would think an entire human city must have lived there until last week.

"How do all of these people know about this place?" I asked. "We only found it because we are very lost."

"I don't know, Oscar. I'm starting to wonder if maybe we're missing out on something living in a place where you can't even find a parking space without somebody telling you to scat. More than forty percent of the western states is public land. Wouldn't it be great to explore it all and have our own picnics in places that no one will ever find us?"

I looked out over the sea of mountains, and remembered the times when I looked at the desert like that, too. Trying to hold all the exploring possibilities in my head at once made me a little dizzy. But then I thought that if I didn't try to explore them all at the same time, and spread the exploration over my whole life, maybe that would be a pretty great way to live.

We would have liked to camp up in the Nowhere, but Mom said that we needed new ice to protect my cheese, so we should probably come down to civilization before bed. So instead of sleeping in a private spot on top of a mountain next to a beautiful lake, we slept in a rest stop on the interstate outside of Eugene. Mom was thrilled because it had people bathrooms and picnic tables and trash cans and running water, which we would normally pay money for. But I didn't like it because I had to keep interrupting my nap to bark at the trucks driving by. I thought that the forty percent of The West that was public was like the infinity of mountains and trails we'd seen this afternoon, but interstate rest stops are public lands too. Sometimes life is just less interesting than you expect.

The Cloud Sickness

We slept right outside the best running city in the world. We could have run on the same trails that some of the second best runners in the world got fast on. But Mom forgot all about The House that Pre Built, and the University of Oregon, and Nike, and instead we drove too many hours to Mt. Hood, which is the place where sweatshirts were invented. It was definitely sweatshirt weather, but if there was a mountain in all that gloom, we couldn't see it.

Since we have learned how to "do our homework" before we go to an unfamiliar trail, we knew that one of the bridges on our route had gone for a swim and drowned.

Mom and I are crackerjack river crossers, and we are always very careful to protect Mom's socks. We know how to use stepping stones, and leaping stones, and wobbling-but-finally-catching-your-balance stones, and I'm a great log dog. So weren't worried until we got to the "stream" and found that it was a blustering, roaring, raging river. This river was definitely not the walking-through kind. The logs weren't the big, wide redwood logs that are easy to balance on, but tiny little pencil-logs that were okay for two-legged runners who could use their front feet to grab things and balance, but not so great for four-legged runners who can't use railings. I thought that I could probably do it, but Mom was afraid that if she let me cross with responsibility then

I could slip and get carried down the river. If she kept me on leash, then I might make her slip and then we would both get carried down the river. We went up and down the bank looking for a bigger tree or a dry rock in a narrow place, or a spot the water was slow enough for Mom to just take off her shoes wade through it with me. But we couldn't find anywhere safe. As Mom learned from playing Oregon Trail, even big oxen can die crossing rivers in Oregon, so we decided this trail wasn't for us and turned back to the Covered Wagon.

Now we were in a pickle. We were surrounded by trails, but The Witch wouldn't tell us about any of them or even how to get there. We didn't want to pick the wrong trail that didn't allow dogs, or a trail where we would get swallowed by the white dirt, or one with another obstaple we couldn't cross, so we drove all the way out of the park to where The Witch could do research. Mom picked the first trail she found, and then drove back into the park to explore it. Mom was in such a hurry that she hadn't even given The Witch enough time to memorize the mapp properly, so it took us a long time to find the woods we were aiming for in the middle of all that woods we weren't looking for. Meanwhile, Mom was starting to go a bit batty.

One thing you need to know about Mom is that she's allergic to clouds, and when it's overcast or rainy she goes cuckoo. "I didn't like that river, Oscar," she said. "Something bad could have happened there and now I'm spooked. I want to get out of here..."

"Mom. We're fine. Look! This trail is perfect! It's not too steep and not too rocky and there's no one here to harsh our mellow."

"This place gives me the howling fantods."

"The what?"

"The screaming Mimis."

"Excuse me?"

"The willies! The heebie jeebies. I don't like all the green. It means that it rains here a lot, I can feel it in the air. It makes my skin crawl. Something bad is going to happen if we run into those woods by ourselves."

"We've been running in the woods by ourselves for years. Why don't we just run a mile or two and see how it goes?" I suggested.

"No, I think that we should get out of here. Let's go home. I don't know what I'm doing on this stupid trip, living out of a stinky van like a homeless person rather than working. What the heck do I think I'm doing? I'm a loser! I'm one of those crazy people who thinks my dog talks to me. I hate this trip. I want to go home and lock the door and never explore a new place again."

Just then, an opportunity to distract Mom ran by. It looked a bit like an Oscar-sized dog wearing a wolf costume. "Hey!" I shouted, running after him. "Hey! I'm Oscar. My hiking partner is being a party pooper. Can I run through the woods with you instead?" I had almost caught up with him, but Mom was screaming and making such a fuss that I hesitated and my new friend went on without me. So I returned to make sure that Mom hadn't hurt herself with all that screaming.

Unlike Mom, I do great on cloudy days. If you've ever read *Twilight*, you might recognize the character that's based on me because he's irresistible to the ladies, runs faster than the wind, and has to avoid the bright sun. And just like Edward Cullen I have a whiny girl who follows me everywhere. Mom didn't let me finish *Twilight* because she said that the writing was so bad that it might give me brain damage, but I'm sure it turned out great for everyone, just like this run surely would...

Soon Mom settled down a little bit, and we ran three uneventful miles up the mountain together. The trail went through a forest of trees that were all from the same litter. Once we went around a switchback we couldn't see the trail above or below us, so the whole thing felt like the scenery was on a loop like in an old movie, but not in a boring way. If we had kept going, we would have reached a lake in a few miles, but Mom was getting hangry, and with the cloud sickness I didn't want her getting any grouchier. When we turned around, we were rewarded with a perfectly graded, ankle-friendly flowing descent that even put Mom in a good mood.

We had talked about spending the night near Mt. Hood, but once we were finished and I had fed Mom she said, "Can we please get the heck out of here now?"

"Are you going to make us go back to California?" I asked. I was loving Oregon, and I knew that if we could just find Mom some sun that she would come around too.

"No, but let's keep going to Washington. If it's still gloomy there, we'll hurry east until we get out of this rainforest. I don't like the way it makes me feel." So even though we had resolved to avoid the freeways, Mom got on the interstate and we hauled butt for two hundred miles toward Seattle.

Once we got to the edge of the Olympic Peninsula, the clouds had mostly cleared and Mom was feeling more like herself. "Isn't this place wonderful, Oscar?" she said. We were in a forest with views of a bay, and white-hooded mountains in the distance. "And look at how great this campground is! It's got a little stream running by our campsite, and we're across the street from the beach, and all the trees are covered in this green, fuzzy moss."

"That's the same moss that they had in Oregon that gave you the 'galloping fantods.'"

"No, I think this is sun moss. Don't you see how bright green it is? This place doesn't feel haunted like Oregon did."

"Is that because it never rains in Seattle…?"

Since Mom was feeling better, she took me across the street to the beach. What gives me the "screaming Mimis" is water that moves on its own, but this water was calm and smelled like sea boogers and adventure, so I went swimming without Mom even throwing a stick to get me excited. The beach was covered in the ugly grey sea booger shells and Mom put one on my head like a fascinator and took my picture. I don't get Mom's obsession with putting things on my head, but because my head is big and flat to make room for my big brain, she is forever trying to balance things there. I love her, so I just stand still and let it happen.

I had been swimming almost every day, so my fur was shampoo-commercial shiny and silky, but Mom's head fur was such a fright that she could never cover it with even the biggest sea booger in the world. So Mom used the treasure coins we'd been saving in the treasure chest between the coffee cups to buy herself a shower at the campground and wash off all the fantods and heebie jeebies from Oregon. Then we snuggled up to enjoy our first night in Washington.

Wowie Zowie

It sure does rain a lot in Washington. At home, if the weather report says that there's a seventy percent probability that it's going to rain, then it will definitely rain with seventy percent intensity. If the forecast is for a ten percent chance of rain, then that means it's going to rain, but only at ten percent intensity. But here in Washington it's kind of hard to tell the difference between when it's raining and when it's not, because sometimes it rains and you don't get wet, or it rains when the sun is shining, or the air is soaking and you get wet when it's not even raining. And it stops and starts again and again, so you have all the weathers in just a few hours... and then the loop starts over.

The trail we found was one of the most beautiful trails that we've ever run. Mom is the kind of person who rarely leaves positive reviews, but this trail was so great that it inspired Mom to leave a Six Star review on Alltrails, which is like the human version of loving something so much you roll around in it before peeing on it. I told her that she should start her review with "Wowie zowie," but I guess that's an expression that is professional for dogs to say, but sounds different to humans, who only say it deep in the wilder-ness where no one but dogs can hear them.

And wowie zowie, I can't wait to tell you about it! The trail climbed up a slope that was perfect for humans because they can run it without wishing for death, and a fun for dogs because they don't have to spend the whole time waiting for their human. Hills are important on trails, because places look the most beautiful when you look down at them from above. This trail had all of the beauties in it: pretty trees with green fuzz on them, exciting rocks doing big rock things, streams falling over rocks, wooden bridges stretching over the water that was falling over the rocks, and a beautiful grey-blue lake with no boats or docks or any other human stuff in it. It started raining a little bit when we got to the lake, even though the sun was out. The sun was shining through the cloud in stripes, and the rain sparkled in the air and made the lake twinkle, and on the other side of the lake there was a mountain covered in dark grey trees that smelled like green. Even Mom, who gets sick when she sees clouds, was charmed with the place. Only The Witch that lived in Mom's Phone said that it was nothing special. When Mom asked her to take a picture we saw why. When we looked through The Witch's eye, she could only see three quarters of the beauty. The rest you need a sense of wonder to see, and since The Witch is such a know-it-all she misses the best part of things.

We liked this place so much that we decided to stay for an extra night. The home we found for the night was a campground the size of a campcity that even had its own three-mile hiking trail. Mom was wearing flip flops and I was wearing my city leash, but we decided to explore the camp trail in our town clothes anyway. Mom thought that since most of the people in the campcity were old people, "how difficult could a hiking trail around a campground really be?" Once Mom had tried to coach her flip flops down the steep slopes, and to balance flippily and climb floppily on the big rocks, she admitted that these camping types must be "tough old coots," which is a way of saying that they are sturdier than a flip flop.

Suddenly, I heard a sound in the brush below us along the trail. I looked down and saw... *A DEER-COW!* I tried to pull Mom down the hill after it, whining heroically. Maybe because she was wearing flip flops, Mom wouldn't chase the deer-cow with me and pulled me back. As I watched, another deer-cow stepped out from behind a bush. I couldn't contain my excitement any longer, and a bark exploded out of my mouth, "I'm Oscar. I'd be coming to getcha, except I can't have responsibility so close to tough old coots!" I shouted at them. "Come party with me later. I'll be in the Covered Wagon. I love waking up suddenly in the middle of the night to bark at stuff."

That sure startled them, and they started to jog away... which is when about a dozen more deer-cows came out of the brush to follow them. Of all the things we've missed on this trip, I think that missing my chance to chase the deer-cows will be my biggest regret. But Mom said that there would be plenty of deer-cows in Montana, and I might get another chance. She just requested that if it happened, that I please not get kicked in the head. I guess if my head gets stove in, then it will really ruin all the portraits she's been taking...

If a Dog Runs in the Woods and Doesn't Tell the Internet...

We woke up in the morning to a very unpleasant surprise: my Facebook fan page had disappeared without a trace! Mom searched frantically for it, but it was as if it had never existed. How would I tell all of my Friends and Oscar fans about what I discovered in Montana?

"Don't worry, Mom. The Wetlands that Smell Like a Fart are right next to Facebook, and I bet they've been waiting for a chance to repay the favor of all the patrols I've done in their back yard," I reassured her. "I'll just call Zuck and have him recover it for us. In the meantime, let's go run." Reluctantly Mom let herself be dragged into the driving chair so that she could take us to the trail.

Since we were on the Olympic Peninsula, which is a very famous place that is also easy to get to from a city, we were afraid that the trail might be busy. But it was so well hidden down a dirt road that we could hardly find it ourselves when we were parked right on top of it, so Mom didn't even bother with the leash. Now that we're both getting very comfortable with responsibility and Mom trusts me to come when she needs me, we don't need the leash much and only use it when we might run into dog-aggressive humans.

Instead of distancing us, I think it has made Mom and me closer to be off leash and more than six feet apart. When we run near our stuck house, we already know where all the excitement is, so I can leave Mom behind I know she'll follow me. I also know what all the dangers are, so I can bark at them before they even happen. But out here in The West everything is new, and I never know what's going to happen next, so Mom and I need to rely on each other a lot more. If I run after a bunny, Mom might not be where I left her when I come back, so I have to stay within barking distance. In the wilder-ness where everything is exotic and strange, I don't always know how to tell danger from excitement without Mom's help either, so I pay closer attention to Mom in the wild than I do at home.

Also different from home, Mom's and my routines are in synch when we're on the road, so Mom pays a lot more attention to me too. I get food when she gets food, we drink water from the same bottle, we both share the dog bathroom, and every night we get together and write down our story, and then snuggle up and sleep in one ball. It has made us so close that sometimes Mom doesn't even need to say anything or show me the sign language for what she wants. She just gives me a look and I can read her mind. Who needs a leash to tie you together when you've got that kind of bond?

At the start of the trail there was a sign that said that this trail was an ancient route that had been used for hundreds of years by the people who lived in these mountains long before the Microsoft, and Amazon, and Starbucks tribes were formed. I liked to imagine what it would be like if Mom and I had to run this trail rather than the freeway that we have at home to do our errands every day. I decided that would be a very nice way to live, and even though ancient people didn't have Witches in their

Phones to tell them things, or delicious McRotguts for special occasions, they probably had pretty great lives. The sign also said that the trail was remodeled by something called the CCC in different ancient times.

"Mom, what's the Cibillion Consternation Core?" I asked.

"Civilian Conservation Corps," she repeated, because she always has to sound smarter than me. "Back in the Great Depression they created jobs by building what are still many of best and most famous trails in the country. That way people without jobs could earn money to bring home the bacon. Because of their work, anyone who visits the wilderness can see how beautiful it is without having to do dangerous exploring."

"That's what we're doing!" I said. "We're curing your Great Depression and giving you something to do by traveling and writing about it. Is it paying for bacon?"

"No, we don't make any money doing this. But maybe if we create something really great together, then people will be impressed that I'm your assistant and will want to hire me." I liked the idea that I was helping by being such an interesting and handsome dog. "...But no one looks at what a beautiful thing you've created if you don't have a lot of followers, and we just lost your Facebook page..." she said, and I could see the Great Depression take over her again.

Just like Mom uses the leash to tell me what to do, The Witch that Lives in the Phone has a leash on Mom. The Witch had been good about giving Mom responsibility on this trip, and Mom had been good about having that responsibility, not looking at The Witch unless she needed to navigate or take a picture. But not today. For two miles Mom talked to The Witch and ignored me and her surroundings. I could tell that I was going to need to be a hard core life coach today.

"It's okay, Mom. Just because no one can see the pictures, it doesn't mean that you weren't there... We're in a beautiful place right now, see?" I said, running ahead so that she would surrender her staring contest with The Witch and look at the nature around her.

"But Oscar, you're just The Talent. You don't know how much hard work goes into being your webmaster. And anyway, we can't be on this trail forever. Isn't sharing it with other like-minded runners through pictures and stories a good way to prolong the experience?"

"Sure, but you're not experiencing this trail at all with your face stuck in your phone like that!"

"But I need to see if our friends at Facebook get back to me about what's going on... and the cell signal is good up here..."

I could tell that ordinary, everyday brilliant life coaching wasn't going to get the job done here. I was going to have to do something really drastic. So I came up with a plan...

In addition to the dozens of dog portraits Mom had been taking every day, she had also been taking video to relive the experience in even more detail when we got home. I love taking video because it means that Mom gets me very excited, and then we run back and forth while she laughs and tells me that I'm ruining it. The next time she started setting up the lights, camera, action for a video I saw an opportunity for a teachable moment. While she was picking moss off a log to balance The Witch in a perfect place, I ran into the woods to chase An Exciting Thing. Because she didn't yell at me right away, I kept running and running until I was very absorbed in sniffing after The Exciting Thing and Mom seemed like a distant memory.

Off in the distance I could hear Mom's shouting getting more frantic, but who wants to hang out with someone who can't pay attention to the handsome dog whose butt is right in front of her? I chased and investigated The Exciting Thing until it turned into a Boring Thing before I came back to Mom. I think I was only gone for a few minutes, but Mom said that it felt like a lifetime.

"Here I am!" I announced as I ran up like a thunderdog to let Mom smoosh her face into my noggin.

"Oh, Oscar. I thought I had lost you for good! At first I thought that I heard you playing in some water, but then I realized that the noise was just a drainage pipe. I had no idea where you were. My whole life passed before my eyes!"

"So you were paying attention to your surroundings?" I asked, making sure that she got my point.

"Yes! And I didn't want to be up here if I couldn't be here with you. I would have rather been anyplace with you than this beautiful place without you. But I would stay up here forever looking for you if you were lost."

"Was it more or less scary than when you lost my Facebook page?" I asked.

"Much, much more scary. The Facebook page is nothing. It's just a place where I post photos and let people know that you've told a new story. But it's not the memories themselves. The blog is still there with all the memories, and I still have all the photos backed up... somewhere. We can rebuild the Facebook page, but I could never replace you! Without you, who would I take pictures of?"

"And what about Instagram?"

"Oscar, I turn thirty-five this week. I'm from the generation when the internet used words. I don't know if I will ever understand Instagram..." she wailed.

"Instagram has words in it... They're just real small, in an ugly font, and have hashtags in front of them. You can learn to use it..." I wasn't sure if that was true because Mom's so old, but she was getting so upset that I thought that I should make her feel good about something.

Now that Mom had learned her lesson about her phone-leash, we resumed running. We were running down the far side of the mountain now, where The Witch couldn't get to us, and the scenery was even more beautiful than before. Everything smelled even greener, even the dead trees were prettier, and we had to climb over really scary log bridges that only had railings on one side, and certain death on the other. At first I was scared to cross because Mom made it seem like a Scary Thing, but then I realized that she was just doing that crazyperson thing that she does in high places. So the next log bridge we came to, I ran across as Thunder Dog to collect my kisses and pats on the other side.

When we were finished, Mom said that we had to hurry to our next destination. She had found a "fancy" RV park with electricity and wifi. "And then we can spend the evening creating a temporary Facebook page and posting all of your good photos to Instagram." She seemed excited. "You're good at words, so give me some good words and I'll put some hashtags in front of them, and then we'll win Instagram."

"And make sure to use emojis in your captions, for the people who can't read..." I reminded her. I wasn't sure Mom was really understanding Instagram, but she was enthusiastic and offered me some McRotguts as a reward for the long trip, so I guess it couldn't hurt.

It didn't quite work out that way, because all the people in the fancy campground were using up the not-fancy wifi to watch movies rather than enjoy the

 nature. Every time we tried to upload an image, my handsomeness was so overwhelming that the wifi lost control and shut down. That's how I know that the wifi must be a lady (hashtag ladywifi).

Gotcha Day

The next day was a very special day in our family, because it was Mom's "Gotcha Day." Four years ago Mom went into the pet store where I was The Talent at an adoption fair. I was an irresistible ladies' man who knew how to work it even then. To hear Mom tell it, she "accidentally" adopted a puppy, but I knew that I was going to take her home as soon as I saw her. To celebrate our special day, Mom got me a very fancy breakfast of Starbucks ham, egg and cheese pucks and we went to an off-leash trail for a long hike-run up a mountain.

Before Mom and I started exploring The West, I didn't know that there were so many different kinds of mountains, but now I know that I need to be more specific when I tell you that we climbed "a mountain." This mountain was the pointy, rocky kind where you can see a lot of things in the distance. Some mountains are loners like me and Mom, but this mountain was the social kind that likes to have other mountains that dress the same close by. Every direction that we looked in there were more spiky mountains wearing the same white hoods. It was also the kind of mountain that grows out of a river. I had never seen a river like this one before. It was enormous and frothy and loud, a little bit like a temper tantrum, and not good for swimming in at all. You wouldn't believe how much water flowed by. It seems awfully selfish for Washington to have all this water even in the dry parts of the state when there are rivers in California that have only had water one year out of the last lifetime. But apparently just like smarts and beauty, water isn't evenly distributed in this world.

Some "hard" trails aren't all that challenging when you get there, but Mom had chosen well for our special day. This trail was very steep, with lots of things to climb over and step on to keep the brains in our paws and legs interested; not like there was any risk of getting bored. The higher we climbed, the better this trail got. At the bottom there were wildflowers and shade and trees, but as we ran higher the wildflowers gave way to bushes that sometimes hid birds' nests for me to rouse, and the trees turned into naked white bone-trees. By the time we were up on the ridge, almost four thousand feet above where we'd started, even the bone-trees and bushes had almost given up and it was just white dirt and regular dirt and rocks with chipmunks underneath them for me to chase up and down the naked mountain. Mom really took care of every detail so that we would have a great Gotcha Day!

There wasn't as much of it as we have seen on other mountains, but this white dirt was hungrier than the stuff in California, Nevada and Oregon. Rather than only swallowing half of Mom's leg, it kept taking giant bites all the way up to her waist. The white dirt further south didn't eat gorgeous dogs, either. Sometimes the southern white dirt nibbled at me, but it always spit me back out. But this Washington white dirt would take a bite and start chewing. Every time I stepped out, it sucked me back in!

Finally Mom had had it. The trail was under a long stretch of white dirt, and we were practically within view of the top. "This trail may be covered in snow, but there is plenty of open ground if we make our own path," Mom said. "Let's see how high we can get if we go straight up." I was proud of Mom. I always explore the mountain outside the trail, but she's usually less curious. The West is a land with a history of explorers who had to break their own trail, and it seemed a shame to explore the whole of The West by always going where someone else had gone before. So we climbed wild for another couple hundred feet, Mom taking more roundabout routes to stay away from the white dirt, and me chasing chipmunks all over the mountainside, and then catching up to her when she stopped to rest. Finally we got to a place where Mom couldn't or wouldn't go any further. We were still a couple of hundred feet below the summit, but I don't think that either of us really minded.

There is such a thing as too much scenery. I know because Mom was suffering from it. I could smell a little bit of anxiety and a little bit of sadness coming off of her, along with the other stinks of dirt and sweat and homelessness. "What's wrong?" I asked.

"There is just so much out there to see, we could never see it all from all the angles. Even if we hiked and ran every day for the rest of our lives, we would still miss stuff. It seems like such a waste to spend five out of every seven days working. Worse still, it seems like a real shame to commit to being in one place when there are so many things to see that are too far to drive to."

"Don't worry, Mom. We've got plenty of time, and we've got the Covered Wagon now. It hasn't even broken down yet. We'll figure out a way to see it all..."

"Even if we could see it all, hiking and trail running are only one way to experience The West. There's also road biking, and mountain biking, not to mention backpacking and through hiking. And did you see all those climbers heading into the woods with crash pads on their backs?" I had indeed seen lots of people with arms bigger than their legs with mattresses on backpacks hiking into the forest. "...those people were going to climb the mountains in a totally different way: up close and with their hands, like lizards. There are women all over town with arms like GI Joes. They must climb every day..." Mom explained whistfully.

"But Mom, you're afraid of heights. Even little ones. You would make a terrible lizard."

"Okay, then what about the kayakers and rafters?"

"You hate being cold and wet."

"Good point. So I'll get a mountain bike. Anyway, the point is, I feel like I'm wasting my life. I don't want to go back to a place where everyone is talking about two million dollar two-bedroom homes, and whose startup is valued at what, and I'm the only woman I know over the age of twenty-five that hasn't had plastic surgery. That's not how I want to get old. I want to let my hair go grey and let my wrinkles happen without botox, and I want to drive an old, beat-up car that doesn't cost much and that I can get banged up and dirty."

"Why can't you do all those things?" I asked her.

"Because if you let yourself get sunburns and tan lines, and let your hair go grey, and drive a beat-up ugly old minivan people think something's wrong with you.

The people with the money and the nice cars and the botox don't think you're worth as much as they are, and they don't consider you for the good opportunities."

"You got all that from looking at some mountains?"

"I do have a tendency to overthink things... But yeah, I feel like I need to choose between the mountains and security."

I thought about my Gotcha Day, and how my life could have been different if the wrong family had taken me home. What would my life be like if an indoor mom had been captivated by my soulful eyes instead? When we came back to our stuck house, Mom would be going to a kind of job adoption fair, and she isn't nearly as handsome as me. Without buttocks on her face, what if people didn't think she was cute enough to adopt? Not every life coach gets adopted by their soulmate...

"But Mom, what if after a few months of camping and wandering you got sick of it?" I asked. "Why don't you find a job where you can work from anywhere? Then we can live in a log cabin in the woods and still travel?"

"Because you have to give up a *lot* for those jobs, Oscar. What if the sacrifice isn't worth it?"

I was beginning to understand why Mom wanted to run off into the mountains and not come out again. Humans need to plan things to survive, and a lot of times the things you plan for don't happen, and things that weren't in the plan happen instead. Mom wanted to run into the woods so that she could be more like a dog. Dogs don't need to decide where the car is going. They just sit in the back seat and nap, then they pop out at one adventure after another and follow wherever the trail or a chipmunk leads them, and it's always fun in the end. Dogs don't have to worry about 401Ks and health insurance and mortgages. This problem was going to take more than one run to fix...

Mad George

The next day we decided that we would do a flat-ish run called the Mad River Trail. The trail didn't climb anything, it just followed the Mad Riverbank through what Mom called a "George," which is the word for when there is a river on one side and a steep rock wall on the other. I could see that the river was frothing, roaring mad, but I didn't think it could attack, so I ignored its tantrum the same way the person answering the Comcast phone ignores Mom's tantrums. The idea of running twelve miles next to a river felt like nothing compared to some of the steep and tall mountains that we had been climbing lately, so both Mom and I let down our guard and relaxed into an easy run.

The Mad River attacked us for the first time early in the run. It ran up and over its banks and made a deep puddle all the way up to the George wall. Mom avoided getting her socks wet by climbing up on the George like a rock climber, and just like a rock climber she stayed stuck up there with one leg blocking the other leg, and had to think about her next move so she could get down. Since I don't wear socks, I was already on the other side cheering her on. When I saw that she might need help, I jumped up on the George with her, but it was steep and slippery and I fell off again. The second time I managed to stick to the wall with her by crowding in real close to Mom's feet. "Shove over, you're in my way," I said. And then, "Okay. Now what?"

"Aaah! Get out of here! I'm going to slip and squash you… and get my socks wet!" Mom screamed. She wasn't more than two feet off the ground and she was still afraid of falling? How ridiculous! So I jumped off, and then Mom jumped off, and the Mad River lost the challenge.

The Mad River learned that we were too strong to attack as a team, so for its second attack it waited until Mom and I were separated and ambushed me alone. I had run ahead because of Excitement, and Mom was still around a bend behind me when the river said, "Aren't you thirsty, Oscar? I'm so cool and I taste so good! Come stand on this bed of soft pine needles and drink from me while you wait for Mom…"

That sounded like a great idea, so I walked out onto the bed of pine needles that was sitting at the edge of the river… but it was a trap and I fell right in! I didn't see that one coming…

It turned out that the pine needles were floating on top of the river, but underneath was water deeper than an Oscar. Thank goodness it was in a calm spot, because I had time to drag myself up onto the trail and was shaking off the water and pine needles by the time Mom came around the corner and saw me. If it had been in another part of the river, all Mom would have seen was a handsome blur float by, and then she might not see me again until I popped out somewhere in Seattle.

The Mad River attacked us for the last time with an all-out blitz. We were less than halfway to the turn-around spot when the river jumped furiously over its banks and ran over the trail with a white, frothy war whoop of a rapid where we were supposed to be running. We looked for a place to climb around, but the river was right up against the George. We had no choice but to surrender and turn around.

Since we were finished early, Mom decided that we could take the scenic route rather than pushing straight to our next stop in Idaho. This was a great idea, except that it meant a lot of extra time in The Covered Wagon, which turns into an Easy Bake Oven in the sun. We stopped for a little while at a lake so that I could take a swim, but after a couple more dog hours of driving even Mom was drowsing in the heat.

Since we're explorers, we thought about how we could use our environment to help us. In the distance we could see a mountain covered in a coat of white dirt that the signs called Mt. Sherman. That would be a perfect place to hide out during the hottest part of the day! Mom checked Alltrails and saw that there was a trail called "Mt. Sherman Peak" (... on second thought, it might have been "Mt. Sherman Creek..." But anyway...) It was less than a mile from the highway and looked shady, so we stopped there to hike through the hot part of the day.

Once we saw it, there was something very un-trail-like about this trail. "This is just a dirt service road!" Mom said.

"Why are all the trees wearing neckties?" I asked.

"This isn't a trail. This is a logging road!" Mom said.

But the air was cooler up here, and somewhere off in the distance we could hear running water, so we decided to follow the logging trail and see where it went. We could see white dirt on top of the mountain up ahead, so at least we would be cooler when we reached it.

Mom was not impressed with the logging trail, but I thought it was swell. It was covered in sticks to chomp on, and there were many squirrels and other unfamiliar critters for me to chase. One squirrel ran up a tree that didn't start to grow any branches until higher than a telephone pole. I danced around the tree and squealed, "I'm going to get you, Mr. Squirrel! Come back here! My next jump is going to be so high that I'm going to be up there in the branches with you, and then you'll really be surprised! ... Okay, maybe I'll just climb the... Okay, maybe not... Hey? Did you maybe hide in this bush behind the tree and just confuse me, Mr. Squirrel?" I never did find him, but I bet I was real close and I gave him a good scare.

We had walked further on the logging trail than we had run next to the Mad River when Mom checked the mapp. "Hey!" she said. "The mountain is on the other side of the highway. This trail doesn't even go there! We're almost done and we haven't even reached the snow line. Let's go."

It's funny how sometimes you can have so much adventure in such a little distance like we did in the Mad George, and then sometimes you have long, long stretches where nothing happens and you can't find any excitement. Life is kind of like that too, I guess. You might start down a path thinking that it will take you to the top of a mountain with all the best things like scenery, air conditioning and excitement, but soon you find that it isn't what you thought it was going to be. Some people are like Mom and feel disappointed because they wasted an afternoon, but even if you find yourself somewhere you didn't expect to be, you can still find joy if you look for it. There is always something exciting on every trail, like a squirrel to chase, or some mysterious poop to investigate, or a fun game you can play like Who Can Bark at the Most People. Isn't it terrific that it isn't luck that decides if you have a good day, but a decision you make for yourself? I think that that was the secret that Mom needed to learn: that your happiness isn't the trail you're on, but what you decide to do while you're on it. I had no idea how I could tell Mom all that, I would have to show her instead.

Distance

Even though we were very far north and spring was supposed to come late to this part of the country, it had been dog-meltingly hot for the past few days. The Witch said that it was only eighty-two degrees, but she lied as usual, because all of the thermometers that we passed on the road and who ought to know the truth said that it was ninety-two degrees, which by my math is twenty-two degrees hotter than The Witch said. If The Covered Wagon has to work hard (like climbing a hill, or driving on the freeway), or even if it sits still in the wrong place, it gets even hotter on the inside than it is outside. To make sure that I stayed in a solid state, we had to do some extra planning, which is why we had to wake up super-duper extra double-dog early to drive the last few hours to the trail in order to run before it got too hot.

Mom had planned to run a ten-mile trail that climbed two peaks of the same mountain, then turned around on the second peak to climb over the first again on the way back. Even though we started at 7:30, it was already a hot morning. Even though it was a hot morning, there was still ice blocking the dirt road for the last quarter mile to the trailhead. Mom tried to drive over the ice, but she got the Covered Wagon's front paws stuck in the white dirt, and the back paws stuck on some ice. Then the Covered Wagon wouldn't move at all.

"What would happen if we just left the Covered Wagon here until the cold melted?" I suggested.

"We're blocking the whole road," Mom said, like

my idea was stupid.

"Well so is the ice."

"Oh, wait… I have the emergency brake on," Mom said, reaching down by her knees and doing something that made a pop deep inside the Covered Wagon. "How did that happen?" Then we backed up like normal and parked the Covered Wagon in a less road block-y place.

Despite our mishap, we didn't see any more white dirt for the first mile and a half of our run. Most of the mountains around here smelled green, so I was afraid that I was going to miss a chance to cool off by rolling around in the white dirt. Mom was afraid that I would melt and she would need to carry me back to the car-house in a bottle. But then, all of a sudden, we turned a corner and there it was spread whitely all over everything. From then on I did all the running while Mom hiked more deliberately on the white dirt all the way to the summit. Mom didn't complain much, though, because this white dirt was a vegetarian that didn't want to eat either one of us. Instead, it was friendly and let Mom walk on top of it just like normal dirt does.

We played in the white dirt on the summit for a very long time. Mom lay down and waved her arms and legs. Because she was being cute, I did what she does to me whenever I do something charming: I ran around her barking about how silly she looked, and then kissed her in the face a lot. When she got up she said it was supposed to look like an angel, but all my running around had ruined it.

"Oh, well you can make another one," I said.

"Nah. My back is soaked. Let's explore."

There were all kinds of strange things on the top of the mountain, like an old mattress that was just a rusted skeleton, and some very large pieces of concrete bigger than an Oscar, and large planks of wood the size of an entire tree. I wondered how they had gotten up there, since there were no roads for them to ride up on trucks, and no higher mountains that they could have fallen down from. Finally I realized what should have been obvious: Giants did it.

Part of the reason that we could walk through the white dirt up to the first peak was because there were lots of footprints for us to follow. When we looked for the trail to the second peak, we found a sign pointing the way where the trail must have been, but there were no footprints or breaks in the trees to tell us where to go. We stood there for a long time studying the spot and looking for clues.

"We're leaving now, right?" I asked. We never have had much luck in the white dirt on our own.

"I just hate that we keep quitting every time we run into snow," Mom said.

"But you hate the white dirt. Remember? Your socks."

"Yeah, sure. But we're not finishing what we started."

"How far away is the finish?" I asked.

"Three more miles. Ten miles total. If we turn back here we'll only have gone like four miles."

"Is there a big difference between four and ten?"

"Sure. There's a whole other mountain between here and ten."

I looked around. There were lots of mountains around us. Did we have to climb them all before she would let me eat lunch? "What are we going to see on the second mountain?" I asked.

"I don't know… all the same mountains that we can see from here, only at a different angle. And maybe we'll also see where we're standing now, only by the time we get there, this spot will look far away."

"Well if we're not going to see anything new, and we can't climb *all* the mountains, then what does it matter if we don't see the second mountain?"

"Alright. You got me. It's because I woke up this morning planning to run ten miles, and I don't want to turn back after running only four."

"Why? You've accomplished everything in four miles that you planned to accomplish in ten."

"Because… ten is better!" she said, throwing up her hands like I was the one being daft.

"Okay. So why don't we just shorten our miles today, and say that ten of them fit into the distance we go before lunch."

"Math doesn't work that way, Oscar. We need to use the same miles every day so that we can compare ourselves to others."

I straightened my life coach collar and said in my best therapist voice, "Why?"

"Because we have goals! Because we have to run and hike two thousand miles this year."

"But aren't we way ahead of schedule?"

"Yeah. But I also put money into a savings account for every mile that we run, and that's how we pay for stuff like this trip. If we don't run enough then we'll be poor and vulnerable and won't be able to go on vacation."

"Hang on, so someone's been paying you to run with me?"

"*I* pay myself to run with you… Or, if you prefer to think of it this way, I pay you to run with me, and as your trustee I put that money toward adventures for us."

"But it's our money either way. Why don't you fire us and take me on runs for fun, and then just save up for vacations whether you ran a lot or not?"

"Because then I might get lazy and fat and have to spend all of your vacation money on snacks and new clothes…"

"Well then why don't you just eat less food?" I asked.

"If I could answer that question, Oscar, then we could sell the answer and we would be so rich we wouldn't have to worry about money."

Since we were near a lake, Mom suggested we avoid the hottest part of the day by finding a beach and eating a picnic lunch in the shade, then finding a hike that went along the lake so that I could take a quick swim if I got too hot. And that's just what we did, except that everything is way more stressful when The Witch won't cooperate. Without her help, we didn't know where the roads were, or how long they were, or if they were made of dirt. Once we finally found the trail, it did follow the lake, but there was a big cliff between us and the water. So even though we were hot and dusty, we still couldn't go swimming.

Since it was too hot to run, I walked slowly next to Mom and picked up our coaching conversation where we'd left off. "Mom, have you ever noticed that you have a lot of rules?" I asked.

"Well if you don't have rules, then how will you know the right things to do?"

"Yeah, but your rules aren't to avoid danger. 'Don't – under any circumstances – eat Mom's dinner when her back is turned' is a rule about safety. Your rules are made-up things where you are both the boss and the worker and no one but you knows or cares if you follow them."

"But if I don't follow the rules, then I'll be a loser."

"What will you lose? Are you playing a game?"

"Maybe… Maybe life is a game?"

"Are you winning?"

"No, I don't think so. I smell bad, I'm living out of a fifteen-year-old minivan that smells like a diaper pail, I spend most of the day lost, I'm about to turn thirty-five and I have no job, I'm divorced, and I imagine elaborate conversations with my dog."

"What's wrong with having a strong and honest relationship with your dog?" I asked. "Who else is playing this game anyway?"

"No one, I guess."

"So you're the only one playing the game and you're still losing?"

"Well... I mean... I guess I'm not losing. We're better off than those people with an acre of trash in their front yard, or those people in the twenty-year-old Pontiac in the McDonald's drive-through whose entire back seat was filled with sun-faded trash. I'll be able to get a job as soon as I want to, and we do have a house to live in, and this has been a pretty rad vacation that we can take because I saved for a rainy day... But I don't like the feeling of not knowing what's going to happen in the future."

"Mom, NOBODY knows what's going to happen in the future. Not even me and I know like everything."

By the time we got back to The Covered Wagon we were both hot and cranky, and we still had a lot of getting lost to do before we could go to bed. "How far did we go?" I asked Mom.

"Five miles."

"Is that good or bad?"

"That's bad, because the trail was only supposed to be three and a half, but we got lost."

"Hang on, this morning you wanted to go ten miles today, but you were frustrated because the trail was too short. And now we've gone ten miles and you're upset because the trail is too long? Your game is definitely a lousy one if you lose even when you reach the goal..."

"Okay, I'm convinced. I've got to change something. You're a happy, handsome, popular and successful dog. How do you do it?"

"You're going to have to live like a dog. Are you sure you're ready?"

"Sure, let's give it a try," she said, and this time I think she meant it.

Rrrruuuuuuuunnnnnn!

The story for the next day's run started that night, when we camped along the dirt road on the way to the next trail. We were getting a little more comfortable with the idea that no rangers were going to wake us up in the middle of the night and tell us to leave the public land, but Mom would still get a little nervous that there were some country rules that we didn't know about. So when the Sons of Anarchy rode by on their macho golf carts and gave us strange looks, Mom just waved at them like, "Howdy neighbor." She tried to act like making a salad on a TV dinner tray out of the back of a mail-man van ten miles from the nearest paved road is the most natural thing in the world.

Anyway, so we were making dinner, and all of a sudden I noticed this buzzing that wasn't coming from mighty golf carts. "Mom, what's with this flock of medium-sized birds?!" I asked, trying to bite them out of the air one by one. For every one I swallowed, ten more swarmed into its place.

"These..." Mom said, doing an angry interpretive dance with her arms, "...are mosquitoes, and they are among the most irritating things on earth."

"Where did they come from?!" I asked as they swarmed around me like a bunch of adoring fans asking for my pawtograph.

"They are born in fresh water like lakes and ponds, and come out to ruin warm nights. At home we don't have lakes or warm nights, so we don't have anything to attract mosquitoes." Then something flew by Mom's head that was so loud that it made her flinch like someone had thrown a stick at her face. "What the duck was that?!" she said. "It was the size of a flying tampon!" I know all about tampons. They seem like a great snack, but they're kind of big for swallowing in one gulp, and then you get punished with a trip to the vet if you eat one. I was glad that it had flown for Mom's face and not mine.

The real trouble was that when we do chores like dinner, we need to leave all the doors to the Covered Wagon open. So when we were ready to go to bed, dozens of the hum-bugs had moved into our bedroom. Mom spent the evening lunging and diving around The Covered Wagon, clapping and squishing until most of the hum-bugs were dead and our home was decorated with their squashed bodies.

In the morning, when Mom gave up and parked The Covered Wagon at an ice bank more than one but less than two miles from the trailhead, the hum-bugs were back. I looked out of my window and could see a frenzy of them trying to get at me through the glass, like hungry zombies in fast forward. "I thought you said they only came out at night!" I shuddered, cowering inside the car-house.

"Out! Out! Hurry! So I can close the door!" Mom squawked. They weren't so bad when we were moving, but as soon as we slowed down, the hum-bugs crowded in around us like a crazymaking cloud. The hum-bugs were worse than the ticks, who at least gave us a relaxed kind of hysteria. The hum-bugs made everything feel like panic. When we reached the trail and nature crowded in closer, the hum-bugs got even worse.

"Mom, what are you doing checking your phone at a time like this?!" I asked over my shoulder as I ran down the trail.

"This is the first time I've had reception in two days... *Gah!* ...and I want to see... *Bah!* ...if I've missed anything." She wasn't just waving her arms at this point, she was snapping her head back and forth, and even her shoulders and waist were getting into the action of swatting the hum-bugs. "But I can't... *ugh!* ... hold my hand still for long enough ... *godSLAM it!* ... to read anything."

"Okay, Happiness Coach Lesson Number One: In an emergency, put down your stinkin' phone!" I said as I ran, trying to lead by example and convince her to follow me.

"What?" *Swipe. Swat.* "Crap! I think I just deleted something!"

I left Mom to her fool's task and ran into the woods to explore. I could smell something big, and there were recent tracks in the white dirt that looked like deer hooves, but were way bigger than any deer's feet I'd ever seen, like a deer Sasquatch. I remembered about the flying tampon last night, and the mystery of all the big things on top of the mountain yesterday, and concluded that there must be all kinds of giant things roaming in the hills of Idaho.

When I next came back to check on Mom, she was still twitching like she had a taser stuck in her, but at least she had put her phone away. She had a cloud of hum-bugs around her that you could practically see from the next mountain over.

"You've got to run, Mom!" I said.

"This is no time to be a marathon coach, Oscar! This whole trail is covered in snow, I can't run on it!"

"But the more you walk, the more hum-bugs you collect. They can't keep up with you if you run. You don't have to run far, just *RUN!*"

So we ran. Mom didn't flow fleet-footed over the snow like me. Her fleeing looked more like a stumbling drunk person trying to catch a tennis ball bouncing downhill, but after a minute or so of running she had shed most of the hum-bugs and could hike until she caught her breath and collected another swarm and it was unbearable again.

At one point Mom had collected a really huge cloud and was about to run away when she reached a tree that had fallen across the path. The tree was too low for her to crawl under, but too high for her to jump over. Desperate, she tried to give herself a lunging start. She had one foot up on the log and just needed a little boost from her down leg to get her weight up and over. But when she pushed down on the white dirt, it gave out underneath her and she somersaulted backward and landed like she was trying to make another snow angel. Mom didn't even hesitate to brush the white dirt out of her socks. She just screamed about ducks and then got her butt onto the log and threw her legs over. While she was scooting, her shorts got caught on a branch and I thought for a moment that she was going to let the shorts tear off her butt, and then run pantsless into the wilder-ness rather than stopping to untangle herself.

We were supposed to climb three mountains, but after we had climbed one and were running down to start the second one Mom said, "Oscar, this is horrible! Can we please go now?"

"Are you going to complain for the rest of the day about cutting our run short?"

"No, there is absolutely nothing that makes me want to continue doing this run!"

"Even the other two mountains and the fact that this is the first time you've been able to hike any real distance on the white dirt this whole trip?"

"We can talk about it in the car," she said, leaving me behind as she bumbled and lurched back in the direction of the ice mound where we'd left the Covered Wagon.

We didn't do any more hiking or running for the rest of the day, but Mom did make me take a swimming break to cool off. There was a little lake with a walkway that started at the car kennel and stuck out into the lake. The walkway moved with the water, which I found interesting and a bit scary. There was a black lab there, and she kept jumping off the walkway into the water. I was curious about how that worked, but decided that it was best to let the dumb lab take the risk. So every time

Mom threw a stick, I barked instructions at the lab... who ignored me and let the stick float away.

When the lab left and everything was quiet, I thought I would investigate the water in a little more detail. I cautiously leaned over the edge of the walkway to sniff the lake...

...when suddenly something came up from behind, scooped me up by my shapely bottom, and flipped me face-first into the lake. I had never been in water over my head unless I had cautiously walked out there myself after weighing the risks. I splashed and flailed for a second, trying to get my bearings. I thought for sure that I must have been attacked by a giant. I turned to warn Mom, when I noticed that she was standing in the spot that I had just fallen from, and laughing her butt off.

"Did you do that?!" I asked.

"I did. I'm sorry." When I swam to the land, she squeezed the water out from my face fur and kissed the hard spot between my eyes.

"That wasn't very nice!" I sulked. "Happiness Lesson Number Two: we don't do mean things to people we love! Mitten-god! What's the matter with you?! You're acting like you've been taking happiness lessons from a cat..."

"It was mean. I know. I'm sorry," she said, still laughing. "But you should have seen your face though...! That little prank made me very happy indeed. You are a great happiness coach."

I think we need more work on Rule Number Two.

Leash Aggression

We finally reached Montana, and stopped to hang out in a city called Missoula because Mom said that we had a lot of city chores to do. Cities are hard because they have things like traffic, and rules, and lines to wait in, and other people to deal with. But they're nice too because they have things like paved roads, and car kennels, and ice cream restaurants, and the kind of air that lets Mom's electronics reach the outside world, which she finds relaxing.

Trails in a city aren't usually as wild as the trails in the middle of the wilder-ness, but sometimes that can be nice too. The drive to the trail on our first morning in Montana was so short that Mom didn't even have time to finish the coffee in her cup. She called leaving behind hot coffee "uncivilized," but I think she was joking. There was a large car kennel at the trail, which we agreed was much more convenient than having to stop in a pile of white dirt and hike a mile or two to the trailhead. Best of all, this trail was crawling with Friends, both the furry and fleshy kinds. Unlike Mom, I'm a real social guy, so I always appreciate the opportunity to meet new Friends to tell me how great I am.

Another great thing about this trail was that even though it was in the city and very crowded, I could still let Mom off leash.

Now that I was so good at responsibility, it made me grouchy to have a leash to tell me where I needed to go and what I needed to do. It made me lose patience with sharing the trail, just like Mom does. Mom gets quiet and judgy when she is territorial, but I bark at Frienemies that bother me, which is called being "confrontational." If I need to follow the rules these people make up, then they should have to follow the rules I make up too.

I'm starting to think that I had it backward about the leash: maybe the leash is really what responsibility feels like, and the responsibility makes you serious and a lot less fun to be around. That made me think about something. "Mom," I said. "I think that I understand why you were so grouchy all the time when you were working. It was because you had to be on a leash all the time, following rules that other people made up. And you could never go off trails and chase chipmunks because someone might call you to heel at any moment."

"I suppose that you're right, Oscar."

"Do you think that that's why everyone at home is always so aggressive and unfriendly? Because they have too much responsibility and have to walk around with their faces in their phones, and can't get away from each other's rules, so they have leash aggression?"

"That's a good point. Leash aggression comes when you feel trapped and can't get away from something dangerous. If I see someone making a scene in an open place like the street I can escape quickly if I don't want to get involved. It's only when I can't get away from someone like in traffic or at work that I growl and snap at them."

"Mom, I like it here. No one is leash aggressive. Even when I run up to someone like a bowling ball, barking that I don't like the fur on their face, they always smile and say how adorable I am. When you tie me up outside the Starbucks at home and I have to screech and scream to make you come back out again, people always look at me like I'm ruining their morning. But here when I had my manly meltdown outside the ice cream store, all the ladies at the table next to me thought it was the cutest thing they'd ever seen."

"It's true. People do seem happier out here, and they have more time. I can tell just by the way they drive. I don't think that we could live in Montana, or any of these states next to the Canadian border, though. There's too much snow in the winter. And you know me and snow…"

"Mom! The things you come up with! The white dirt is a *summer* thing. I have lived through four winters and never once has it snowed in the winter. It only comes out on a warm day in the mountains. Obviously, the mountains grow it in the summer so that they can stay cool and don't get a sunburn. Haven't you been paying attention? Any idiot could figure that out."

"Whatever you say, Oscar…"

Even though Missoula is surrounded by mountains, the trail that we were on only climbed a little hill, and so we ran for most of the time, only stopping for me to meet a Friend or for Mom to record how handsome I am. We ran past a pair of ladies, and I smiled at them to let them know that we were all having fun together. After they told Mom what a handsome devil I am, they said that we must be very fit to be running up this mountain.

Were we fitter? I didn't feel fitter, I just felt like the mountains were getting smaller.

Another thing about city trails is that the people tend to stay close to the car kennels, so it didn't take very long for Mom and me to run far enough to find a place to run by ourselves.

Now that we were alone, I picked up our conversation. "So why do we live in a place where everyone is leash aggressive, when there are so many nice places in the world?"

"Well, that leash pays a lot more money than I can earn in other places."

"What do we get with that money? Can we buy more time with it?"

"No, that leash also costs us a lot of our family time."

"So... do we get a better house with it?"

"Definitely not. We could get five to ten times the space – and two bathrooms – for the same amount of money if we lived pretty much anywhere else."

"We have two bathrooms already."

"I wasn't counting the dog bathroom. We could have two people bathrooms."

"Why would we need two people bathrooms? You can only use one at a time..."

"You're right, we don't even need all the things that our money could buy somewhere else."

"So... why the leash then?"

"I guess because it creates better opportunities?" Mom said, sounding less convinced.

"Opportunities for what? To climb more mountains?"

"No, you need to stay within cell range in case someone needs you on the weekends. The opportunities are for more responsibility, I guess."

"But why would you want a *bigger* leash, when all it does is keep you away from your family, away from the mountains, and in a house that's so little that there's no room to wrestle? How much money would you pay to have more time to be in the mountains with your dashingly handsome, intelligent, fit and snuggly life partner?"

"I would pay quite a lot for that..." Mom said, and I could tell she meant it. "...But the less money I make now, the longer I have to work before I can stop working for good and have adventures full time."

"What's the hurry? Is it a race? Do you win something if you get to that finish line first? I thought you weren't going to do any more races."

"It's a race against when I'll be too old and slow to go to these places, I suppose."

I thought for a moment. "Speed isn't right for all adventures. Do you think that our expeditions on this trip would be better if we ran them faster?"

"Well, we could see more, I guess."

"That's bad human math logic," I pointed out. "We don't turn around because we've run out of time or energy for adventure. Most days we stop because The Covered Wagon can't get to the trail, or because we lost the trail under the white dirt, not because we've seen all the things there are to see. If you were faster then it would just be over sooner... And then what? More time in The Covered Wagon? More time sending pictures? Wouldn't you rather spend that time in a place that inspires you to take more pictures than a place that has a better signal to send those pictures?"

"True... So what do you suggest?"

"Isn't the answer obvious?" I asked.

"No..."

"Well if you don't see it, I'm not going to tell you..." I said. Secretly, I didn't know the answer, but sometimes Mom comes up with something good when she thinks that there's something there for her to figure out. I wanted to see what she came up with...

Water

There is so much water in Montana in the spring that they hadn't found a place to put it all yet. We weren't jealous, even though we're from California where people fight over water because there isn't enough to go around. The problem with Montana's extra water was that it was in all the places that we had come to see, especially the big skies and the trails. We had planned to explore Montana a lot more, but a big storm followed us into the state and planned to stay for so long that we wouldn't have time to get back home if we waited for the sun to come back. So we picked a couple of trails on the way back to Idaho and hoped that the rain would break by the time we got there.

Lucky for us, Montana rain is like Washington rain that sometimes doesn't even get you wet. Or perhaps the rain just isn't as wet when you're tougher and more confident, just like the mountains aren't as high when you're fitter. For whatever reason, the rain let us be and we explored the full length of both trails without getting rained on. But that didn't mean we didn't get wet...

The first trail we visited climbed up to a waterfall. Except that there was so much river trying to get through its George between the mountains that the whole river acted white and frantic like a waterfall for the full length of the trail! This river was much more furious than the Mad River, but in its thrashing it had dug itself into a pit far, far below where we were hiking, so it couldn't reach us to attack like the Mad River had. But that doesn't mean that it didn't try!

There were two places where the water didn't look before it leapt, and tumbled a long way down to where the ground was there to catch it again. The first waterfall was the taller one, and it fell a distance taller than four giraffes balancing on each other's horns. The problem was that the waterfall was kind of far from the trail and hidden behind the trees. There was a bit of rock that stuck out right in front of the waterfall, and it would have been a perfect spot for a strapping dog to look tough and flex while his Mom took a picture of him, but that spot was barely larger than a couple of butts and sat at the bottom of a very steep slope. Mom and I put on our leash, and like a couple of rock climbers we helped each other down the slope toward the ledge. You may remember that Mom is not a very good rock climber, so she didn't know that the safety doesn't come from being tied together, it comes from being tied to something stuck in place. You may also remember that Mom is mortally afraid of heights. As we were getting close to the ledge, Mom's paw slipped. It probably only slipped a millimeter, but that was enough to turn her into a screaming fool. The trouble was that the path was steep enough that when she turned around to flee, she found her nose right in my manly chest hair. Since there was a handsome dog blocking her escape, she screamed even uglier. Since she had tied that handsome, trail-blocking dog around her waist, he couldn't get out of her way, no matter how ugly her screams were. Luckily for both of us, we weren't actually in real danger, just Mom's imaginary danger, and after a very loud and long second, we were both back on less steep ground, where Mom took some really unimpressive pictures of our bravery.

On the higher falls, the water ran wild outside its coral, and we could practically walk right up to it. Up here, all the rocks were rounded like an egg, and the water just slipped off the edge like it had nothing to hold on to. Mom said that most of this water came from little streams that were only a couple of inches wide at first. All over the two mountains to our left and right, thousands of little streams were joining to make brooks, which met other brooks to make creeks, and the creeks got together to make rivers, and all those rivers came together at this spot where we were standing to rush out of the mountains.

"Is this all the water in The West?!" I asked. With the amount of water falling off this cliff, it seemed like there wouldn't be any more left in all the oceans of the world.

"Nope. There are rivers like this coming off of all the mountains right now." There must be more water in this river than there was in the whole state of California. Every second a Lake Berryessa of water was falling off this cliff, and when I thought about all the seconds there were in the spring, and all the mountains we'd passed in The West, and how they each could have their own river for sweating off their white caps, the thought of all that water made my head swim.

The next trail was supposed to be a very easy one; just seven and a half flat miles around a lake. We had picked this trail just in case we needed something easy to do, but we were finding that things are very seldom easy in the wilder-ness.

Like a dog that only uses the couch when he's home alone, the lake had taken advantage of the lack of weekday hikers to take over the part of the trail furthest from the car kennel. In some places the water ran right down the center, turning the whole trail into a stream. In other places where you could tell that people usually jumped easily from rock to rock, rivers had swallowed up all of the rocks, and to protect her socks Mom had to leap across like the photo on an inspirational poster. When we were close to the very tippity top end of the lake where it nosed into a notch between the mountains, we had to cross a brook that was so high that there was no way to get Mom's socks across safely. The water in the middle was deeper than an Oscar is tall, and flowing pretty fast – not scary fast, but fast enough to change color.

Mom looked at the river for a long time, and then sat down on a rock. "What are you doing?" I asked.

"We can handle this, Oscar. We're going to ford the river," she said, pulling off her shoes and tucking her socks inside.

"We're going to what?! We don't drive a Ford. Let's Dodge the river!"

"We're going to walk across."

"But...! But...! Whenever you try to ford the river in Oregon Trail, someone in your party **always** dies, and a few oxen **always** drown. There are animals in *our* party too! Handsome animals that don't want to die here."

"Don't worry," Mom said, pulling out the leash again. "You won't drown if you're wearing this." And then she hooked me up, and I had no choice.

I stood on the bank for as long as I could while she slowly picked her way across. I gulped as I watched the water climb high enough to get the butt of her shorts wet. But I wasn't going to let myself get dragged into the water like a big baby, so right when the leash was about to run out, I splashed in and dashed across. Other than being wet and a bit cold, neither of us had had any real problems with fording the river, and no one drowned. Once Mom's shoes were back on, she pulled out her phone. "People are going to want to see a picture of what the river looked like where we crossed," she said. "Sit here, so that we can see the river in the background."

I sat cockeyed where she asked me to so that I could block the view of our crossing spot, and then stared at her balefully so she would know that I didn't approve of subjecting a loving and loyal dog to such life-threatening adventures against his will. She moved around a bit to line up her shot, and then looked up. "Hunh. What's that?" She pointed behind me to something about fifteen yards upstream.

I looked. "It's a bridge, Mom. A bridge. Across the river."

"Oh, well if we had used that bridge, you would sure be struggling for a story to tell about this run, wouldn't you?" she shrugged, tying her shoes and continuing down the trail.

Many hours later we had left Montana and were driving through the butt of Idaho when Mom woke me up from my nap. "Oscar, come here, I want to show you something," she said, pointing out the windshield. The mountains had gotten shorter, but they were also cliff-ier. From below they looked like a bunch of surfboards all lined up next to each other. "Do you remember how the river looked like it was stampeding as fast as it could, and then when it reached the top of the waterfall it didn't have time to stop its momentum before it fell off a cliff?"

"Yeah," I said. "But the river is on the ground here, not up there on top of the cliff."

"True, but the people who lived here before the eastern explorers came to this part of the country used to use that spot to hunt buffalo."

"What does that have to do with waterfalls?" I asked.

"Well, that's the interesting part," she said. "They dug a long trench, kind of like a river gorge that ended in one of those slots you see up there. It would take a lot of people a lot of work because they didn't have back hoes or Caterpillars, but when they were finished they could start a buffalo stampede and direct the animals into the

216

channel that they had built. By the time the buffalo at the front reached the cliff, there were too many stampeding animals behind him, and the whole herd would fall off the cliff and die. That way the people had more meat and buffalo skins than their entire tribe needed."

"That's really sad..." I said, thinking of all the times that I had tried to run on a slippery floor and crashed into stuff.

"True. It wasn't environmentally friendly, but it is interesting, don't you think? There are buffalo jumps that were so effective that there are centuries-old bones piled twenty feet deep and buried at the bottom."

"Mom, I don't want to scare you, but I think that you should be more careful when you run in some of those big races... You never know when they might build a runner jump instead of a finish line."

King of the Potato Beasts

The next day was going to be an easy day, but then Mom saw a really amazing-looking trail on our wish list that was on the way home. When I say "on the way," I mean generally down and to the left. We didn't really have a plan for how we're going to get back, so anything that was down and to the left of us and had a road nearby was "on the way."

"Oh Oscar, look at those mountains!" Mom said, showing me the picture. "And there's a lake, see? And a river? We can't miss this!"

"But Mom, it starts above six thousand feet and then climbs to above seven thousand feet. It's going to have white dirt on it."

"It'll be fine! We're way south of where we were when we came through this range the last time, and it's had another week to melt. And rain makes snow melt even faster... Look! The picture was taken at sunset!"

"Will we be there at sunset? Do we have lights for the way back?"

"Well, no. You're missing the point..."

It was cloudy as we drove to the trail so it was hard to tell what the mountains looked like, but from what we could see through the breaks in the clouds, they looked rocky and pointy... and had lots of white on them. "Oh look, Oscar! They're going to be breathtaking. Like that day in Washington... only better because there will be trees and a river and a lake too!"

"But Mom... the white..."

"We're experts at snow now, Oscar. It won't be a problem," Mom said to shush me.

The white dirt wasn't right at the bottom of the trail. It took us a few minutes to reach it, but then it was everywhere. There was regular dirt everywhere too, though, so Mom could pretend like this trail was a good idea. I didn't bother to be as careful, even though this was dog-eating dirt. Every time it swallowed one of my legs, I just said, "You like that?! Here! Take another one! I've got more where that came from!" When I had no more legs left for the white dirt to eat, I would sit on the surface like a legless potato for a second, and then burst out all at once barking, "I'm Oscar, King of the Potato Beasts, the best mountain runner in the world!"

It took a couple of miles, but eventually reality caught up with Mom when the white dirt started sucking up her legs like a couple of pieces of spaghetti. Every time she tried to climb out of the hole, *sluuuurp*, her leg would get sucked back in up to the shorts line. With each step she let out a roar that was a little bit like a gladiator going into battle, and a little bit like someone whose leg was being bitten off by an alligator.

Trying to be helpful, I said, "I just heard about these special shoes that let you walk on top of the white dirt…"

"I don't want to hear it, Oscar."

"Well I was just thinking that…"

"…I was just thinking that we're going about half a mile an hour, and it's probably time to turn back."

"Speak for yourself, I've sprinted about a mile through the woods in the time it's taken you to get to here from that tree over there. Anyway, about these shoes…"

"Oscar, I hate snow. If I bought snowshoes, then I would be committing to spending time in the snow. Since one of my goals in life is to spend as little time in the snow as I possibly can, then snowshoes are against my core values. See?"

"But if you had those special shoes, then you could see this lake, and the summit of Gotcha Day mountain, and all the other things that we've missed because the way there was covered in white dirt."

"I'm entitled to my opinion. Stop challenging me on my beliefs!" she said, and stormed off inchily back down the mountain.

As we walked back down, the clouds started to clear and we could see the mountains that we would never see reflected in the lake at sunset. They were the kinds of mountains that you see in jigsaw puzzles and computer desktop backgrounds; all black and white, and rocky, and pointy enough that you could see sky on both sides. Once we got back to the highway and could look at them from a distance, we saw that they were all clumped together like a bouquet with lots of open sky and lit-up clouds around them. Mom stared at them longingly from the porch of the Visitor's Center as her gadgets sucked their lunch from the plugs on the side of the building, and the stories and photos from days-old adventures rode the bad wifi up over the mountains and soaked slowly into the sky.

Since we didn't have a plan for where to go next, we just continued down and to the left through the mountains for hours. Each bend in the road was more beautiful than the last, and there were campgrounds and trailheads every few miles along the road.

"How did I never know this was here?!" Mom asked. "Why isn't Idaho as famous a tourist destination as Tahoe, or Aspen, or Jackson Hole?"

"Where?" I asked. "Those all sound like dirty words to me."

Mom ignored me. "...All I knew about Idaho was potatoes. But these mountains don't look like potato farms to me!"

"Idaho is famous for potatoes?!" I said. "I'm a potato beast! I knew I belonged here!"

We were very excited to find our campground for the night, and then explore more Idaho mountains the next morning. But then, an hour or so before we planned to stop, the mountains quit on us.

"Gross. This is all ag country," Mom said, squishing up her face.

"I smell cows! So many cows!" I said, sticking my nose out the window.

"Maybe, but these aren't the bucolic, open range kind of cow farms. This must be the potato part of the state."

"We get to camp on a potato range?!" I barked. "I get to meet my subjects!" I couldn't wait.

"There aren't going to be any campgrounds in the potato fields," Mom said, giving me a weird look. "I have a feeling we have a lot of driving left to do."

We had to drive and drive beyond the border of the Potato Kingdom to find a place to sleep. We drove until Idaho turned into Oregon, and "Ag Country" turned back into cattle ranges, and the cattle ranges turned into something like desert. "I had no idea Oregon was so big," Mom said. "I think that this close to the end of the Oregon Trail."

I looked around at the bald little nubbins of hills, and the dry scrubby shrubs. "Well that would be disappointing, after all the cool things the Oregon explorers had seen on their journey through The West."

"I think they were into a different kind of scenery," Mom pointed out. "They didn't have snowshoes or four wheel drive, remember? Some people aren't into adventure scenery. All they want is predictability, safety from danger and a place to grow lots of food."

"Oh, well I guess you would get that here..." I said. But secretly I wondered if maybe the Oregon Trail explorers, once they got here, might be a little bit disappointed that they hadn't done something more exciting like die of dysentery instead.

The Magic Mountain and the Moon

We finally did it! I've lost count of how many times we'd gone toe-to-snow with the white dirt, but one day we actually made it to our destination! And boy oh boy was it worth it. We almost didn't go to this trail. It was called "Strawberry Lake," and Mom thought that it might be too girly for a couple of tough adventurers like us. After some time, I convinced her that even two manful ruffians could have fun on a trail that was pink and sweet and cream-puffy, and golly am I glad she finally agreed.

At first the trail was pretty mild; not exactly a cream puff, but not nearly as rugged as a lot of the other stuff we'd hiked on this trip, so there was no reason not to run. One of us was wheezing from burning lungs and woofing from being out of breath, but I felt great and zoomed around the trail like The Flash. The only hard thing about the trail was that there were a bunch of trees lying down across the path, and we had to push branches out of the way to climb over them. Mom could use her front paws to clear a path, but I had to crash through like Bigfoot.

Once we had gone a couple of miles, Mom looked around and said, "I think we should have reached the lower lake by now…" Then she looked at her phone. "Shoot! I think we're on the wrong trail. How the heck did that happen?!"

"Mom! You have *the worst* sense of direction! You couldn't find a trail if it were a five-lane freeway."

"That's not fair! I don't remember a single place where we could have turned!"

We about-faced and retraced our steps, and Mom watched the little blue dot on her screen the whole time to make sure that we were going in the right direction. Finally, after half a mile we came to a spot where huge tree had fainted, blocking the whole trail. This tree was so big that when it came down, it took a whole section of forest down with it. "Ah *hah*!" Mom said triumphantly. "The trail intersection was hidden under this tree!"

"I know this game," I said. "This is where you make me go around in circles through the bushes for a few minutes, and then we go back to the car-house and you make a cup of tea."

We carefully climbed over the trees on the ground, and much to my surprise, there was another trail that we hadn't seen before crawling out from underneath the fallen monster tree. We followed it, and a few minutes later we were at a lake. This was a very pretty lake with all the regular pretty lake things like big rocks and trees going right up to the edge, but it also had pointy, black-and-white mountains in the background that made it extra nice to look at. There was still more to see on this trail, so we ran around the lake to where the mountain sat, and climbed some more.

Up ahead we could hear static from another angry river. We came around the corner, and then suddenly Mom sighed, "Oh, Oscar!" She actually said it like that, out loud. She sounded like some little girl all tied up in ribbons in an old fashioned movie from before they invented attitude. She said it like she was opening a present and inside was a Strawberry Shortcake doll. 'Too tough' for a girly trail indeed! The thing that had turned Mom into a cream puff was that there was a perfect waterfall falling from right above our heads and spitting out a mist that made the air sparkle. It was small enough that its roar wasn't scary, and you could look at it all at once without moving your head. All around the waterfall were shiny rocks with bright green furry moss decorating them, and next to the big waterfall were smaller neon grey ice waterfalls. On the ground there were giant chunks of ice that were perfectly clear and looked like soccer-ball-sized diamonds. We felt like we were in a fairy land for tough people, like that elf city in Lord of the Rings (obviously, I'm Legolas and Mom is Gimli). I was glad that I wasn't too manly to come here.

The white dirt began right after the waterfall, and within a few minutes it had swallowed the trail whole. This was the hungry kind of white dirt that ate feet and paws in one big bite. Mom used a set of old footprints to help her navigate and also keep her socks dry. She placed her feet where the other feet went, even when the footprint went as deep as her thigh. When we lost the tracks (which was often), Mom used her phone to find what direction we needed to go, and then we climbed through bushes and over rocks in a straight line until we found the tracks again. We had a good laugh about all the signs at the trailhead that told us to stay on the trail to protect the plant life. "I would love to stay on the trail, if I could find it!" Mom said. *Hardy-har-har-har.*

Finally, after close to a dog hour of wandering leglessly through the white dirt, we came out of the trees in a giant bowl with mountains on all sides. These weren't lame, lumpy mountains that you can walk up, but sharp, straight up-and-down kind that would hurt God's butt if he sat on them. I knew that God had been there, because there were giant boulders sitting in the middle of the bowl that were the size of a house, and they were way too big to fall from anywhere but God's pocket in the sky. If we had wanted to climb to the top of those prickly mountains, we would have needed ropes, tools, and a lot of skill and experience that Mom didn't have. But lucky for us, the lake we were looking for was sitting under a cape of ice right behind a boulder the size of a Starbucks. We didn't need ropes and spiky shoes to finish, we had made it!

On our way back down Mom leashed herself to me, just like a mountain climber buddy. I thought maybe it was for safety, but it could also have been because I was barking at some turtle-hikers in front of us and "scaring" one of them. The problem was that we were still in the deep white dirt, which meant that I had to sprint and roll a lot, and Mom was still trying to balance and place her feet carefully in the foot holes. It seemed like whenever I pulled to get at something interesting, she had been trying to balance on one leg and the leash made her fall over in the white dirt. Finally she gave up and unhooked me. "Just bark yourself out," she told me. "I'll apologize when I catch up."

By the time we had finished, we had turned a 6.2-mile moderate trail run into a 7.7-mile expedition. And then we went to the moon.

...At least I *think* it was the moon. We came down from the mountain and in no time at all the world looked like desert, with stripes on the rocks and those funny hills that look like squashed totem poles. The road took us through a narrow slot between two mountains just wide enough for a roadway, and when we popped out, we were on the moon.

There is a rumor that the moon is made of green cheese, but that is untrue. The moon is actually made of green tea and toothpaste. Here on the surface of the moon someone had squeezed out a giant tube of toothpaste in big, sloppy globs, and then covered it in the powder that they use to make matcha at Starbucks.

At this trail we had a choice between walking a very short museum-walk with stuff about fossils, or doing a longer scenic walk on the ridge so that we could look down on the moon, and the desert on the other side of it. "Tell you what," Mom said. "If they're cool fossils like dinosaurs then we'll do the fossil walk. If they're lame fossils like invertebrates then we'll do the scenic walk."

"What's an inverberate?" I asked.

"They're living things that don't do anything interesting like attack each other, or grow long necks or very short arms."

"What are fossils?" I asked.

"They're the dead bodies of animals that weren't eaten up by time because they got covered by a volcano and turned into rocks instead."

"Oh, well that sounds exciting..." I said.

So we walked to the first sign, which showed a picture of a fossil of a sort of very large wombat, or monstrous and muscular chinchilla. "Is this an interesting fossil or is it an inverberate?" I asked.

"I don't know... It's a mammal, so it doesn't seem very exotic to me," Mom said. "Let's go up to the ridge." So we turned back and climbed up the hill, but when we got there it was kind of hot, and we could see that we were in the desert, which was not very interesting after our mountain trek in leg-eating white dirt this morning. When we stopped for Mom to take a picture of me looking artistic, I lay down and refused to get back up again. "I'm hot and this is lame. Can we go back to the moon, please?"

When we got back down to the moon there was a lady sitting on a bench looking tired. I could tell she wanted to scratch my butt, so I joined her so that we could sit in the shade together. She loved me, obviously, and so did the rest of her family, who came a minute or two later and melted onto the bench next to us with a fainting sigh. "He must be a very fit dog to do this hike," they said before we parted ways for Mom and me to walk up the museum trail, and the family to walk back to the car kennel.

Once they were out of telepathy range, I asked Mom, "Is this hike going to be very difficult?" I didn't know if the moon was covered in difficult terrain, but I thought maybe not.

"No, it's less than a mile, hardly climbs at all, and has walkways so you don't have to climb over rocks," Mom said, looking a bit confused.

"Then why are they having so much trouble?"

"I don't think that we're particularly fit, but I guess that some people are just very, very unfit. I'm not sure where you go wrong in life to where walking a mile and a half on basically level terrain in seventy-degree weather is exhausting. Let's just be happy that we fell into a different kind of lifestyle so that we don't miss things like magic waterfalls and secret lakes and walking on the moon."

We walked up the trail and saw a dead turtle that looked like a regular rock, and a saber-toothed cat that was smaller than an Oscar, and something that the scientists said might be an aardvark-like-thing or a horse-like-thing. As we were walking back to the car, another person on a bench wanted to talk to us.

"The moose-skeeters are coming out," the man said.

"Mosquitoes are hatching out of that stuff?" Mom said incredulously, pointing to the little puddles of matcha latte on the ground.

"Well I've been bitten three times already," the man said.

"You must smell better than I do…" Mom said as we walked away.

"Mom, I thought you said that hum-bugs were only in places with still water," I said, alarmed. "We're in the desert!"

"Oscar, I don't think that man knew what he was talking about... not everybody's a naturalist."

"Well he was right about one thing; you *are* pretty stinky..." I said.

Pupportunity Cost

The trouble started that night. After we left the moon, Mom wanted to find a place that had a shower, but we were getting close to a city called Bend, and cities are never good places to live in a car-house. We planned to find a place about an hour outside of the city, but Mom miscalculated and we were sucked into the Gore Tex of the city before we found a place to stop. I had resigned myself to smelling Mom's stinkiness for another day, and we were on our way to The Ritz of Parking Lots when we found a car-house park with an opening. I thought it was a good place, but Mom said that it wasn't because:

- the shower was "revolting"
- the after-hours check-in didn't give her the wifi password
- you couldn't use the water if you didn't bring your own hose
- our view was of the Wendy's drive-through
- there was a streetlight that shined right into the Covered Wagon when we slept
- and they locked the toilets overnight

"...And this dump costs twice what that palace in Missoula cost!" she fumed.

Our trail for the day was like the Motel Six Stars of trails, with all the comforts and amenities like a paved car kennel, one-bar cell service within only a fifteen minute drive, and a little stinky Christmas ornament that smelled like pine tree farts in the people potty. As Mom was getting everything ready for our run, she discovered that one of her shoes was missing.

"Don't you feel so lucky that you brought an extra pair of shoes?" I said. Mom has been using her spare pair whenever the white dirt makes her good pair too wet to wear for two runs in a row.

"But these shoes are falling apart!" she complained. "The left one has like five rips in it. I'm going to bust out the side of it one of these days."

"Well we can get you a new pair," I said. "See? We're in a city where they do lots of outdoorsy things, I bet they sell lots of trail shoes."

"But I have freakishly small feet. I have to order these ones online because no stores carry my size."

"Well I'm sure that we can find another brand that you don't know that you like yet," I tried.

"Truthfully, Oscar. We're running out of money. I don't know if spending a hundred and fifty dollars on a new pair of trail shoes is the best use of the money we have left." Dogs can't have credit cards, so I didn't know how to answer that. Instead, I kept quiet and strained at my leash to go make friends with a bunch of mountain biker ladies who were also getting ready to leave the car kennel without commenting on what a good-looking dog I am.

The trail turned out to be an easy seven-mile flat route that followed a giggling river through the pine trees to a waterfall. "Isn't this great, Mom?" I said. "No dirt roads to get here, no mountains to climb, no big trees blown over the trail, no dog-boiling weather or

Wagon-stopping white dirt... Just a nice, easy run through the pine trees."

"It's alright, I guess," Mom said, like it wasn't so great at all.

"Oh brother, what is it now?" I asked.

"I'm bummed out about my shoe."

"Don't be bummed. We're almost home. I bet your foot won't rip all the way out of your shoes for at least another week."

"No, it's not that. I hate the feeling that because I need to buy new shoes, I can't buy something else I'll love with that money. Those ladies in the parking lot had those beautiful mountain bikes... I would like to buy a mountain bike and make friends to ride it with, but there are so many other things to save up for..."

"That's silly, Mom. I can't ride a mountain bike, so obviously buying The Covered Wagon was a better purchase because it lets you spend more time with me."

"It's not just bikes and shoes. It's also this trail. It's nice and everything, but wouldn't you rather be seeing something spectacular today that not everybody gets to see? I mean, for heaven's sake, you can drive right up to the waterfall at the top, and there was a big railing blocking all the dog views. I'm sure we could have found something better and more dangerous if we'd tried."

"It's okay, Mom. I could smell the waterfall through the railing. Don't be a trail snob. Isn't it relaxing to run on a trail that is easy on the Covered Wagon, and easy on your legs?"

"But doesn't it ever give you anxiety?" Mom asked.

"It gives me anxiety to be left outside of Starbucks not knowing if you're in there with a murderer. Exploring natural places never makes me feel like Starbucks. Why would it give me anxiety when I'm not missing anything?"

"Because we can't possibly see all the beautiful places and do all the cool things. When we pick one trail, that always means that we're missing another trail. That's called 'opportunity cost.' Even if we could see everything, we would eventually get tired, and then we would be spending our time in beautiful places wishing that we weren't there. Missing beautiful places, and not enjoying beautiful places while I'm there make me feel like I'm wasting my life."

"Being a dog isn't about seeing all the beautiful places, it's about knowing that no matter where you are, it is a beautiful place if you are with your pack and know how to sniff out adventure. Remember The Loneliest Road in America? Most people think that desert is boring, but we couldn't have been happier because there were bunnies to chase, and you were inspired by the Pony Express, and that was the moment our whole adventure changed from bad to great. Remember?" I looked at Mom, but I could tell she couldn't remember how exciting that day had been for us. So I changed the subject. "Why don't we go back and look for your shoe so that you don't have to be anxious about spending our adventure stressing about it."

"But we'll have to backtrack. We'll be wasting my life… I mean, we'll be wasting time."

"Today was supposed to be a rest day anyway. What's more relaxing? Finding your shoe, or spending the day in a shoe store?"

So we drove back to the crummy car-house park where Mom asked the man at the desk if he'd seen her shoe. He hadn't. "Oh well. Thanks for trying," she said, looking down at the floor in sadness. She was still looking down when she turned around to walk out. Then she said, "**MY SHOE!**" Someone had left it on the floor with a note in it! "Oh Oscar," she said when we came back to the Covered Wagon. "You were right, it wasn't my shoe that ruined our run, it was me! I did all that worrying for nothing. I'm going to live the rest of today just like a dog. No FOMO for me, let's just drive south until we sniff out a good campground. There are bound to be a ton of them; the map is practically solid green from here to Bakersfield. We'll stop early and then we can build a fire and relax all day! We'll be stopped in time for lunch!"

Mom doesn't make a very good dog, because it took us six hours to find a campground. First we had to escape the Gore Tex of the city. There was plenty of open land around Bend, but now that Mom remembered that she can set things on fire, she wanted to go somewhere where she would be allowed to burn stuff. We drove and drove, but the wilder-ness never came. We just found one gas-station-depressing-restaurant-and-used-car-lot town after another. Then the rain started. There was no reason to stop if it was raining, so we continued driving south…

It rained all the way back to California, where we were held up by a bandit looking for nature smugglers. The highway robber wasn't very intimidating-looking because he was dressed like Russell from *Up*, but that was probably part of his hustle. Hustle-Russell was undaunted by my barking and stole Mom's perfectly ripe avocado, saying that it was unsafe to bring a perfectly ripe avocado from Oregon into California. Mom was almost as upset about having her avocado stolen as she was about her shoe, because a perfectly ripe avocado is even more rare than a trail shoe that fits your freakishly small paws perfectly.

Now Mom was getting even more upset because she was hangry and Hustle-Russell had stolen her lunch, and there was still nowhere to stop because we were in farmland where they don't build campgrounds with fire pits. We finally found a campground when it was nearly dinner time. My disappointment mounted as Mom and I collected a whole bunch of sticks that I was hoping that she would throw, but she just set them on fire instead. Then she finally began to make us some food.

Right when our breakfast-snack-lunch-snack-dinner was about to be ready, a car stopped at the campground so that the people inside could use the potty.

"Are we in time for dinner?" asked the man. He asked in that way that you'd look like a boob no matter what answer you gave, so you're just supposed to laugh even though it's not funny. But Mom wasn't in a laughing mood.

"This is lunch, and breakfast too," Mom mumbled, but the man already wasn't listening. He thought that his funny joke should be the end of the conversation. So she killed the man and we had to eat him to destroy the evidence.

The Trail that Goes Forever

By now we had fallen out of Oregon and landed in a familiar place in California, so Mom said that it was okay for us to go on without a plan. According to Mom, when you find yourself in the same very remote place five times in a year, and your soul feels like it gets belly rubs on every visit, then you ought to sniff that place very closely to see what it's trying to tell you. She said that maybe it was trying to tell us that we should buy our forever stuck house up here. I looked around and wondered if I would be the same Oscar if I lived in a place with cows and mountains in my backyard rather than a little place where eight cars share my driveway and I have to bark at all of them when they come home. What would I bark at if I had no neighbors? Would I bark at the cows, or would I not need to bark at all? Would I be myself if I didn't bark?

Another reason that we didn't have a plan was because the last weather report we saw before the air stopped feeding The Witch in Mom's Phone said that it was supposed to rain. But the first good surprise that our special place gave us was that it was a perfectly sunny, clear, warm day. When Mom saw a sign at the side of the highway that said that there were views, picnic tables, and hiking trails in the same spot, she decided that that would be our adventure place for the day. The sky was so clear that when I looked left I could see a pointy white mountain far in the distance that looked just like the mountain emoji. When I looked in the opposite direction, there was another pointy, white mountain emoji. I felt like we were living in an Instagram caption. We knew that the first emoji was called Mt. Lassen, but we were surprised to find out that the other one was Mt. Shasta, which we had seen on one of our first days of adventuring, when we weren't good at it yet. Back then Mt Shasta had hidden from us, but now that we were in our happy place, it wasn't scared anymore and came out to show us its pointiness and emojiness.

The trail left right from the end of the car kennel and went toward Mt. Lassen. It wasn't the toughest trail we'd ever done, but we weren't looking for tough that day. It would have been easy running, but Mom kept stopping and walking, even when she didn't have to. "What's wrong with you? Don't you want to run so you can see as much as possible?" I asked.

"My legs are tired, Oscar, and today they would enjoy the trail more if we walked."

"But we might not get to see the whole thing. I know how much you hate when we don't get to the end."

"There's no way we could finish this trail, Oscar. It goes south all the way to Mexico, and north all the way to Canada. In fact, we're standing only a few miles from the midpoint right here. We've crossed this trail a bunch of times in our travels. We were near it in Washington on your Gotcha Day, and on the way out of Death Valley, and that day we got lost and had to drive seven hours to the Devil's Punchbowl, and that day that my hydration bladder exploded, and even yesterday in the enchanted wilderness."

My imagination lit on fire when I thought about that. "Has anyone ever walked the whole thing?!" I asked.

"Oh sure, hundreds of people hike the whole thing every year, and even more people hike the whole length in stages over several years."

"But then where do they leave their car-house? Do they have to go back for it every night?"

"They don't use a car-house. They carry everything they need on their backs, like a turtle."

"Is that something that we could do?!" I asked, staring off into the distance and imagining walking all the way to Canada.

"Unfortunately not," Mom said, looking sad. "A lot of it goes through National and State Parks where they don't allow dogs. That's why we couldn't go to Glacier or Yellowstone in Montana... or Yosemite, or Big Sur, or Olympic Park, or Crater Lake, or lots of the other places that people recommended." We both sighed when we thought about all the places that I can't go just because I'm a dog and I poop in the bushes, bark at people, and chase bunnies. It really doesn't seem fair, because Mom does all those things except chase bunnies. "Anyway, it gets really hot in some of those places and you have to hike in the middle of the day. You probably wouldn't like it," Mom said. Then she pointed at an old dead tree that had its butt sticking up in the air. "Look! That tree looks like an octopus's cloaca! Go stand on it so I can take a picture."

"Mom, don't be silly. Octopodes don't have cloacas. Where did you learn biology?"

Another reason that Mom was walking was because her phone worked on this mountain. It was the first time since yesterday morning that we could get our questions answered about where we were and where we should go next. "Do you want to go to Tahoe tomorrow?" she asked.

"What's Tahoe?"

"It's a lake with mountains around it. It's real pretty, but it would take us another three or four hours of driving to get there. Either that or we could relax here and then just go home tomorrow and recover."

I thought about it. "Is Tahoe close to home?" I asked.

"Yeah, it's only about three or four hours' drive, same as here."

"Then let's come back when your legs aren't tired of running, and your eyes aren't tired from mountains, and the white dirt has soaked into the mountains and buffalo-jumped through the rivers a little bit more. We're not going to stop adventures, are we?"

"No, let's promise not to stop adventures."

"You swear? You promise that if we go home that we won't stay there forever and get bored again?"

"I swear on the Covered Wagon that cost me the chance of becoming a mountain biker that we will not stop having adventures."

"Okay, then let's relax."

So we drove not a very long way to our maybe-future-home, where Mom threw sticks into the river so that I could bark at them, and then she set more sticks on fire while she wrote in her thinking book.

Our Special Place

For our last adventure of the trip, Mom and I finally realized a dream that we'd had since the summer before: running on the trails around Second Dog Valley. This was my third time int the Valley, and Mom had been there four times, but until that day something had always kept us out of the woods. Now that we had survived in the desert, traveled through time, climbed tall mountains, walked in and on, and fallen through white dirt, explored hundreds of miles of trails by paw, and driven hundreds of miles on car trails (and thousands more on regular roads) in a Covered Wagon, we hoped that we had finally proven ourselves worthy to see the trails of Second Dog Valley. The day we finally made it to Second Dog Wilder-ness we drove eight miles up a mountain on a dirt road to get to the trailhead. Car trails are always risky because we never know when the trail will be too difficult for The Covered Wagon, but this dirt road let us through, and at the trailhead we found a secret campground next to a lake. That's the cool thing about these mountain places: sometimes you think that you're so far into the wilder-ness that you'll be lost forever, and then you find a people potty, or a campground that shows that someone loves this corner of the earth enough to build a place for anyone who visits to poop in privacy.

The trail ran around the lake that was so clear that we could see fishies swimming inside. "I wonder how fish get up here above five thousand feet..." Mom said.

"That's easy," I said. "They're mountain climbing fish. Like dirt roads are trails for cars, rivers are trails for fish."

"You've seen some of those rivers. How's a one-inch fish going to swim up something like that?" Mom asked, doubtfully. Sometimes she can be so dense.

"Haven't you been paying attention on all of our wilder-ness expeditions?" I asked. "You can get up anything with four wheel drive." But Mom is a suburban person, so she's clueless about how tough and determined nature is.

Once the lake was behind us, we climbed up the side of the mountain. The mountain was made of one enormous rock that was covered in smaller but still giant rocks that had fallen off of it. At first it looked like we were climbing wild up the mountain, but when I got close I could see that someone had made steps out of the boulders. Even though all the different steps were too varied to run, we had an easy time getting up the steep side of the mountain. "See how easy hiking can be when there's no snow blocking our trail!" Mom said. "Imagine everything we could have seen if we started this trip a few weeks later..."

"Oh, look! There it is!" I said, running up to where the mountain got closer together and the rock hid under some trees, and the trail hid under some white dirt. But this white dirt wasn't as serious as the stuff we'd hiked through earlier in the trip. It nibbled at our feet, but mostly we could walk safely on top of or around it.

Once we were in the trees, Mom got really antsy and insisted that I stay close to her.

"Don't worry, Mom. I don't think that there are any other hikers up here today. It's a Tuesday. Remember Tuesday?"

"I'm not worried about hikers. There are cats that hide in these trees. They jump down and before you know what's happening, they've grabbed you by the head and are dragging you into the bushes to eat you up."

"Oh! I love cats!" I said. "They are great fun to chase! I hope one drops on me."

"Not these cats..." Mom warned. She gets so scared of the silliest things.

After running through the trees growing on the back of the mountain's head for a couple of miles, we popped out on the forehead of the mountain. We walked around see a menu of other mountains to climb in all directions. I could tell that Mom was starting to get jittery like she does when she tries to climb all the mountains at once, so I jumped to the rescue. "Sit!" I told her. She sat on a rock right at the edge of the mountain.

"Now put your hand on a dog," I told her. She put her arm around me and started scratching me behind the ear and banging on my chest. I licked the salt off her face.

"Okay, now don't look for the roads and trails," I whispered in her ear. "Just look at all the mountains at once, as part of one big picture." I could feel her getting a little anxious, so I leaned in a little harder so she would hug me closer. She started to relax again.

"See how those other mountains are what makes the top of this mountain beautiful?" I said. "That means that you are doing all the mountains at once. See? You did it. You can relax."

"You're right," Mom said. "We can't be on top of all the mountains at once. It would be very sad indeed if we ran out of mountains to climb."

This place had tried to keep us away with cold and rain and lost-getting, but sometimes you just need to come back enough times to show that you really want to be there for a place to let you in. We were like Meatloaf on the porch in *Fight Club*. We stood there for a long time to show that we were serious, but now that the mountain had let us in I could tell that it was going to let us back whenever we wanted.

Finally Mom stood up and turned back to the trail that would take us down the mountain. "Let's see if we can finish this trip in a relaxing way and get back in time to miss rush hour," she suggested.

The Witch in Mom's Phone gave us a gentle reintroduction to the human world. Rather than taking the highway, she took us for more than fifty miles through a back mountain road that turned into a dirt road for a pawful of miles. We fell so steeply out of the mountains that the Covered Wagon shuddered, but eventually we reached the hot, dusty farms, and bit by bit I started to recognize the places that we were driving. Finally, we got to our stuck house, where Mom unloaded our adventure out of the Covered Wagon. Mom showered all the wilder-ness smells off of her, and we were back to our old life by the time the sun set.

Melting

After everything that Mom and I had done and the things that we had seen, it was hard to go back to finding adventure at home. Mom's knee was doing a "weird thing," so we looked for places where I could run and she didn't have to. One day we went to the off-leash hiking place. The off-leash area used to seem really big, but now that I'd climbed mountains in eight states, it seemed silly to go bananas just because Mom took the leash off. I couldn't find anyone to bark at or chase anyway. It was a hot day, so maybe all the dogs were hiding in the shade or something. We walked all around the off-leash area looking for dogs under all the trees and behind all the rocks, but they weren't anywhere to be found.

It wasn't until we had left the off-leash area and were walking back through the leash-y bit that we passed all the dogs that had come to play with me. They had all been turned into legless potatoes on the way to the playground, and now were lying lifeless in the shade at the side of the trail.

First we came to a poor yellow lab puppy that had lost all of his legs. "Help me!" he pleaded. "I was just walking along with my lady, and then suddenly here I am on the ground. I know I used to have legs to walk on, but now I'm a potato."

"Ah, you melted," I told him, sagely. "That's what happens in the summer. There's nothing you can do to prevent melting, it just happens and then you're stuck being a potato for a minute or two till your legs grow back. I've found that it helps them grow if you drink water."

Next we passed a mutt whose legs had just grown back after drinking some water. He looked like a fine, upstanding guy that maybe I could bark at and chase. But he couldn't play because his person had been turned to stone. While he drank out of his bowl at her feet, she stood stock still. She wore her head fur down over her neck and shoulders in the way that real people never wear it on hot days, and she was wearing big sunglasses that covered half of her face, which is how humans hide their antisociability on sunny days. I wondered if maybe her brain had boiled under all that hair, and now she was a potato-head. Then the potato-head looked at its phone, and I realized that she wasn't a potato, she was just a boring person. This poor dog probably had to spend half his life watching his lady watch herself in the mirror and putting different disguises on her face, and then watching her watch herself in her phone taking selfies for Instagram. She wasn't even smart enough to know that no one wants to see a photo that's just a human face, and Instagram is made for looking at cute dogs. Some dogs enjoy that kind of glossy life, but Mom and I would rather get dirt on our faces than stay indoors and look pretty.

Next we met a very handsome gentleman dressed in a tux just like mine. But only Oscar and James Bond can wear a tux on a hot day without panting, and this poor guy was struggling. As I came past, he rose up from being a potato to say hello and sniff my butt. "It's a miracle!" said his lady. "He was too hot to walk down the hill, but now that he's smelled your irresistible butt, he has legs to stand on again!" I was happy for this dog for getting his legs back, and happy for this lady for getting her dog back. But "miracle?" Nah, I'm just very, very inspiring.

If you try to walk away from a dog that just got his legs back because of you, obviously he's going to follow you. "He's walking again! Praise Oscar!" the lady gushed, only she pronounced it, 'good boy,' and come to think of it I'm not positive she was talking to me.

We walked on, me with the swagger and him reaching out his neck to sniff my butt, like my butt had him by the leash. Then we came to the end of the shady patch, and as soon as we were back in the sun, his legs crumbled to dust and he went back to being a potato-beast, and Mom and I walked the rest of the way back to the car on our own like the only two survivors of a spud-pocalypse.

Oscar the Bug Snapper

Mom had found a foster job that would give her a place to go during the week and a few more months to figure out what she wanted to do with our lives. But after a couple of weeks of showering every day and putting on "real pants," Mom had ants in her slacks to get out of the Stuck House and a stuck routine. So once she finished working one day, Mom and I got in the Covered Wagon and drove to a trail just outside of Big Sir. We arrived at the bottom of the trail in the dark and spooky part of the night, so we had no idea what it would look like when we woke up.

The way weather works in California is that the cooler and wetter it is at the ocean, the hotter and drier it is on the other side of the mountains. That means that the hotter it is at our Stuck House, the colder it will be at the beach. Since the weather had been roasting at home, I hoped that meant that it would be nice and cool in Big Sir.

When we sleep at our Stuck House, there are always people making noise, so I need to bark at all of them, even if that means barking from bed in the middle of the night. And then Mom needs to bark at me to stop (even though I don't pay much attention, I think it makes her feel better to join in). The result is that neither of us sleep very well in our Stuck House. But when we're camping there isn't usually anything for me to bark at, so we sleep like rocks. That's how Mom messed up our early morning plan and slept and slept until the sun had already been up for awhile.

"Mom! You've ruined it! We're going to die now," I said when I stepped out into the warm, sunny morning.

"It's only seven in the morning! It's been this hot all night. Anyway, I kind of thought we would be near the ocean and it would be foggy..."

I looked around. All I could see were the kinds of plants that you get in hot places, and grass that smelled like brown and yellow and ovens. "You missed the ocean. By a lot," I told her.

"Yeah, well... apparently Big Sur has an inland side. Who knew...?"

Mom packed lots of water into a packpack and we started hiking. I sprinted in loops through the foxtail and tick grass, but Mom could only run for a few seconds before she had to walk. "Come on!" I insisted. "We've got to hurry so that we can be done before the heat."

"I don't know what's wrong with me," Mom said. "Maybe I have some sort of neurological disorder, or a nutrient deficiency, or maybe I'm aging at an accelerated rate... but my legs feel wobbly, and I feel terrible when I try to run. I wish that I could check with a doctor and find out what's wrong with me." She meant consulting The Witch to look at WebMD for the most dramatic and scary thing that she could find. But The Witch had no bars, so the good doctor wasn't open for consultations.

"Oh, I know what that is," I said. "You're just melting. Come on, it's not permanent. You'll be fine. I mean, not today, but when it cools down you'll be fine. Drink some water."

"Okay, but I'm still trading in some of our runs for yoga sessions. I mean it this time!" she said, and tottered on.

This trail was like nature's storage room, where all the cool things were in one place, but disordered and piled on top of each other in a way that made it hard to look at them right. Big bits of sandstone with holes scooped out like swiss cheese stuck out of the ground. There were slabby sheets of rock fanned out on the grass like someone had knocked over a giant stack of mattress sized pancakes. In shady glades crouched little villages of boulders that definitely had gnomes living behind them. We found a tractor that had been abandoned in a grove of dry trees after the Revolutionary War. A patch of leafy plants wore a layer of white fuzz and looked like they were covered in frost as a fashion statement. Wildflowers grew in all the shades of grey in the rainbow. As we climbed higher, there were views of the mountains in every direction that I looked. I could even see off in the distance where the mountains fell into the ocean and the cool, grey fog clumped like a bad mood.

What made it hard to enjoy these things was that this trail also had every single kind of bug ever invented, and they were all obsessed with me. There were the bugs that buzz in your ears, and the bugs that dive for your eyeballs, and the bugs that crawl all over your skin, and the bugs that leave webs that stick to dangling tongues and human sweat, and at least one tick. Mom's front paws were never still, alternating between swatting and trying to get the spider webs out of her goopy sweat, in an endless loop like a gif left open on your screen. If I stopped to enjoy the scenery or pose for a picture, the bugs would descend on me like crazed fans. I couldn't sit still for a picture because I needed to snap at flies constantly. Mom couldn't take good pictures because at the critical moment she needed her paws and arms for swatting, even when she didn't mean to.

As we got higher up the trail, another infestation started in addition to the bug problem: a plague of shrubbery. The trail was so overgrown that we were almost constantly being scraped and strafed by leaves the shape of steak knives, poked by sharp sticks, or raked by branches reaching out into the path. Then Mom marched right off the trail and directly into a bush.

"Mom, what are you doing?"

"I think the trail's this way."

"Are you sure?"

"Yeah. See? It thins out just right on the other side of these two bushes." Mom tried to walk through the bush, but the branches were holding hands so thickly that she got stuck. They grabbed onto her shorts and the packpack straps and pinned her in place, and the steep, sandy ground slid backward every time she tried to take a step.

Finally she broke through the bushes and I followed her into a clearing. We were surrounded by a wall of Oscar-high bushes that went all the way around us in a ring.

"This sucks," Mom said. "Let's go back." It wasn't until we'd pushed back through the bushes for about a hundred yards that we saw that the trail had turned where Mom had not. Since our excuse to leave was gone, we kept fighting the bugs and bushes on the way to the top.

We were within a quarter mile of the tower on top of the mountain when we somehow got turned around again and found ourselves walking back down the mountain the way we had come. "I'm not having much fun, are you?" Mom asked.

"No, [snap] not really [snap]," I said with my tongue hanging around my ankles.

"Forget it, this is close enough," she said. But "forget it" doesn't make you magically land at the bottom of the trail next to your car-house. We still had more than five miles to hike back, and it was getting seriously hot.

I hoped that it would be easier hiking back down, but the bushes were just as grabby on the way down as they had been on the way up, and the ground was steep and sandy, with lots of loose rocks that rolled away like a conveyor belt under Mom's feet as she lurched down the hill. So even though down is supposed to move faster, we were still making slow progress, as the sun blazed hotter every minute.

I jogged from shady spot to shady spot where I lay down and snapped and panted while Mom marched resolutely on, not even bothering to wait for me. I looked forward to drinking from the little streams we had crossed on the way up, but they were all gone by the time we got back to them. I'm not exaggerating! It was so hot that entire streams had disappeared in a single morning. Mom kept pouring me water, but most of the time the bugs distracted me before I could drink it. In my thrashing, I threw the water on the ground more often than not, which made Mom stomp off in a huff.

It took us almost five hours to complete the eleven mile trail, and by the time we got back to the Covered Wagon, the temperature was over ninety degrees. All I wanted to do was lay on a cool floor somewhere and pant, but there was nowhere cool for miles around, least of all the Covered Wagon, whose air conditioning was broken. She offered me lunch to say sorry for cooking me, but I refused. All I wanted was to lay in the dust and melt.

I melted in the dust and watched Mom take off every bit of clothing she was wearing until she was standing in the parking lot in nothing but her skin and flip flops. I wondered if maybe there was a shower somewhere that I didn't know about, or maybe she was just crazed by the heat? But my hopes of a cool swim were dashed when Mom pulled dry clothes out of a bag and put them on before signaling me to climb into the back of the Wagon. Then we rode our rolling oven for hours through the world's hottest afternoon. I'm a pretty positive dude, but I had to admit that it was the least fun adventure we'd ever been on.

Oscar the Heckler

Mom wasn't the only one who had gone back to work once we got home from our walkabout. Now that we were back on Our Trails, I was back to going on patrols and barking at all the guests as a Mayor must do. You can't be the Mayor when you're adventuring because there are too many new things to explore, but My Trail was still familiar and boring. Mom and I had to stay leashed together anyway, so there wasn't much exploring to be done within three feet of Mom's waist. During one morning patrol, your brave and handsome hero (that's me) was attacked on his home turf.

We were running on one of our favorite trails very early in the morning, and other than the ghosts that hide in the June Gloom, we had the mountain to ourselves. Suddenly I felt a zippy pain on my ankle that spread quickly through the back of my whole leg. "What the..." I thought, and snapped my head around to kill whatever had caused this torture. I couldn't find anything, so I resumed running when ZAP! it happened again, and I whipped my head around the other way.

"Ugh! Oscar, stop it!" Mom said without turning around to see why I kept tugging on the leash and breaking her stride. I was under attack by some invisible ghost jellyfish that kept shocking me with stinging electricity, and this ogre was yelling at me for slowing her down! Every few steps a fresh pain burst on my leg, and I had to stop and whip from one side to the other to try and catch my attacker.

"What the heck is wrong with you?" Mom said, finally turning around to see her faithful and loving life partner not sniffing at a flower, but thrashing around like a fish in agony. "Oh, Oscar. I'm so sorry!" she said, as she found the wasp that was hiding in the hollow groove of my ankle and knocked it off with a leaf.

Once we had climbed the mountain and were on our way back down, we came up behind two hiking humans that needed passing. When we were within range, I sped up to catch them, which always makes Mom a little tense. To soothe herself, she talks nonsense in her tea kettle voice. She acts like she's talking to me, but I think she really does it to warn the humans that I'm coming and trick them into thinking that she has control over the situation. When I got to the right distance away, I barked, "Hey, strange humans! I'm Oscar and I own these here woods. That means that you have to play a game with me."

"I'm sorry," Mom said. "He barks but he's friendly, I swear."

"...Hey! Are you listening to me?" I barked, jumping back and forth to get their attention. "Here are the rules of the game: I bark all ferocious, and then you have to stop and say how cute I am. Then I'll wag my tail, but you've got to keep complimenting me until I stop barking..."

"Oh, he's just being protective," the lady said.

"Protective of whom?" I barked. I jumped forward in a pretend lunge, and then jumped back like I was going to cut and run to give her a chance to chase me. I wanted to get her attention by showing that I was a really fun guy who knew how to play lots of games. "Don't change the subject. I'm not done," I went on. "You've got to keep saying nice things about me until I stick my butt at you, and then you scratch it and say, 'awwww.' Got it?"

I barked and barked, but the lady must not have understood the rules because she didn't say her lines. I even gave her a chance to pet me by sticking my head real close to her hand, but she didn't get the hint. So I ran past her and got behind the man.

"Did you hear the instructions?" I asked him. "This is the part where I bark a lot, so that's your cue to say nice things."

"Don't eat me, buddy," the guy said in a friendly voice.

"Why would I eat you? Are you made of cheese?"

"Yes, Oscar," Mom said. "We all get it. You're very ferocious. Can you please shut up now?"

"You're playing the game wrong, you big galoot!" I said, running up beside the man and barking right at his butt without breaking stride. "Your line is, 'Oh! He's so cute!' Repeat after me... 'Oh...'"

"Settle down, big guy," the man said.

"...'he's so...'" I went on.

"Okay, you've showed him. He's quaking in his boots. Now quit it," Mom said.

"...'cute!'" I finished for him. But then he was behind us and we had an open trail again.

"Gol-*ly*," I said to Mom, after barking one more time over my shoulder for good measure. "I don't know why some people are such rude guests. Did you see that couple? It was like they thought they owned place and I was interrupting their good time. How very rude!"

Spaghetti Monsters

One afternoon Mom and I got in the car and drove a medium-long way. The sky got more and more grey and cold as we drove, like it was warning us of danger. Mom gets agitated when she sees these kinds of clouds, and calls them "mominous," which is her word for danger that only she can feel. Even though I'm not scared of a fluffy cloud, it makes me anxious when Mom is anxious, so I felt mominous too.

When she stopped the car I could smell dogs, and people, and sheep. This must be a doggie amusement park! I was so excited to get out and meet all of the dogs and people and especially the sheep that I ran around to all the windows to get a better view of the party. Then I barked at the partygoers to let them know I was coming as soon as the car opened. When Mom opened her door, I pushed my head into her back so that I would be ready to jump out behind her to a trumpeting *tadaaaaa*!

"No, you've got to stay in here until you can be cool," Mom said. Then she went to where I couldn't see her, leaving me all alone in the car for like six years. I barked and barked that I was already cool, but no one was paying attention to me!

Eventually Mom came back and got me, and I barked in person at every one of those people and dogs standing around and politely waiting for me to liven up the place. The sheep stayed in their bathroom behind the fence, but the best surprise of all was that the Dean of my puppy university – the lady who taught Mom doggie telepathy and taught me all of the cool tricks that make the ladies go, "Aaaaaawwww!" – was there!

The Dean may be the best teacher of dogs and humans in the whole wide world, but she sure throws a lame party because none of the dogs were running or wrestling or even sticking their faces in each other's butts. They were all just wearing leashes and waiting around patiently with their humans. Every few minutes, a man came and took one family at a time into a penned-in area.

When it was my turn, The Man gave me some pats and then put this really big and clunky collar on my neck. "It's okay, dude," I said. "I already have one, and mine has lobsters on it. See?" But he wasn't into my preppy New England look, and put his tacky collar on me anyway. Then he clipped on a really, really long leash and took me to the stage to perform for all of the bored dogs and humans. I wasn't sure what I was supposed to do, but I was pretty sure I'd be great at it once I tried it.

First, the man walked me away from Mom and I watched him closely to see if maybe he had treats. Then he stopped walking. "What?" I said, tilting my head and looking at him with question marks in my eyes. He tapped his boot on the ground. "What?" I asked again, searching his face for a clue to what he was on about. Then I looked at Mom for clarification. "Look at this weirdo," I said smiling and winking at her. "Is he trying to make music?"

"Oscar," The Man said, holding out his hand with just one finger pointing out. "Look!"

"What?! Do you have treats in your hand?" I asked, trying to get a good sniff at what was under his fingers. "You may not know this..." I said, following his hand around as he waved his finger. "...but I love treats. Would you like to share one with me? Look how cute I am when I sit."

Then The Man threw something on the ground a few feet in front of us. In case it was a treat, I looked where it fell, and... "ZOINKS!" I said. "There's a spaghetti monster sitting right next to where you were tapping your boot a second ago! Hang on, let me go check it out."

The spaghetti monster was about as big around as a rope leash, and had mean eyes on one end, and a shaky thing that made noise on the other. I knew from experience that this was called a "battlesnake" from when Mom and I saw a bigger one the day that I took every tick in Lake Berryessa with me to the Motel Six Stars. Maybe the spaghetti monster was why Mom was so anxious this morning? I was very interested to sniff what could make Mom scream and run away like she had, so I leaned in to get a better sniff and... *OW!* Something zapped my neck right under that big, borrowed collar. It felt like when Mom pets me after walking on a carpet in socks. The zap was so strange that it distracted me for a second, but soon I remembered about the spaghetti monster and leaned in again. I was so filled with suspense that when the spaghetti monster zapped me again I screamed like a little girl (but only for a second) and jumped two feet in the air. I was afraid that someone in the audience might have seen me get startled, so I hid behind The Man for a few seconds so that no one would see me being embarrassed. I'm no fool. There was no way I was getting near that spaghetti monster again and letting it zap me for a third time.

Next, The Man took me to a different corner of the pen where I smelled another spaghetti monster and heard a noise like rocks shaking in a plastic bottle. Every time I heard that noise, I felt another zap on my neck. It didn't hurt, but I didn't like that I never knew when it was coming. All I knew was that it had something to do with the spaghetti monster and that annoying sound it made. I was *really* starting to dislike spaghetti monsters.

Next, The Man took me to a place where someone had made a little flag out of spaghetti monster skin. It smelled like a spaghetti monster, and it had the same pattern, but there was no spaghetti monster inside of it. It was like when Mom leaves her sweatpants on the bathroom floor, and they smell like her but there's no Mom inside. I thought that this was my opportunity to learn about spaghetti monsters from their dirty laundry, but even this spaghetti monster jacket could zap you if you sniffed it or looked at it too long. Take it from me, spaghetti monsters are bad news, and I recommend that you avoid them.

Finally The Man let out the leash to its full length and Mom called me from across the pen. I couldn't wait to see her and tell her all about the spaghetti monsters and how scary they were, but how I wasn't really all that scared... when I noticed that there was a gigantic spaghetti monster on the ground between me and her! "Leapin' lizards!" I whistled deep in my throat. This wasn't the same little spaghetti monster as before. This one was as big around as my tail and much, much longer. "Oh hell no!" I said. "I'm not passing that thing! No sir-ree Bob!" I ran a wide circle around it and refused to even look at it as I passed so it wouldn't zap me again.

When I got to Mom, she petted me like she was already very proud of me. "Mom, you'll never guess what happened!" I panted, wagging my tail in excitement. "I met four spaghetti monsters, and three of them attacked me, but I was very brave, and only a little bit scared. I think that you should stay away from them on our runs, okay? You may not know where they are because your nose is so blind, but don't worry. I know what they smell like now, so I'll keep us safe."

Mom gave me lots of treats and lots of pets for being so brave, and The Man took his ugly collar and long leash back. Then he explained to both me and Mom that if we ever saw a noisy spaghetti monster again that whoever saw it first had to scream and run away. It was very important that we act so scared (even if we are actually secretly being brave) that whoever hasn't seen the spaghetti monster yet won't miss it and step on it by accident and get zapped. "Deal!" Mom and I agreed.

Déjà view

One day Mom came home smelling like work, but instead of taking me for a patrol of the neighborhood like she usually does, this time she took me right out the door to the Covered Wagon. We have the best adventures in the Covered Wagon, but the worst drives because the Covered Wagon's ancestors were Easy-Bake Ovens. This time our Wagon adventure was even more harrowing because we had to do a lot of sitting still in the hot sun while we waited for other cars to get off our roads. Because Mom believes in lifetime learning, she used the extra time in traffic to teach me new vocabulary words like "despair" and "existential crisis," but I don't remember what they mean because I was too hot to think.

I couldn't wait to see where we were going, but after three hours of mostly sitting still and only like three dog hours of movement-driving, Mom pulled the Covered Wagon over at the side of the road and let me out. "What kind of bullplop is this?!" I asked, looking around outside the car. "It's dark out here and I smell monsters."

"We're not going to make it tonight," Mom explained. "Let's sleep here."

"I don't like it here," I told her. "It gives me the howling fantods. It smells creepy and there are things in the woods." But Mom just pretended like she couldn't hear me and lay down. She also forgot to close the windows, so I could smell and hear all the creepy things casing The Covered Wagon, figuring out how to get inside and gobble us up. I thought about letting Mom sleep, but every twenty minutes I had to bark at a noise or lick her face to say, "Hey, did you hear something?" Luckily, thanks to me keeping watch and letting her know every time A Thing did something, Mom didn't need to go all the way to sleep at all before she got up at three in the night to keep driving.

Finally the sun came up and we pulled up to our adventure spot. There were trails in every direction! We picked one trail and started running. Then we stopped running. Then we started running. Then we stopped again. Apparently humans make lousy pack animals, because Mom kept complaining about having to run with ten pounds of water on her back. So instead of leaving the water in the car and running the whole way like swashbucklers, we slowed down and hiked instead.

The place we were in was very beautiful. There were flowers that smelled like red, and purple, and yellow, and white, and the sky smelled like it was the same colors with a big, white moon in the middle of it. The Covered Wagon had done all the climbing so that we didn't have to, and we were already high enough to see all the mountains around us.

After about four miles of gentle climbing, I started having *déjà vue*. "Mom," I asked. "Do you ever get the feeling you've been somewhere before?"

"Don't you recognize it?" Mom asked. "We were here on the last hike of our last road trip. The peak is less than a mile that way." She pointed over some shrubs on the right. "It just looks different because there was snow up here the last time we were here, and we came from a different direction." This was Second Dog Valley?! It blew my mind that there were mountains so big that there was more than one way to climb them. And how could it have white dirt on one day, and then no white dirt just a few weeks later?

"Why do we keep coming back here, Mom?" I asked. I thought that maybe Second Dog Valley was famous like Paris, or Disneyland, or Disneyland Paris.

"I don't know why I'm drawn to this place, Oscar. All the people are always nice, there are a million places to camp even though no one knows this place is here, and I never get the howling fantods when we're up here. I think that this is our special place."

Part of the reason that we had woken up so early was because we wanted to be done before it got hot, but we might have gone too far. Once we started walking downhill on the shady side of the mountain, Mom (whose heart pumps ice rather than blood) started to turn blue. Every mile or so, I had to come back and block the path in front of her so she would stop and bang her hands on my tight, firm butt until she could feel them again. It wasn't that cold, Mom is just made with lizard parts.

Suddenly Mom froze solid. "Oscar!" she said in a hot voice. "Did I bring my wallet when we left the house yesterday?!"

"I don't know, Mom. But you don't need it, remember? When we're in the Covered Wagon we don't need money or other people."

"Well… that's not strictly true," Mom said. "Like, for example, if we ever want to get home again, we need money."

"Do we need to go home again?" I asked. "I thought this was our special place. Maybe we are home."

"Um, yes. I think we need to go home again. I've got milk in the fridge that will go bad, and a doctor's appointment that I'll miss next week if we don't. Plus, I only packed three pairs of socks."

"Uh-oh spaghetti-o!" I said as the seriousness of the situation sunk in. "In that case, how do we know if you forgot your wallet?"

"We'll have to get back to the Covered Wagon."

"And how far is that?" I asked.

"Maybe nine or ten more miles…" Mom said.

"Oh. That will take a very long time. Do we need money before we get there?"

"No, I suppose not."

"Then you should enjoy the hike," I said. "Look! A bird just hopped. Let's chase it!" But I don't think she took my advice about enjoying the hike, because she stopped taking pictures after that and looked worried.

Mostly we hiked, but also we climbed over giant trees that had died and fallen across the path, and we climbed over tiny streams which are what happens when white dirt dies and falls across the path. We walked and walked for hours, until the day started to make its own warmth and Mom started to turn people-colored again. Then we popped out at a beautiful lake that was just as perfect for drinking as the streams on the mountain had been. We walked for miles along the lake, and then we left the lake and still kept walking. It was so beautiful and exotic, I hoped that the suspense about Mom's wallet could keep building forever.

Mom had put me back on leash. She said it was because she didn't want to have to yell at me, but I think it must have actually been because she was lonely, because she kept yelling at me anyway. Every time we met other people on the trail, I ran up to the Friends and barked, "Hi! I'm Oscar! I bark. It's kind of my thing."

And then they would look scared and Mom would say, "He barks. It's kind of his thing." And then the people would smile and tell Mom how cute I was, except the people puppy who whimpered and folded herself up whenever I barked. She was extra fun to bark at, but Mom pulled me away before I was done turning her into a pocket square.

Finally, after many, many hours and more than fourteen miles of hiking, we found the Covered Wagon. "What are you going to do if you don't have your wallet?" I asked Mom.

"Well, nobody will get lunch, and we'll have to walk into a gas station and hope that a AAA card will... Oh wait. The card's in my wallet too..."

"NO LUNCH?!?!" I said, and pretended to faint in the shadow of the car while Mom checked the wallet slot, where the wallet had been waiting for us to come back and find it the whole time. We celebrated by not spending any money anyway and eating the food that we already had in the car.

Infestation

Since Mom and I didn't need to panhandle for gas money, we decided to drive up deep into the mountains and hide out at the secret spot where I could swim and Mom could pretend that there weren't other humans in the world. We knew about this spot because it was where we parked the last time we visited Second Dog Valley, the time it had finally let us in. Six miles below, where the dirt road left the pavement, there were no signs telling people that there was camping to be found up there. You had to drive up, up, up the mountain on a dusty dirt road to find the secret campground, and since we hadn't told anyone the secret, we thought we were the only ones in the whole wide world who knew it was there. Last time we were there, the only two other humans within miles and miles of wilder-ness were two men sitting in a pea pod boat in the middle of the lake.

The men in the pea pod boat must have spilled the beans, because when we arrived at our special place the afternoon that Mom didn't forget her wallet, there were people and cars making noise, shouting to each other, and leaving their engines growling in all the nooks and crannies. The people puppies were running back and forth in that way that makes me excited and barky, and stresses Mom out because when I bark at people puppies I "scare people." After a quick swim to cool off and make Mom's shorts less stinko, we sat in the Covered Wagon, which was wedged illegally into the car kennel. As we sat there trying to decide how to spend the rest of our afternoon, we watched three big cars with even bigger wheels pull up. Then all the people inside the cars shouted out their windows to each other about parking and waved their arms wildly at all the other big cars with big wheels. Then they drove in all sorts of funny, distracting, and dog-squashing shapes with their big cars until their monster wheels were sitting on top of nature. Then the big cars stopped growling, and the people got out one by one. One of the people puppies ran back and forth shouting the same question over and over to every human in her pack. We hoped that they would take their commotion further out into nature where they couldn't distract us, but the full-grown humans kept forgetting things and going back to their cars, and all the still-growing ones only remembered that they had to go to the bathroom when everyone else looked like they were ready to leave. Mom and I had wanted to take a nap in the Covered Wagon, but it wasn't relaxing enough with all the bustle and hubbub... and anyway, the Covered Wagon was in Easy-Bake Oven mode. "Let's get out of here," Mom said once the chaotic pack of people had finally started hiking and we could move freely without having to bark or get squashed.

We drove about a mile back downhill, where Mom found a perfect napping nook for us. It was shady and had a little brook flowing by for me to drink from, and for Mom to throw her sweatshirt in when she spilled tea all over it. That's the great thing about our Covered Wagon. We don't need a tent or a permit or a plan. We can make home wherever we want to. Sometimes it doesn't work out so great because we find that we've stopped in a place with hum-bugs or one that's haunted with howling fantods, but usually it's a good thing.

When Mom and I woke up the next morning, we were feeling much more refreshed, and ready to have a great adventure. We drove back to the not-so-secret spot, where most of the people were gone. Just like the secret of having a car-house, another one of our secrets is to sneak into the world early in the morning when the world isn't open yet. Almost no one knows about the early morning, and because we don't share the secret, we often have the world to ourselves.

Well... mostly to ourselves. We were running through the skirt of the mountain where the boulders and bushes fight to see who can win the trail, when I came around the corner and saw a turtle-person right in front of me. "What are you doing here? Let me see your early morning permit!" I barked. She looked suitably scared of me, so when Mom called my name, I figured it was okay to turn my tail on the turtle-person to go get Mom to show her what I'd found. When I came back around the bend, this time with Mom, the turtle-person held out her hand. I was about to bark instructions for how to scratch my butt when Mom grabbed my collar and gave me one of those leg hugs that squeezes me in place. Since I couldn't reach her anymore, I had no choice but to use my voice to ask the turtle person if she was cool. "Hey," I said. "Are you cool?"

"He's a good boy, he just barks a lot," Mom explained. The turtle-person looked scared again and scuttled on by. I guess she wasn't cool after all.

"Why did you do that?" I asked. "You scared her."

"No, Oscar, *you* scared her."

"She was about to make friends with me," I told Mom. "But then you grabbed me like I was dangerous or something."

"I wanted to show that you were under control."

"What's to control?! Potato beasts are loud and friendly creatures."

Soon the boulders won the fight to control the mountain, and Mom and I made stairs out of the rocks. This part of the mountain was so steep that Mom had to decide between having control over me, or controlling her own position on the mountain, and she chose to set me free from the leash again. Since Mom is a slow rock conqueror, that left me plenty of time to find the best spots at the edge of inner space to stick my nose in the middle of the air current and smell all of Eastern California blowing by.

One fun thing about this trail is that when you reach the top of the hill, you get to keep running along the edge of the world. To one side there is forest, and to the other just sky and all the world below us. We ran for two miles along the edge of the world, which was covered in wildflowers where there had been white dirt before. There were lots of kinds of wild flowers, but they were the sort that look better on wallpaper or the Lands End summer collection than at the center of a photo all their own. Finally we reached the bow of the top of the world, and I stood on the edge of it like a drop of sweat hanging off of Mom's nose. I could see all the way to Mt Shasta in one direction, and all the way back to where there was reliable Witch service in the other.

"Hey, Mom," I said. "Remember when I learned about responsibility, and we found that secret trail with the bat cave over yonder? And then remember that time when I won Second Dog in the half marathong down over there? And that time when we were standing somewhere over there and you taught me about the longest trail that ends up in Canada one way, and Mexico the opposite way? And remember how we've walked up this mountain before, both from the front and the back?"

"Yeah..." Mom said.

"And now we're looking at all of it from the sky, like a cloud would."

"That's true," Mom said.

"And remember how you used to get sad because you couldn't climb all the mountains?"

"Sure," Mom said.

"Isn't that kind of what we're doing?" I asked. "We have memories on so many of these mountains already. It's kind of like they're all ours."

"I guess you're right..." Mom said.

"So... You can relax now?" I asked. This was a very important life coaching moment that I had been waiting for a long time to teach her.

"Yes, Oscar. I think I can relax now. At least for today..."

Welcome Back, Oscar

A few weeks later we came back to Second Dog Valley to celebrate Welcome Back Oscar Day. Not only had they named the place after my achievement last summer, but they were also throwing me a half marathong parade to thank me for helping raise money for their stray people puppies! I would have raised the money anyway, but I do love it when people come out to stand by the side of the road to watch me run and shout what a good job I'm doing.

Mom and I were almost late to my parade because Second Dog Valley is so very far from our Stuck House. After Mom finished working, we raced out to the Covered Wagon as fast as we could and drove without stopping until the middle of the night. We still weren't there yet, but we parked the Covered Wagon in a rest stop and did our resting for the night. Resting is different from sleeping because it takes less than four hours and you have to make sure to wake up and listen to all the people who stop their cars to shout to each other on the way to the bathroom. We finished resting before the middle of the night was over so that we could be at the starting line when the sun came up.

The one thing that I didn't like about my parade is that it is a tradition at this festival for four-legged runners to wear face socks in the start and finish area. A face sock is a kind of mask that goes around your snout so you can't open your mouth, bark, or lick things. Mom says it's not nice to criticize other cultures, but I don't think it's nice to humiliate your guest of honor or keep him from making speeches by holding his mouth shut. And how are you supposed to do fun things like eat chips, or lick strangers' legs when you're wearing a face sock? Everywhere I looked, there were four-legged runners smooshing their faces on the ground or punching themselves in the nose trying to get the face socks off.

Then something very embarrassing happened. A lady in a very pretty skirt said, "Is that Oscar?!" I had never been recognized before! This was my first appearance as a celebrity, and here I was wearing this dumb face sock. I was too embarrassed to even jump on her or try to bark a bit. Since my face was shut, I let Mom introduce me to my fan, whose name was Lynn. While they were talking about human things like how slow they each planned to run, I gave Lynne my butt to scratch so that she would have something inspiring to think about when she was tired from running in my parade.

When we finally started running, Mom let me take the face sock off so that I could grin at all the runners who had come to be in my parade, and all the spectators who had come to cheer for me. Since everyone here had come to celebrate me, and we were all running to the same place, that meant we were all on the same team and I didn't have to worry about barking at anyone or being what Mom calls "scary." I smiled at Lynn one last time so that she would know that she was doing almost as good a job as me, and then I pinned my ears back and started racing.

I'm an expert at racing, so I know all rules like how you're supposed to chase the runners in front of you. Every experienced racer like me also knows that you should poop before the race starts, but I passed some poor nincompoops who didn't know to "poop first" and had to stop and squat right in the middle of the parade route. Those were two dogs that wouldn't be winning the parade today. Suckahs!

The dog right in front of me was a horse-colored vizsla that I knew was named Cinnamon because her running buddies kept telling her she was a "good girl, Cinnamon." Cinnamon was very pretty, but she had no brains for racing. Instead of pulling her human steadily in a straight line so he would run faster, she kept running side to side and confusing him. It's a good thing she was so bad at racing, though, or else she might have run too far ahead of us and I wouldn't have had anyone to race with. Without Cinnamon's butt to chase, I would have been so bored that I would have run at Mom's pace, and we would probably still be out there today.

One of the reasons Mom and I loved this race is because the concession stands catered to all the runners, not just the human ones. Each concession stand had a pool for either swimming or drinking, and most of them had yummy treats to keep humans and dogs from getting so hungry they would have to lie down in the street and give up. The first concession stand was my favorite because not only did I get some jerky, but there were also baby goats! I ran up to one of them and sniffed at him. "Hi! My name is Oscar and I'm a big fan of your work!" I said with doggie telepathy. Then I puffed up my hackles, whimpered a little bit, and wagged my tail at warp speed to let him know how excited I was.

I don't think the baby goat had done media training, because instead of letting me sniff his butt, he backed away from me like I was some big, scary beast or something.

"Daaaaaaad. We have an encounter...!" said the people puppy behind the jerky table when he saw me having my brush with greatness.

"Come on, Oscar. Let's keep racing," Mom said, pulling me away from the baby goat right when I was about to get my nose in his butt hole.

"But Mom, these are *real live baby goats!*" I said. And when I turned back, the shy baby goat was straining at his leash to get even further away from me. He was obviously one of those kid stars that can't handle the pressure, and will wind up going wild when they get older, like Britney Steers or Michael Jackasson.

We left the baby goat behind us and went back to chasing Cinnamon for a few more miles. She ran at about the same distance ahead of us until the tenth mile, when we climbed the biggest hill on the course. I thought for sure that Mom would walk because she's slow now, but instead Cinnamon's fit-looking people walked, and I dragged a jiggling, chugging Mom right past them. At the top of the hill there was a rest stop, and Cinnamon stopped for a swim while Mom kept running down the hill, dragging me along with her.

Now I was conflicted. Isn't racing about chasing? Weren't we supposed to stop and wait for Cinnamon to chase us now that she was "it?" What was the point of passing someone if you weren't going to give them a chance to chase you? For the next half mile I kept checking over my shoulder waiting for Cinnamon to come back and give me some motivation, but she never did. So I stopped helping Mom with my pulling as a punishment for her being such a spoil-sport.

When we got close to the finish there were lots of fans there to cheer me on, but since I didn't have anybody to chase, I took my time running past all of them so I could soak up as much attention as possible. I guess that wasn't exciting enough, so the director of the people puppy shelter that I had raised money for came down and ran across the finish line with me to give me someone to chase. She was so dedicated... Some runners needed someone to chase, while others were just lonely, but she accompanied each and every one over the finish line and gave them exactly what they needed, like the best hostess ever. Did I mention that we love Second Dog Valley?

After the race it was starting to get warm, but instead of finding somewhere shady to park the Covered Wagon and nap, Mom decided to drive us back home in the heat of the day. "This way I can buy you lunch on the way home," Mom promised. Usually that means that I get McRotguts from the drive through, but this time Mom took me to a very fancy sit-down restaurant called The 76 Station and bought me a delicious treat that was also named after me! It was called a "hot dog," which is a very special meat tube slow-cooked on the rotisserie for many, many hours, or maybe even days. The hot dog was so delicious that it was better than hanging out in the mountains all afternoon. Maybe.

Busy-ness School

After awhile Mom stopped going to her foster job and started hanging out at the house again. She took me on lots of extra walks and gave me lovins in the middle of the day, so I hoped she would never get adopted by a forever job. But one day she told that she'd accepted her Forever Job, so we had better spend some time in the Covered Wagon before we won't have time to be strays anymore.

"Where will we go?!" I asked. "Somewhere new and exciting, like New Jersey?"

"Let's go back to Second Dog Valley," Mom said. And because Mom's are the legs that reach the driving pedals, her choice always wins.

So we got in the Covered Wagon and I sat in my copilot's seat between the chairs with my head in Mom's lap as we drove through all the traffic places, past all the ugly metal trees that spit smoke into the air, through the ground clouds that come up from the farm dirt, past all the signs about how happy we'll be when we visit the casino, until we were in the mountains again. We drove straight to our secret campground that wasn't so secret anymore without stopping at any of the human places along the way. When we parked the Covered Wagon at the bottom of the mountain, I headed to the lake to get a drink. I had to run a long way, on grass that I had swum over the last time we visited, and past a boulder that used to be an island. "Mom, where is the lake going??" I asked.

"Well once all the snow melted, it stopped being fed."

"But where did the water go that was already there?" I asked.

"It went into the sky to become rain storms in Cleveland or Toronto or something."

I looked around at all the mountains and trees. Even though the white dirt was gone, this still seemed like the most beautiful place in the world. Cleveland or Toronto must be even more beautiful than anything that I had ever seen in all eight states in this country for a lake to want to get up and fly there rather than staying here.

We kept hiking until we found a trail that we'd never taken before to a place called Gold Lake. I was expecting a quiet lake with fall trees right up to the lake's edge, where the smooth surface of the lake would smudge the fall greys back at us. But when we arrived at Gold Lake, it was like a lake at the bottom of a low-flow toilet bowl and we were standing all the way up on the seat. Someone had flushed the lake so low that we couldn't figure out how to get down the bowl to drink from it. I wanted to keep exploring, but Mom said that we had to get back to the Covered Wagon before the sun set.

When we got back to the car kennel there were a bunch of trucks parked next to the Covered Wagon, and a group of hunky, handsome men that looked like human Oscars were sitting at a picnic table eating a snack. Mom looked really interested in them, and since we had our own exciting snacks already, I figured that she must be so interested because she wanted to be a firefighter too. Maybe that was the new job she got?

The last time we were up here it was July, and the Covered Wagon was so hot that we couldn't even sit in it. But now the sun took the heat with it when it sagged behind the mountain. I let Mom wrap me in a blanket like an em-pup-nada while she read a book, but once it was lights out and no one could see how cute I was anymore, I took the blanket off so that I could jump up and bark if I needed to. It sure was cold with the lake and white dirt gone. I snuggled up close to Mom to keep warm, but most of her warmth got stuck in the two sweatshirts and two blankets she was wearing. By the time Mom finally woke up almost half a day later, I had turned into a pup-sicle. It took a long time with the Covered Wagon blowing heat at us while Mom drank her poop juice for me to defrost back into a supple beefcake again.

Mom said that we could "mellow out" on this trip, which means that she was too lazy to run and she'd be walking up the mountain. That was okay with me, because while she walked I could run even more miles through the brush and practice my plyometrics, sprinting over logs and jumping on rocks.

Once we started hiking, I left Mom to chase critters in the bushes, but she called me back and asked me to stop. "That's the silliest thing I've ever heard," I said through the mouthful of salmon jerky she paid me for coming when she called. "The whole point of hiking is to chase critters."

"Well, there was a sign back there that there's been an outbreak of 'the plague,' and to watch out for fleas."

"What's 'the plague?'" I asked.

"Well... 'a plague' is just when a lot of people get sick at the same time. But when people say 'the plague' they usually mean the one where black blobs called buboes grow on you and then you die. It was a big deal like seven hundred years ago, but I don't think it's really a thing anymore."

I looked at Mom's weird boxy body that's flat in all the places where humans are sometimes curvy, and then I looked at my sleek, athletic frame that was black, but not blobby at all. "Well I don't have any boobies, and neither do you," I said. "And if one of us is going to chase contaminated critters, it should be the one of us that is up to date on his flea meds, don't you think?"

I ran to and fro, chasing critters and sniffing in all the nooks and crannies to see if anything interesting had happened while I was away. Every time Mom called me, I came running back to her with a big grin, and she was always laughing when I found her.

"I wish that we could keep doing this forever," she said.

"Why can't we?" I asked.

"Well, because I have to feed you and the Covered Wagon, and pay for our Stuck House and lots of other things. So I have to work."

"We've been wandering through the wilder-ness for six months, but you still haven't told me why all that stuff is so important."

"I don't know. I guess I want significance. I want the world to be a different or better place because I'm in it, and to do that I have to do things for other people."

"You could be a fireman, like those guys we saw yesterday. You seemed really into them, and they save lives. Even better, they get to chase cats that are stuck in trees. I have spots, so I bet they would let me be a dalmatian and ride in the fire engine with you."

"You can't be a firefighter," Mom said. "Firefighters are brave. You're afraid of everything."

"I am too brave," I said. "Name one thing that I'm scared of!"

"Well, sirens for one," Mom said. "And balloons. And watering cans. And men with beards. And chihuahuas. And Halloween decorations."

"Wait, are you talking about that dead guy in the neighbor's yard that wouldn't stop pointing at me, even when I barked at him? He wanted to kill me though! Murderers are scary."

"The point is, firefighters aren't scared of things that other people are scared of. I'm afraid of blood, and you're afraid of stuffed shirts with masks on top."

"I'm not afraid of the plague," I pointed out.

"What if I told you that I found us a job where neither of us had to be in danger?" Mom said as we walked along the edge of the world with all the human things like jobs and cars and houses so far below us that they seemed imaginary.

"What do you mean 'us?'" I asked.

"Well, they said that you could come to work with me, but... well... they haven't met you yet."

"What's that supposed to mean?" I asked. "I'm irresistible."

"Oscar... you bark a lot. Business dogs know how to use their indoor voices."

"I haven't barked all day!" I pointed out. It's true. I don't bark all that much. Only when there are strangers, or Friends, or Frienemies, or noises, or runners who take walking breaks, or occasionally some other times. When there aren't any of those things, like in the mountains, I'm a real quiet and introspective dude and mostly just sniff stuff.

"You know how I decided that I didn't have to be the most ferocious runner in the world so that I could save my energy for other things?" Mom asked when we got to the end of the world and looked out at all the mountains between us and Oregon, and Nevada, and Toronto.

"Yeah," I said. "It's why we almost never run more than five miles anymore."

"Well, I want that kind of peace for you too," Mom said. "You don't have to always be competing for top dog. Maybe if you were a little more tolerant of things like people coming out their front doors, neighbors parking their cars, recycling trucks, dogs that ignore you, or waiting outside Starbucks, then you wouldn't feel so anxious all the time."

Going through life not worrying about whether something dangerous would happen sounded awfully scary. "But Mom, if I don't bark at those things, how will I keep myself from getting scared?" I asked.

"The point is that maybe you can learn not to be scared of those things at all anymore. Wouldn't it be great to not get the bejesus scared out of you so many times a day? Maybe if you chill out, you could use all the energy you save to become successful business dog. Business dogs get butt scratches from all kinds of different people. Do you want to be stuck in a dead-end security dog job and spend all day home alone forever?"

I didn't think that this was time for me to bring up The Other Woman who comes and takes me on adventures while Mom is away. "Okay," I said. "I'll give it a try."

As we drove home from the mountains, Mom described my new training plan. Instead of intervals and long runs and hills, we would go for walks downtown where there are lots of scary people coming out of doors, and practice not having a melt-down outside Starbucks, and not jumping up and putting my front paws on counters in stores like the humans do. It would mean a lot of hard work, but you don't get to be a busy-ness dog without training. That's called busy-ness school.

Oscar the Mooch

This was my first full time job as a busy-ness dog. I had temped a few days at Mom's last office, but that was the sort of place where they didn't appreciate things like chasing the mailman around the lobby and screaming your head off, or accidentally pooping on the carpet. But Mom's new job is in a place called The City where everyone is accepted, even dogs. In fact, in The City there are plenty of people who even act like dogs, sleeping on the floor and pooping in the open air. There are other things on the ground other than dog wannabes and human-doo too, like stuff that used to have food in it, and still might have a little nibble left if you try swallowing it. I loved my new job right away, and I hadn't even gotten to the office yet.

I brought treats for all my new coworkers so that they would like me, and left them in the kitchen with a sign that said, "To my new Friends, Love Oscar." Then Mom asked everybody to repay the favor by telling me to sit and giving me a treat before giving me pats and butt scratches. I wasn't so sure about letting so many people besides Mom boss me around, but Mom explained that everyone is your boss when you start your first job, and you have to do what they say. I met so many new Oscar fans who gave me pats and butt scratches that sometimes I couldn't give them all the attention that they wanted. Work is really stressful!

When no one was paying attention to me, I looked around and saw that everyone was looking busy, so I grabbed the bone that Mom had given me and started earnestly chewing on it so that I would look busy too. A few times I spotted one of my new Friends and shouted hello at them. Mom always gets mad when I bark, but this time she got stern with me so quick that I started to think that maybe I was doing something wrong. I looked around, and noticed that no one else was barking. Maybe a busy-ness dog doesn't holla when he sees a Friend? So instead I let my tail wag so hard that my butt almost hit me in the face, and ran up to my Friend like a silent bowling ball.

A few times during the day, Mom took me out to the dog bathroom for a break and I got to explore The City a little more. The City is mysterious and full of clues, like rude messages written on paper plates on the sidewalk. I sniffed at a plate on the ground to see if it had any foodishness on it, but the only thing it had on it was words. "Well that's rude," Mom said, pulling my nose away from the plate while I was still trying to figure out what it said.

"What does it say?" I asked. But Mom wouldn't explain to me what "bick" was. I find it quite soothing to suck on things when I'm stressed out, so the message written on the plate seemed like reasonable life coaching advice to me...

Being a busy-ness dog sure is tiring. You're not supposed to fall asleep at work, so I didn't get any naps all day long. By the time Mom took me back to the car, I was pooped-with-a-capital-P. But Mom was so proud of me that she kept waking me up the whole drive home to tell me what a good boy I am, and that I'd passed the interview. My new Friends said I could come back and be a part time busy-ness dog!

"Does this mean that I'll get to do important things like participate in board meetings and manage client relationships?!" I asked.

"I don't think so, Oscar," Mom said. "I think that you were more of a diversity hire."

"What's a diver city hire?" I asked. I was afraid it might involve swimming.

"It means that they hired you because your picture will look good on the web site."

Well that made sense, I am a damned good looking dog. "Hang on a second," I said after having a think. "Do you mean to say that they didn't hire me just because I'm a good boy? That they think that humans would do a better job at being busy-ness people than me, and they only hired me so that they would look like a progressive company?"

"Something like that," Mom said.

"But they're wrong! I'm a real hard worker, I learn fast, and I'm very loyal!"

"I know you are," Mom said. "So the best thing that you can do is show what a good business dog you are, and not create any office drama. You've got to be a polite all the time, and support everybody in the office. When they see that people like coming to work because they enjoy working with you, then they'll see that hiring business dogs is as good for productivity as hiring an extra person."

"I get it!" I said. "I should give my coworkers lots of kisses, and when they are stressed out and want soothing I should tell them to suck my bick!"

"Hold that thought," Mom said. "Sexual harassment training isn't till next week."

Oscar the Mermutt

I just love working so much! The next day, when Mom stopped the car in The City and I realized that I got to go back to work, I was so excited that I walked to the office with purpose, holding my nose high and dragging Mom behind me like a fleshy, whiny briefcase. Since today was Halloween, Mom and I wore matching costumes. Mom was dressed up as a sailor, and I was dressed as a mermaid with seashells on my chest just like a real mermaid in the movies. At first I wasn't so sure about my costume and tried taking it off, but then when Mom put it back on and I saw that it got me extra attention, I decided to keep it on for the rest of the day.

As soon as I saw my new Friends (Friends at work are called "collies," I learned), I screeched in a very professional voice and ran around trying to greet them all at once. All my collies told me to hush, but they were smiling so I knew I wasn't really in trouble. And anyway, I had already bounced off of all of them and didn't need to bark anymore, for now.

When Mom and I are home we're family, but when we're at work we're collies. So when Mom went to the People Bathroom while I was in a meeting getting scratches from two collies at once, I let her go alone and didn't bark a peep even though I couldn't see her. Not following your collies into the bathroom is called "professionalism." Mom was so proud of me for being professional that she threw me a quiet party of vigorous pats when she came out.

An important thing for any job is that the boss-person be a good leader. My boss-man is a great leader because he brought turkey jerky to our meeting, and immediately he had my undivided attention. I was riveted. Was he trying to inspire me by leading by example? The problem was, he ate all the jerky himself instead. "You are a very handsome man," I told him, laying my head in his lap. "I find you irresistible..." I went on.

"Oscar! No! What are you doing?!" Mom squawked, yanking at my leash.

"I'm twerking, Mom," I said. "Isn't that obvious?"

"Please! Keep it professional!" she begged me.

I was confused, did she expect a piece of eye candy like me to toil my way to success with hard work when I had these natural good looks to work with? Apparently so, because every time I tried to put the moves on the Boss Man, she pulled me back. I've heard that women can be really jealous of the most attractive collie in the office, but I didn't expect this behavior from Mom!

I've saved the best part of the day for last: lunch! One of the things about working at a start-up is that if they want to attrapped the best workers like me, they have to pay them in lunches. If a start-up doesn't pay its workers in lunches, then they get to go outside and buy their own lunches, and then maybe they will get lost and never come back to finish making technology. A bunch of my collies had ordered something that came with poached chicken livers, and can you believe those weirdos didn't want to eat theirs?! Why work hard if you're not going to eat the chicken livers??? So I got to go around the table and eat everybody's liver. Some people think that we're spoiled in The City, but if you had seen how good I was at not napping all day, you would know that I earned all three of those chicken livers.

Cleaning Up

Working in The City is unlike anything else that a dog might do. First of all, you have to smell clean every single time you go. While it may be okay to climb into the bed you share with Mom smelling like the dead bird you rolled in at the park, or like a mermaid from a day at the beach, you can't go to work smelling like anything but Head and Shoulders for Men. Mom has to groom herself differently too. Instead of wearing stinky running clothes or comfy sweats with bits of food stuck all over them, she has to put on fancy clothes that don't fit her like a grocery bag. And the silly shoes! She wears the dumbest horned tip-toe shoes that look like a rhinoceros that rolled over on its back for belly rubs. Not only do the horned tip-toe shoes look stupid, there's no way she could ever run in them. I think they're how they keep her at her desk without a leash.

When Mom took me out for potty breaks, we always had adventures that confused me. That day there was a human lying on the sidewalk in one of those sacks that Mom uses in the Covered Wagon to keep her warm at night. Only this man wasn't sleeping in his, he was singing and conducting an invisible orchestra. He also smelled like he hadn't used Head and Shoulders for Men after the last time he'd rolled in a dead bird. So Mom and I crossed the street.

When we got to the park, I had to poop. When I stood up and sprinted away from my doo-doo like we sometimes do on the trail, Mom stood fast and tapped her pockets. She'd forgotten the bags back at the office, and now we'd missed our opportunity to run away from the scene. This was a place where lots of people took their dogs to play off leash, so I suggested we go find the bag dispenser. At home there is always a bag dispenser so that people won't have an excuse for leaving poops behind to be found by other people's shoes. So Mom stuck a stick in the ground to mark the poo as ours so no one else would steal it, and we set off to find the nearest bag dispenser.

"Mom, why are all those people staring at us with mean eyes?" I asked. "Everybody poops. They all poop. Even that guy over there eating a whole apple pie with his fingers poops."

"They think that we're not going to pick it up," Mom explained. "And so they think we're evil."

To prove that we weren't evil, we walked all the way around the park looking for the bag dispenser. We checked next to all the water fountains, trash cans, and signs about things you can and can't do in the park, but there were no bags! "That must be why all the humans leave their poo on the sidewalk after they go," I explained. "No bags." I was sure that this meant that we could leave the poo behind now.

"That's not how The City works," Mom said. "They give you tickets for leaving your car somewhere for too long, but don't have places where you can park for more than two hours. Because the police are so busy giving parking tickets, they don't have time to prevent car break-ins. They give you a huge fine if you leave your recycle bins on the street for an extra day. I'm sure we still need to find a way to pick it up." I thought about explaining to Mom that this situation is exactly why we're supposed to learn how to eat our own poop, but now didn't seem like the time to start *that* old argument again.

Mom walked into the street and picked up one of those advertisements that they put in your mailbox so that you'll think it's a newspaper telling an important news story about a sale on Scandinavian furniture. Maybe somebody had tried to throw it out, but since the recycle bins have to hide every morning, they probably couldn't find a place to put it, so they put it on the ground just like the orchestra conductor, and the greasy napkin snacks, and the human poo, and all the other out-of-place things.

"Ohhh! Furniture!" I said. "Are we going to redecorate the Stuck House? I think we should replace the dreadmill with a couch I can stand on when I bark out the window at the squirrels."

"No," Mom said. "We're going to use it to pick up your poo."

She marched back over to where the stick was still marking my poo castle, and made a big show of using the advertisement to pick up the turds so that all of the mean-eyed people could see what she was doing. As we turned and walked toward a trash can, I felt a tug on my leash. I turned to find Mom teetering on one paw. The ground had slurped up the entire horn of her rhino shoe, and held it tight when she tried to walk away. Now the shoe was lying on its side in the grass and Mom was waving her bare paw around in the air trying to free the shoe so she could put it back on. With the leash in one hand, and my hearty, wet poo cradled in a fancy furniture ad in the other, Mom tried to get her shoe back from the grass without falling over or dropping the poo on her dumb outfit.

Later, Mom explained to me that if anybody asked me what it was like to work in the City, that I should tell them, "It's like trying to hold it all together while balancing on one foot in high heels with a handful of dog doo." That sounded like it could be fun, but the way she said it, I guessed it wasn't supposed to be.

Oscar the Action Hero

Something funny started happening all of a gradual. When something happens all of a gradual, it doesn't start happening one moment, or day, or even week, but it creeps into happening so that you can't tell when you first noticed it, and the first thing you do notice is that you're not noticing anything else.

The smell came first. In the beginning the smell was so faint that perhaps I was just thinking about camping, but soon there was no denying that the whole world was thinking about camping because that's what it smelled like everywhere we went. It smelled like camping in the stuck house, and in the car, and at work, and everywhere else that we went.

Then, when the sun came up one day, I discovered that someone had gone through and erased the world overnight. All the nearby stuff was still there, but anything in the distance had been rubbed out, leaving a smudgy grey-white in its place. Usually when Mom and I go for a walk we see lots of people outside, even when we're running in the dark at a time that's so early that it can't decide whether it's night or morning. But suddenly, when the world got erased, all the people disappeared with it.

And then, after a day or two without a world or people to live in it, the people were replaced by aliens. Everywhere we went, there were human-like monsters in the street with things covering their faces. At first the bottom half of their faces were covered with things that looked like the giant macaroni shells that doctors wear over their faces on TV. But soon they molted the macaroni shells and grew fancy faces in all different colors of grey with one or two breathing holes. Most monsters had one breathing portal in the middle like a mouth, but some of the monsters had two big gills on either side shaped like amputated tusks.

One night, one of the tuskless monsters came sprinting out of the smudgy distance with a dog running beside him. I thought that they were definitely coming to get me, and I barked like I'd never barked before to show them that I wasn't a good abducting dog for their experiments. I must have scared them off good, because they kept right on sprinting to find somedog else to attack. But I don't mind telling you that I was spooked! It took a long time for me to settle down after that. I barked into the dull air the whole walk home, just in case.

That was in the beginning, but pretty soon there were so many monsters that I stopped barking at them and hardly noticed them anymore. And then I realized what was going on; I was starring in a science fiction movie, obviously! It was the only thing that made sense. With my sleek muscles and handsome face, I had the perfect looks to be an action star. The movie was about aliens that land in the wilder-ness and try to act human, so they make a campfire to stare at and think deep thoughts. But aliens are no good at camping and they burn the wilder-ness down by accident. To cover their tracks, they go around erasing all the mountains and the trees with Nature's Miracle so that no one will be able to smell who burned down the forest. Then, finally the aliens erase all the people and achieve world domination.

But they didn't realize that the Handsome Dog and his human sidekick had survived, and it was their job to get the world back to normal... *but how???*

Mom was the kind of dummy sidekick in action movies never notices trouble and is always bubbling into dangerous situations. She sleeps right through when there's a sound in the neighborhood at night, and thinks nothing of letting the mail man in the front gate to murder us. So I don't think that she even realized that we were in a science fiction movie where the air smelled, the world disappeared, and all the humans were replaced by aliens. Instead, she kept on living like the world wasn't coming to an end; waking up every morning and saying, "Yesterday was bad, but I bet it's blown out by now so I guess we can go out and run." So every morning we would run in the dark and feel fine. Then the sun would come up, smelling like the red from an apocalypse movie, and we would see that the world had gotten even smaller, and more of the distance had been erased. Then Mom would look around in wonder as she drove to work like everything was normal and say something like, "We were actually breathing this???"

Since it was a movie, it was all make-believe, and that's why it didn't actually hurt us to breathe the poison air. But I guess Mom didn't realize it was all pretend because one Saturday she did her long run on the dreadmill watching true crime documentaries. It was the boringest scene in a movie ever. I know because I had to watch the whole thing, and fell asleep a bunch of times in the middle. I felt like Clint Eastwood in *Million Dollar Baby*. If you haven't seen it, it's a movie about an old man who thinks he's starring in a macho sports movie with a pretty lady, and then three-quarters of the way through, he finds out that it's actually an artsy drama movie and he's so disappointed that he ugly cries in a very unmanly way. I ran around the house barking a lot to keep the plot interesting, but I'm pretty sure it'll be a box office flop.

A Tilt

After all the things I've done in four and a half years of adventuring, I thought I'd already tried all the grand adventures near my home. I had visited all eight states in the country, had been dognapped, had won half marathongs, had climbed to the tops of mountains and down the deepest valleys, had gotten my masters in obedience classes, and become a successful busy-ness dog. But it has never occurred to me to run in The City.

The morning started just like any other work day: Mom and I got up early, she put on her running clothes, and then she grabbed the running leash and we went to the car. But then she also got her work stuff, which was weird. I've never seen Mom run with her laptop, or in her rhino shoes before. Then, instead of just driving a little way to the Jim or The Fart, we drove and drove a very long way like we do when we're going to the office. Finally we got to a place that looked like The City does after work, when the sky is dark and the buildings are bright. Mom stopped the car, put on my running leash, and we went to run just like we usually do at home.

As soon as we got to the sidewalk, we found a man lying on the ground in his camping sack. Next to him was a hideous, hulking monster. "YOU STAY BACK OR I'LL OPEN UP A CAN OF WHOOP SASS!!!" I shouted at the monster, hoping that it wouldn't notice that I took a little hop backward every time I barked.

"Oscar, what are you doing?" Mom asked, doing a terrible job of hiding that she was laughing at me.

"DON'T YOU TOUCH HER!" I shouted at the monster, getting ready to cut and run at any moment if it started to chase me. "SHE'S TOO DUMB TO DEFEND HERSELF, BUT I'LL MAKE YOU WISH YOU WERE NEVER BORN!"

"Oscar, it's a shopping cart covered in a tarp," Mom said, as if there were no danger at all. "Here, do you want to sniff it?" And then Mom – that dufus – started walking toward the monster.

Well if she was going to take dumb risks like that, let her get chopped up by the chopping cart. I changed my plan. I stopped barking and hid behind her. I didn't need to bark anymore anyway, because the man in the sack on the ground had woken up and was barking up a frenzy himself.

"See?" Mom said. "It's just all of this man's stuff. He moves around every day, just like we do when we're camping. This is his covered wagon." She turned back to see if I was ready to sniff, but I was no fool, and fainted to the other side to keep her body between me and the chopping cart. If it attacked, I would let it chop her into little bits while I ran away.

Once we had inched around the far side of the sidewalk and put the chopping cart behind us, Mom and I ran until The City ended and we were running along the water. Instead of big water like they have at the beach, this was little water that let sidewalks and buildings stand right at the edge of it, and lots of boats sit on top of it. Most impressive of all, a big bridge stood high over everything. "I know that bridge!" I said. "Bodie lives on the other side of it!"

"No, you're thinking of the Golden Gate Bridge," Mom said. "This is the Bay Bridge."

"What the heck are you talking about?" I asked. "I recognize it. It's got the pointies with the U's in between and the stripes hanging off the U. It's called a 'suspense bridge' because you never know what's going to  happen when you're reunited with your soulmate on the other side. I've been on that bridge a million times!"

"The one that goes to Bodie's house is red. This one is grey," Mom said.

"You're not making any sense, Mom. First you say it's golden. Then you say it's red. Then you admit it's grey. Gold and red are both shades of grey. Can't you even see? That's why they nicknamed it the Grey Bridge." Mom can be so think sometimes.

'*Tourist*,' Mom muttered.

"What's a tourist?" I asked.

"It's someone who takes a picture of the Bay Bridge, and then stops you on the street to ask 'if they're painting it'," she said, rolling her eyes.

I was having a great time being a tourist, but I was starting to worry about one thing: Where was the bathroom? Mom had already figured out that there were no poop bags in The City, and now I was starting to realize that there were no grassy patches to relieve myself on either. I held it, looking for a nice yard or ivy patch until I thought I was going to burst, but everywhere I looked was sidewalk. After almost a mile, I slammed on the brakes so hard that Mom didn't have time to stop before I squatted. I slid along the pavement a couple of inches, leaving a trail of turds behind me while Mom ground to a stop.

At home we can sometimes leave a poo and come back to it later once we've found a bag, because we know that no one's going to see us. But here in The City there's always someone to witness you run away from the scene of a poo, even before sunrise. Mom looked around desperately, and then a miracle happened: stuck under a gate like a piece of trash was a string of three empty poo bags waiting for us. Mom grabbed one, stuck her hand inside, and groped at the sidewalk until she'd picked up all of my waste. You may be on your own in The City, but The City still provides in its own way.

I thought our adventure was over when we got back to the car, but it wasn't yet. Mom opened my door for me like a gentleman and then said, "Oh duck!"

"What?!" I asked.

"You wait here. I'm going to go into the gym and shower before I deal with this," she huffed.

"Deal with what? Hey, have you noticed that this car is kind of tilted? That's weird, because the floor we're parked on is flat..." But she had already slammed the door in my face and stormed off.

When Mom came back a hundred years later, her hair was wet and she had her phone stuck to her face. Then she got in the car and just sat there without turning it on. "Mom, aren't we going to be late for work? All my collies will be worried about me."

"We have a flat, Oscar. We need to wait for someone to come fix it for us before we can leave." As usual, Mom was confused. The car was normally flat, but today we seemed to have a tilt.

Eventually a man came in a big truck. He looked like a dognapper, so I barked at him through the window. He didn't look scared, but I knew he was because he stayed outside the car and tried to dognap me from there. Since he couldn't drive away with me in the back like the last time I was dognapped, he lay down on the ground where I couldn't see him and tried to pick up the car and carry it away. I could feel him pushing it higher and higher off the ground, and the tilt going from one side of the car to the other. I got real quiet and stared at Mom, trying to warn her of the danger with my eyes, but she just stood there like a dope and didn't do anything to save me. Maybe this was her revenge for me leaving her to be eaten by the chopping cart.

Luckily, the dognapper wasn't strong like me, and eventually he gave up trying to lift the car, and put it back down on the ground. Then he drove away in shame in his big truck. But in the end it all worked out great because by the time he left, the tilt was gone, and the car had four flat tires again. And I was free to go to work.

Christmas Present

Christmas presents are supposed to be a surprise, but I'm a smart dog and I figured out that Mom had a surprise in store when she started packing our Wagon gear. "Mom, where are we going?" I asked.

"You've been such a good boy that you deserve a big present. We're going to spend Christmas in Utah!" she said.

"But you're packing so many sweatshirts! Won't you be hot and thirsty in the desert?"

"The desert gets very cold in the winter, Oscar. That's why it's the best time for black dogs to visit. You'll see...!"

I don't know why people think that Christmas should be all about the North Pole and snow and stuff, because I just found out that it's actually a day to celebrate some dude's birthday who was born in a barn in the desert. I think his name was Chris. Just like Chris's mom, my Mom didn't make a reservation at any motels or campgrounds, and that's why we had to hurry up and drive all the way to Utah without stopping for adventures. If we dilly-dallied, we may not find anywhere to stay on Christmas night.

It had taken us a long time to get to Utah the first time, but Mom said we could get there in two long days of driving if we used the freeways. For the whole morning we drove under a grey and yucky sky that smelled like big trucks and cow poop. Finally, when we'd been in the Covered Wagon for so long that I was sure that

Christmas had come and gone, Mom stopped for lunch and I got out and found that the sky was high up where it belonged, the sun was out, and the air smelled like dry. We kept driving until all the plants were shriveled up into pointy things, the sun started coming down behind us.

Mom pulled over to feed the Covered Wagon, and aimed its nose at the big juice boxes that wagons drink their meals from. At the last moment she veered away from the juice boxes like they were dangerous. "We can get gas like a dollar cheaper just a few miles away in Nevada!" she scoffed. So she parked the Covered Wagon next to some rusty, old-timey farm stuff so the Wagon could talk to the rust heap about what it was like to be old and retired, and left me on guard while she went into the building to use the people bathroom.

The building had signs about the fancy homemade candy and gifts inside, so when Mom came out, I danced my anxiety dance and licked her face as I squealed, "Is this Santa's workshop??? Is that thing with wheels over there Santa's sleigh?"

"No," she said. "That's a tractor, and this is just one of those crummy gas station gift shops that can't decide whether it's a 7-11, an old fashioned candy store, or a tourist trap." I didn't know what a tourist trap was, but I'm glad Mom hadn't gotten stuck in it, leaving me alone in the Covered Wagon forever.

As Mom walked me around the parking lot for my potty break, we came to some strange humans that were standing very, very still. "Push button to start the show," Mom read from the sign. Then she pressed the button.

Suddenly I could hear whooshing water, like there was a river going by. I didn't understand, isn't the desert supposed to be dry? Where did this river come from? We stood there for a few seconds staring at the odd-looking frozen humans, but when they still didn't move we started to walk away. When my back was turned I heard a human voice say, "Yeehaw! I just found gold!"

Mom and I turned back around to see that one of the odd humans was moving only his mouth while the rest of him stood still like a statue. "Mom! Quick! This guy found gold, but I think he's a disabled person. I bet if I bark a lot to create a distraction, you could steal all the gold from him and then we could run away with it and he couldn't chase us because of his disability. Then we'll be rich!" I knew the barking scam would work because I do it all the time to trick dogs into running away so that I can steal their toys and bones. "On the count of three," I said, letting a big bark build in my throat. "One... two..."

Then, the frozen, disabled human went on, "Oh, I don't mean *real* gold. I mean those delicious honey candies I found inside the store. Better hurry before they're all gone."

"Mom," I asked, "did you leave a whole fortune of gold inside that store??? We could adventure forever with that gold!"

"Um," Mom said, "I think it's a lame advertisement for overpriced candy. Did the gold rush even hit this part of California? I'm pretty sure that most of the action was five hundred miles north of here..." Since Mom seemed to think that there was no gold at this gas station, we turned our backs on the California gold mines and continued into the dark and the desert to strike it rich at the poker tables in Nevada.

A little while later I saw more Christmas lights than I had ever seen in one place. It looked like a whole castle covered with white, and colored, and flashing lights on every wall of every building. "Mom! It's the North Pole!" I said, staring out the window and wagging my tail.

"Um, I hate to disappoint you, Bub, but it's just the Nevada border."

"What's the Nevada border? Is that like the customs station for the North Pole?" I asked.

"No, it's just a casino," she said. I didn't know what a casino was, but judging by Mom's tone of voice, it was something that looked exciting but actually was as boring as a ten-hour drive on the interstate.

Finally, Mom pulled off the freeway where an island of lights glowed in the empty blackness of the desert. As we got closer I could read the sign said CASINO AND SMOKE SHOP and below that it said FIREWORKS. Mom stopped the Covered Wagon in a gravel patch across from the Casino and Smoke Shop, Fireworks. When I got out, I saw rows and rows and rows of tombstones. Then there was a loud boom, and a bunch of tiny dots of light like someone had burst a nighttime skyscraper. What in the world was this place? I thought about it... Casinos, lights, desert, Nevada, lots of dead bodies...

"Mom!" I said, "Is this Las Vegas???"

"No, of course not," she said. "We went through Las Vegas like an hour ago, didn't you notice all the hotels and billboards?"

"Oh," I said. "I thought that was just a movie set. It looked so fake. We didn't even find a dead body." If there's one thing CSI has taught me, it's that everyone who goes to Las Vegas finds a dead body. "So if this isn't Las Vegas, then what's with all those tombstones?"

"Um, those are Jersey barriers, like they put in the middle of the freeway" Mom said. "I guess they have to get stored somewhere, and some truck stop in the middle of nowhere is where they store them here."

"Oh yeah, then what's with all the gunshots and lights in the sky?" I shot back.

"They're setting off fireworks every couple of minutes. I think it's creative marketing. Setting off fireworks over a gas station in the desert in the middle of the night is better than those lame animatronics at the last stop..."

Much to my dismay, Mom joined me in the back of the Covered Wagon and started making preparations for bed. It looked like she planned for us to spend the first night of this adventure sleeping in a graveyard outside Las Vegas listening to gunshots and watching exploding skyscrapers. They must leave that part out of the traditional Christmas story.

I didn't know about blankets the first time Mom and I slept in the cold. While Mom had slept under the comforter and sleeping bag, I had kept knocking off my blanket so that I would be ready to jump into action at any moment. Without blankets, I had spent that whole night shivering, and ever since that night, Mom had been training me to use blankets correctly. As the winter got colder, she started tucking the blankets up around my neck like an em-pup-nada when she got up in the morning, and giving me a kiss on the forehead so I would know I was safe. As long as I stayed that way, I felt cozy and warm, no matter how cold the house was. But if I got up to bark at someone in the driveway, my blanket disappeared and I was back to being a pup-sicle. Sometimes I didn't quit being an em-pup-nada until it was time to go to work.

So when Mom tucked me under my Wagon Blanket, and then tucked us both under the heavy comforter that she'd bought just for this trip, I knew just what to do and snored Mom a lullaby. Snug as a mug in a hug[6], we slept for almost as long as we'd been driving.

---

[6] Mom says that's not the right expression, but I've seen how happy humans are hugging both paws around a hot mug in the morning, so I think my way makes more sense than hers.

Desert Wifi

The next morning we left the graveyard outside the Casino and Smoke Shop, Fireworks and after about an hour of driving we pulled into a parking lot. "Are we there yet?!" I asked, looking out the windshield for Utah.

"Um, no. This is the last Starbucks for like two hundred miles," Mom said. "We need wifi."

I looked around, but I didn't see the Starbucks mermaid anywhere. "Where?"

"It's in the casino," she said.

So, as usual, Mom left me alone to fret about her getting stuck in a tourist trap while she went into the Starbucks to get coffee and discover a dead body. When she came out a dog year later holding her coffee, I sniffed her. "You smell like cold smoke and stink sticks," I said.

"A low-budget roadside casino at 8:30 in the morning on Christmas Eve is one of the most depressing things I've ever seen," Mom shuddered. "The wifi in the Starbucks wasn't even turned on, and no one had noticed, knew how to turn it back on, or even knew what the network was called. It's like they'd given up on the outside world. Let's go to the McDonald's across the street. I never thought I'd say this, but that might be less depressing."

"Do I get McRotguts???" I asked.

"Of course. Once I'm done with my emails." She didn't even have to get out of the Covered Wagon to tap on her laptop. "If I'd known McDonald's had free wifi, that would have made life so much easier on our trips!" she marveled. "McDonald's is almost as great a discovery as Wal*Mart!" Then she went into the restaurant to get me my McRotguts and look for a dead body. She came out a minute later looking confused.

"What happened?" I asked, sniffing at her empty hands.

"Apparently they only sell breakfast this early in the morning. McNuggets won't be available for another few hours. It never occurred to me that McDonald's observed traditional meal times." But McDonald's is a six star restaurant, so of course their chefs don't serve fine dining at the improper time, even on special occasions like Christmas Eve.

Since Nevada was such a disappointment, we kept driving through the desert to Arizona and then into Utah, where the flat ground started climbing up mountains. We could see in the distance that some of the mountains had already started growing their white coats for next summer. As we climbed higher, even the mountain we were driving on started to grow a little stubble of white dirt. It was funny to see the spiky desert plants and tumbleweeds sticking out of the white dirt like that. There was even white dirt on the ground as we came down into Roadrunner and Wile E Coyote country, where cracks became canyons and the mountains looked more like wedding cakes than muffin tops.

We finally arrived at a place to park Covered Wagon overnight where Santa could find us and Mom could use the people bathroom. But instead of stopping driving after we'd checked in, Mom turned the Wagon around and went back to the road. "Where are we going??" I asked. "How is Santa going to find us? Is there a star following us to show him the way or something?"

"I think that we have enough time for a short hike before sunset if we hurry..." Mom said.

When we got to the trail, I was so excited that I didn't even care that Mom had dressed me in embarrassing Christmas pajamas. I hadn't run in weeks, and now that I had responsibility at long last, I felt weightless as I sprinted up and down the trail in a hurry to see what was up ahead, and then back to see if Mom was dead. I rolled on the white dirt, jumped on the boulders, and even chased a bunny or two. I could hardly believe my good luck to be back in the desert with all of my favorite things for Christmas.

Best of all, when we were finished, Mom took me out to a fancy Christmas Eve dinner so that I could have the McRotguts she'd promised me. Finally we brought the Covered Wagon back to wait for Santa. Mom left some dog biscuits out for him to eat when he crawled up our exhaust pipe, but I ate them first. I would need the energy for Mom's and my big Christmas hike tomorrow.

White Dirt Christmas

Mom woke me up in the morning while it was still dark out. "Did Santa come?" I mumbled as she pulled the blankets off of my head.

"Yeah, sure," she said. "But also I want to hit the trail early so that we can be on the ridge to watch the sun rise behind the mountains." Mom turned on the heat in the Covered Wagon, and while she drank her poop juice and charged her phone, I opened the only gift that Santa could fit up the exhaust pipe.

"What is it?" I asked, sniffing at it. It was as long as my leg, tube-y and smelled like food.

"It's a beef trachea…" Mom told me. I'd never had a beef trachea before, and believe me, it's even *better* than it sounds. When I'd finished, Mom drove the Covered Wagon into the night and toward the same trailhead we'd explored the day before.

We got to the car kennel at the moment when just enough light leaked out of the sky for us to see by, so we didn't need my spotlight to keep us from falling off a cliff. When we looked up at the cliff wall, it was hard to tell what the mountain had in store for us, since from a distance (and even up close) the trail blended into the rest of the rocks and sand. I couldn't see the path until we were standing right on top of it. "Where are we going?" I asked, looking at the steep wall of rock looming a few hundred feet above us.

"Well… this trail's called Hidden Valley, so I'm guessing there's a valley somewhere that we can't see. I do know that this trail goes all the way up to the rim eventually..." We looked up at the rocks, but we didn't see a single hole in the wall where a trail could sneak through.

After about a mile, the sort-of-stairs that we'd been climbing faded away, and we came to a place where trees and big boulders lived. Things that are too big can't live on steep slopes because they lose their balance and fall off, so even though we could see nothing but cliffs above our heads, this spot was behaving like it was flat. I don't know how it happened, but a few moments later we were suddenly walking in a wide valley covered in white dirt. When we turned around, we couldn't even tell that the steep cliff we had just climbed was only a few hundred yards away. It was like we'd just walked onto Platform 9 3/4.

"Look, Oscar! The sunrise!" Mom said when she looked back across the open air.

I looked through the crack at the end of the valley and saw that the sun was coming up behind the mountains. It wasn't just lighting up the undersides of the clouds in that way that makes Mom go gaga, but it was also poking through the holes between the mountains like a crown of spotlights. Mom made me take a gajillion pictures so that she could remember what I looked like at sunrise in the desert.

I'm used to Mom taking my picture by now, and it wouldn't have been so bad, except that every time she took my picture she made me put on this stupid Santa hat. She said that I looked "adorable," especially since my hat matched my new winter coat, but I hated it. Every time she put the hat on me, I hung my head and froze in whatever position I happened to be in when the hat caught me, and wouldn't re-manimate again until she took it back off.

Mom took her time walking through the Hidden Valley, so I rolled in, and bit, and sprinted through the white dirt while it flew up in a cloud around me everywhere I went. It was real cold in the valley, but my jacket kept me warm like a blanket as I rolled around and covered every inch of myself in white dirt.

Once we had crossed the valley and were back among the rock lumps that look like humongous round potatoes from far away and flakey biscuits from up close, we found the rim trail in no time. Mom wasn't really sure where we wanted to go. There was an eight-mile loop up here, but since we'd already hiked more than three miles up to the rim, and we didn't have any roast beast to eat, hiking the whole thing didn't seem like a great idea. Anyway, we'd hiked that loop when we were here last spring, and Mom said that we should try to see new trails. "But first, let's go take a picture at the overlook," she said. The last time we were at the overlook, Mom had screamed and practically hit the deck when I went to check it out. I was surprised she'd forgotten, because it was pretty dramatic and embarrassing.

The hike up to the overlook was very, very rugged. We had to climb over big rocks, and sometimes we came to the end of a rock to find that the ground continued too far beneath us for me to jump head-first or Mom to drop on her bad knee, so we had to backtrack until we found a place to climb down safely. "I have a confession to make," Mom said.

"What?" I asked. "The beef trachea wasn't actually from Santa?"

"What I was going to say was that I'm not positive that this is a trail."

That's the thing about the desert: It's built like a sloppy stack of books. You can walk on pretty much any of the flat bits and see the same landmarks, so it seems easy to find your way around. What you can't see is where there are gaps between the books... that is, until you get to the end and realize that you're stuck on top of a Russian novel and there's no way down. Or until you come around the side of that towering potato rock, and suddenly it's as skinny as a potato chip and you don't recognize it anymore. Mom and I climbed until we reached the end of the world, and then we looked down to where we expected to see a canyon. Only, instead of the town thousands of feel below us, there was just a sloping bowl of regular desert sitting not too far below where we were standing. "Hm," Mom said once she worked up the nerve to look over the edge. "It's a lot less dramatic than I remember it."

After only a few mistakes where the trail we were following jumped into a ravine, Mom and I found our way back to the main trail. It was wide, and well marked, and every time we were in doubt about where it went, we just had to look for the tire prints where confused drivers had driven their cars off the road and deep into the desert.

After about a mile we reached a dead end where the trail dropped off to Ohio on the canyon floor thousands of feet below. "Oh," Mom said. "I guess this is the overlook. I wonder what trail we were on before..."

"It wasn't a trail at all, chucklehead," I muttered, rolling my eyes. But I was having too much fun being an explorer to really get annoyed at Mom. When I looked out into the distance I could see hundreds of potato-rocks filing through the valley like they were in a protest march. Beyond the ranks of potato-rocks I saw cliffs that looked like someone had cracked the Grand Canyon in half to get a better look. It made me feel like we could just walk on and on forever, exploring our way through the desert all the way back to California.

Before we left the rim, Mom led me to one of the hollowed-out spots in the rock that looked like the inside of a giant seashell for some dramatic portraits. To protest the Santa hat, I stared defiantly in the opposite direction from where Mom was crouching. That's when I noticed a little cave way up high on the rock. "Mom! Mom! It's the Grinch's house! Do you see it??? Maybe Max will sign a paw-tograph for me!" We climbed up the slope to see if the Grinch was home, but when we got to the top of Mt. Crumpet, the cave was only a few feet deep, barely big enough for an antler-wearing dog to sit up in and definitely not big enough for a taller sourpuss like the Grinch. Mom snapped the Santa hat on my head and made me "stay" while she boot-scooted her way back down to Who-ville to take my picture. When she finally came back up to take the hat off, she congratulated me on such a convincing sour Grinchy frown.

Finally it was time to head back through the Hidden Valley to the Covered Wagon for lunch. People mark the path through the desert for those coming after them by making snowmen out of rocks, and then they name the snowmen Karen. We followed the Karens and our old pawsteps back toward the secret passageway that would take us back down the cliff. All of a sudden the trail disappeared again, as if by magic. There was a Karen wedged under an overhang like she was trying to tell us something, but we couldn't figure out what, and then the trail simply disappeared.

We went back and forth over the same tenth of a mile of trail over and over, and couldn't find anything trail-like anywhere; no packed-down white dirt, no shoe prints in the sand, no rock Karens, not even a long stretch without things in the way of walking. Finally we went back to the Karen wedged under the rock to ask her where to go. Mom scratched her head and stared at the Karen. She looked up, but we'd already tried that route. She looked down, but we'd tried that too. She looked back toward the main trail. Yep, we had definitely come down the correct trail to get here. Frustrated, Mom turned around to look at what her back had been facing... and saw a whole parade of Karens marching down the mountain. "Oh..." she said, walking toward them. "Take that as a lesson, Oscar."

"What? Not to let you be the navigator?"

"Well I was thinking that you should always check your assumptions, but you bring up a good point. How is it that dogs can find their way home from hundreds of miles away, and you keep letting me get lost?"

"I love exploring," I said. "Don't you?"

From this direction the Hidden Valley was even more invisible. We got lost a few more times following something that looked like a trail but really was just a dried riverbed or bald slickrock. The problem with looking for a place called Hidden Valley is that it's... well... hidden. Earlier we had found our way to the fake overlook and back because we could always see where we were going, but since we had no idea what rocks the Hidden Valley was hidden behind, we didn't know what to aim for.

"Maybe it's behind one of those hoodoos," Mom said, pointing to the giant potatoes towering above us on the right.

"You just made that word up..." I said. When we walked toward the voodoos, the "trail" was swallowed by bushes and big rocks.

When we next found the trail, Mom pointed to the enormous rock nose sniffing the sky and said, "Maybe the trail climbs up and wraps around at the base of that promontory there..." But when we identified the trail again, instead of going up, it went left-down and away from where she was pointing.

I was getting hungry and tired. "I don't understand how you could keep losing a trail that we were just on a few hours ago..." I growled.

Finally we came around what seemed like a meaningless bend in the trail and found ourselves staring back down the channel of the Hidden Valley. "Oh," Mom said. "Didn't see that one coming… I thought it was to our right. It was behind the rocks to the left the whole time."

As tired as I was, I still found the energy to roll in the white dirt and kick up an impressive cloud as I sprinted through the Hidden Valley. When I barked my excitement, I heard someone barking "Yippee!!!" back at me. I stopped and looked around for who else was there, but there was no one. Then I realized that it was the mountain barking back at me to wish us a Merry Christmas.

Oscar the Lobster-eared Reindeer

You're never going to believe this, but that night it rained all over the Covered Wagon. Mom promised that it was going to turn into snow in the morning and that we could try hiking in it. Snow is when white dirt falls from the sky, and I was excited to see it for the first time, but when we woke up, nothing was falling from anywhere. The snow probably got scared by the cold and ran away. I would have run away too, but the cold snuck up on me while I was being an em-pup-nada, so I didn't notice.

We left the manger where we'd spent Christmas, and drove with the heater blasting to a park called Dead Horse Point. "Mom, what happened to the horse???" I asked.

"Erm, I don't know. I think she died painlessly of old age surrounded by all the horses that she loved."

"Oh good," I said, even though I thought it was still a strange name for a place. Why not name it after her life and accomplishments? "Since it's a place named after a four-legged runner, we don't have to use the leash, right?"

"We're supposed to, but I have no intention of holding anything that might pull me off balance when I'm standing near a cliff. Safety first. Anyway, the government is on a shutdown, so the rangers who give the tickets are home with their families."

As we were driving to the park, I looked out the window and wagged my tail. Someone had decorated the whole park for Christmas and sprinkled white dirt all over everything. It looked like the opposite of a shadow, like instead of the underside of everything being dark, now the sunny side of everything was white. The decorator hadn't missed anything, from the tiniest twig on the twisty candy cane trees to the giant chimney stacks inside the canyon.

Much to my surprise, Dead Horse Point wasn't a horse hospital at all, but a finger of land that stuck out into the canyon so that we could hike in a loop and always look at a new part of the canyon on our left. I liked Dead Horse Point because now that the horse had passed away, we had the whole place to ourselves. Wherever we went, ours were the first pawprints in the white dirt. Mom was taking her time absorbing the sights, but I had to run around to stay warm so whenever she couldn't see me, I rolled around in the white dirt and practiced my snow angels.

We also did lots of looking into the canyon together. What I like about looking at the canyon is that you can see all the distances. Close up I can smell where the bunnies live in the bushes and see all of the little holes in the rock that look like a giant stuck his finger inside just to see what it would feel like. In the medium distance I saw all of the cliffs and towers and wondered about how an adventurous dog might find a way up or down them. And in the long, long distance I could see the bottom of the canyon, and then rim after rim lining up behind each other until the horizon. In the Grand Canyon we could only see the fake far distance and the near distance, which was filled with dumb humans who weren't paying attention, so I liked Dead Horse Point much better.

"What do you like about the canyons?" I asked Mom, expecting her to say something about gift shops or flush toilets.

"I feel like I can see time. It's like watching a story that's hundreds of millions of years old."

"You're weird," I said. "That's why you're not the writer in this family."

After awhile we found a sign for a side trail. It said, "Horse Pharmacy Viewing Area 0.25 mile" and then an arrow that pointed right off a cliff.

"What the heck?" Mom said. "Is this a trap?" She cautiously got very close to the sign, crouched down so that she would stick to the earth better, and then tentatively looked around and behind the signpost. Then she stood up, "Hey, look! There's a whole plateau down this little step. You can see it if you just step off the main trail and get a little closer to the edge."

After that, Mom was very brave about getting close to the edge, and even scooted up close so she could look all the way down a couple of times. She only screamed once when I ran down a slope into a viewing parapet and put my front paws up on the wall between me and the abyss for a better look. I was very proud of her because she only cried for a second after that, and calmed down when I came to comfort her.

As we walked the plank to where the finger of rock ended and open air began, we started to see some people who had been attracted by the Visitor Center and car kennel built at the very tip of the land for all the mourners to leave their horse trailers. "Mom, do you need to put a leash on me? Are we going to get caught?" I asked as we walked in the direction of the strangers.

"Heck no! All of those people are on viewing balconies within inches of the edge. There's **NO WAY** I'm hanging on to you if you do your bowling ball thing. If you jump on them and knock them off a cliff, you're on your own." Then she pulled out the lobster headdress she'd been making me put on for pictures all morning. "I have a better idea…"

"What are you going to do with those???" I asked.

"I know how to short circuit your confidence and keep you from trying to make new friends!" she said, snapping the elastic under my chin that kept the lobsters stuck on my head. We walked the long way around the outside of the parking lot, and I slunk by the Korean couple who were shouting into the canyon without shouting along with them. Then I slunk past the American couple that said I was "such a cutie" without giving them my butt to scratch. I didn't even bark at the old folks that looked like they were scared of dogs. No one will take you seriously if you're wearing two lobsters on your head, so why bother?

The walk back along the west rim was a little bit harder to find because there was more white dirt, and less red-grey dirt to show old footprints. Luckily, there were Karens everywhere to point the way so we could look up at the canyon rather than looking down at where our paws were going. There was even more to see here because the canyon looked totally different on this side. Again and again we wandered off the trail to explore the canyon up close, and every time we left the trail to explore, the helpful Karens showed us the way back.

On a side trail to a spot called Equine Hospice Overlook, Mom stepped over a crack to look down into the canyon. Something about the crack put my hackles up, so before crossing it myself I peeked down into it.

 There was no bottom, it just went down, down, down until it was all black. My eyes followed the crack along the rock Mom was standing on until it ended in open space... and then after an emptiness as wide as the Covered Wagon is long, it started again on the next rock. It looked like a couch with the middle cushion missing. *What had happened to the cushion in the middle???*

"C'mere Oscar," Mom said as I stared into the crack, still trying to figure out where the ground had gone.

"First tell me why there's no more rock over there! Where did the rock go?!" I said.

"Well... it fell into the canyon. Come here. I want to take a picture."

"No way, José! Are you crazy?! This thing could go at any second. And I'm sure you standing on it doesn't help the situation. I saw how many snacks you ate last night."

"Treat?"

"Not for all the beef tracheas in Utah!" I said.

The sun was shining and the cold wasn't as prickly by the time we got back to the Covered Wagon, but Mom (who isn't as tough about the cold as I am) was ten percent frozen solid. It's a good thing that the Covered Wagon's only temperature setting is "sauna" because it took a long time for her to feel her fingers enough to scratch behind my ears properly again.

Our hike was almost perfect except for one thing: I still hadn't seen it snow like Mom had promised, and now we had to leave Utah because there was a "cold snap" starting tonight. As we drove through the mountains of Utah, looking longingly at the signs for all the National Parks that wouldn't let me in, ugly grey clouds gunked up the sky and the road climbed up to meet them. "Look, Oscar!" Mom said. "It's snowing."

I looked out the window, but all I could see was the laziest rain I'd ever seen. On the car commercials and in the snow globes it always seems like snow happens with bright lights to make each beautiful snowflake sparkle, but this stuff was dreary and clumpy and didn't even make that jingle sound as it fell. It looked like someone was just throwing toy guts at us. "This is stupid. I can make snow at home," I said, laying back down in my throne of blankets for a nap.

Oscar the Explorer

Remember when I said that I wished we could just walk across the desert forever? Well, I changed my mind.

Mom and I had tried to hike in Red Rocks when we came through Las Vegas during our first adventure in the borrowed car-house, but the campground was full and we'd had to drive more than an hour into the bush before we found a place to sleep. This time we were wiser and more experienced, and just parked the Covered Wagon by the side of the road outside the park gate and slept there. When they unlocked the gate in the morning, Mom and I couldn't believe our luck. The weather was beautiful and clear, and we had a perfect view of all the spiky striped candy corn mountains to one side, and the lumpy pinstripe mashed potato rock formations to the other side.

Everything was going beautifully, and Mom and I were strolling down a well marked gentle trail through the scrub when mom turned off the main trail onto a trail-like pattern through the rocks. Instead of packed dirt with frequent signs, now we were walking around big boulders in deep, deep gravel that could have been a trail, or could have been open desert. The first time we had to stop and use strategy to get over an enormous boulder, I started to get a little worried. Later, I tried to jump up onto a high rock that was up to Mom's chin, but only my front half got to the top. I tried to push myself up with the powerful muscles in my back legs, but my paws couldn't find anything to push off of. My nails scratched against the rock as I kicked space, and I was about to give up and drop back down when Mom grabbed me by the legpits and hoisted me up. "Are you absolutely sure this is the trail?" I asked once I had checked that all four paws were back on solid ground. "Since we turned off the main trail I haven't seen a marker or Karen or any signs that humans have ever been here. It seems like we are just walking aimlessly into the desert. That never works out well for the dead bodies on CSI."

"I know," Mom said. "I wouldn't believe it either, except that I have been checking the GPS every two minutes and we are definitely on the trail. I think that we just follow this wash most of the way up the mountain."

"What's a wash?" I asked, taking a step away just in case this was an elaborate ruse to get me to take a bath.

"It's a dry river. This is what the inside of a river looks like when the water is gone. Those big rocks that we have to scramble up would be waterfalls. Not big ones, but pretty enough to take a picture."

The further up we went, the more water(less)falls we had to climb. Sometimes I couldn't figure out how to get up, so mom had to show me the places where I should jump. Sometimes I didn't understand which of her paws I was supposed to follow, or I would forget the sequence and had figure out a new path as I climbed. A few times I missed, and to keep myself from falling I had to jump back down, bouncing off of rocks on the way to the ground like a pinball. If I was really confused, I just stood at the bottom of the Oscarfall and barked until

Mom came down and showed me again, tapping on each step of the route and standing by to spot me if I needed a shove. A few times Mom tried to give me a boost, but I'm no wussy dog and so I made her go the long way around to chart a new route instead. There were times when Mom could have gotten through by gripping and pulling with her front paws, or spreading her back legs and climbing up opposite walls like a monkey, but no one who hikes sensibly with four paws on the ground could follow her, so we had to backtrack and find a different way.

Pretty soon we weren't really following a trail anymore, we were charting a course. We would come to a flat spot and Mom would check which general direction the trail went, and then we would pick out a route to the next flat spot in that direction. Sometimes we reached an obstaple that was impossible to get up, down, over or around and we had to turn back. It was like going through a maze. I didn't know that it was possible to be an explorer on a route that was already mapped, but I was starting to figure out that being an explorer was harder and scarier than it seemed from a distance.

After about two miles we found ourselves facing an Oscarfall that was about four Oscars high. The only way up it was to use that funny four-legged climb that Mom could do and I couldn't. Even if I had used Mom as an elevator, she was not tall enough to lift me all the way to the top. Mom looked for another route, but there were nothing but sheer walls on both sides. "I think this is the end of the road for us, buddy," Mom said gratefully. "Let's head back." Even though we were definitely still on the trail, this adventure was starting to get the stink of a very bad idea, and we were both happy for an excuse to turn around without giving up.

So we started charting our way back down the mountain. The way down had its own problems, because sometimes the things that were easy to climb up were harder to climb back down, especially if you happen to prefer climbing with your front legs first and leading with your noggin. We had just picked our way down a very challenging and confusing Oscarfall to a flat spot when Mom looked at the mapp to see what direction to go next. "Oh crap," she said. "This isn't the trail; the trail was up there." We looked back at the Oscarfall we had just come down, but couldn't see a way for me to get back up it. We spent about five minutes trying to find a way, and then Mom climbed back up to see if there was another route we couldn't see from where we were standing. She looked like a fly climbing up a wall with all of her paws like that. When she came back down, she said, "Okay, let's reframe this. Our problem isn't really getting back to that trail, but finding a way back to the car. Maybe the easiest way is to take the long way round."

Mom studied the mapp and figured out that if we followed this new river a short way, then we would find another trail that could take us on a two- or three-mile detour back to the Covered Wagon. After not too much scrambling, we were back on the civilized trails and feeling happy again. The sun was out, it was warm, the scenery was beautiful, and we were going to have an easy walk back home.

Everything was going well and all the trails were exactly where the mapp said they would be, until we reached the last 0.7 mile trail connecting us back to the route to the Covered Wagon. This trail was even worse than the other one: all Oscarfalls with almost no flat spots in between. I was sure that this time we were definitely climbing rocks randomly into the desert, except that on the mapp Mom showed me, this was an even-more-clearly-marked trail than the last not-trail I'd been sure we were lost on. What's more, we started to meet other hikers who were coming down. This death trap was crowded! First we met what looked like a tour group of people hiking in clothes that they had bought at Marshalls and Ross Dress for Less rather than REI or the outdoor store. Next came a pair of fat humans whose faces looked like tomatoes and were shiny with sweat. They looked like they were going to have twin heart attacks. If these two John Candy look-alikes and the milksop tour group could do this trail, why were two experienced hikers like Mom and me having so much trouble? Next we met a group that had a people puppy that was about my age and size, and they had a dog too! "Take me down with you!" I barked to the dog.

"What? This is nothing! Even the baby human can handle this trail. Haven't you ever been hiking before?" said the dog.

Sure, I'd been hiking before! Lots of times. But even when we were very, very lost, I had never had to hike something so difficult and dangerous. Why didn't this trail carry a warning? You may think that everyone in Las Vegas is a murderer, or a murder victim waiting for their turn, but you have to be tough to face death every day! The Las Vegatarians are so tough that they go out and tempt a painful and frightening death for fun, which is probably why so many of them wind up as dead bodies on TV. As Mom and I scrambled up a pile of rocks, we heard the people puppy start howling behind us. I was too tired to bark at the noise, but I whatever had happened to the people puppy, it made me feel better to know that as tough a day as I was having, at least I wasn't howling.

In one spot, Mom and I spent a dog hour minutes trying to figure out a safe route for both dogs and humans. Mom first tried the human-friendly route, but there weren't enough intermediate spots for me to put all four paws and jump to the next step. Next, she tried the slickrock route, but the rock was too slippery and steep. If one of us fell, the drop was high enough to break a dog's or a human's leg, and then we would be howling like the people puppy until we expired and the CSIs found us. Making matters worse, I could smell that Mom was starting to get scared. We were going to have to climb down thirty or forty hard-won feet to try a different route, and what if this was the only way up? As we came down, we met a couple of humans and a grey-beard dog who were trying to decide which route to take. "It's not this one," Mom said, helpfully. So all five of us set off together in a different direction.

With our new companions, it was much easier for me to get up the tricky stuff. When it was just me and Mom, I wanted to keep an eye on Mom at all times, which meant that she always had to go up things before me. But now that I had the human lady and greybeard dog to follow, I could let Mom and the man walk behind me. If I faltered, The Man grabbed my tight little butt and gave me an ally-oop, which really helped. The greybeard didn't need any ally-oops. She just got a running start and bounced her way up vertical walls. "*Psst.* How old are you?" I whispered to her.

"Twelve," the greybeard told me matter-of factly, as she climbed a route that I needed a boost to get up. *Twelve!* Like I said, the hikers from Las Vegas are the toughest in the world. I bet the four-and-three-quarters-year-old dogs there can fly!

With the help of about a hundred effortless ally-oops, we crossed a distance in about ten minutes that it would have taken Mom and me an hour to figure out. Then the Woman said, "I think this is the top!"

"I love you!" Mom blurted out.

It had been thirsty work climbing all those Oscarfalls, so we stopped for a drink of water at the top. But now that we were at the peak, the weather had turned nasty. An icy blast of wind almost blew Mom's hat off her head, and the sun was gone. "Is that snow???" Mom said. The weather was so miserable that we needed to get down off the top of the mountain as quickly as possible, so we hastily parted ways with the greybeard and her family and followed the path back down into the valley.

In the frigid miles back to the Covered Wagon we had to do very little scrambling, and we only needed to backtrack a few times. We hardly noticed the backtracking anymore anyway, just as long as it was flat. After what felt like a hundred lifetimes and seven harrowing miles, we stepped off of the gravel wash and back onto the main trail. Mom clicked the leash back into place, not like it was necessary. My exploring was done and I walked at Mom heels with my head hanging low.

After a long morning of wondering if we were going to die in the wilder-ness, it was a shock to be back with regular people. Next to us there was a clump of three humans all stuck to an impossibly old fourth human. The old human seemed to be having trouble with this flattest and smoothest of trails, and she kept repeating, "I'm a team player!"

"What's a team player?" I whispered to Mom. "Is it someone who is lost in the desert and needs help?"

"I think it's more like someone who agrees to something that they don't want to do out of spite, so no one else can enjoy the experience either. There's a team player in every family." We left the clotting humans behind and caught up to a bunch of dude-bruhs. One of the dude-bruhs had the witch in his phone playing music that sounded like a dirty cloud of static from far away, and sounded like very angry static when we got close enough to hear it better. "Dude," said another one of the dude-bruhs. "It's so hard to text when your fingers are cold."

"Yeah, bruh," said the third.

We were planning to stay in Las Vegas for an extra day and wait to meet a Friend for another hike, but when we finally shivered into the Covered Wagon, Mom asked "Do you want to stay? We can do a walk on The Strip, and relax in the Covered Wagon with the heat on, and maybe get a fancy dinner at McDonald's for you..."

"Nah. These team players and dude-bruhs don't know how to have a good time. I don't want to be near them."

"I agree. Well, do you want to come back here tomorrow and do an easier hike? Something with a real manicured, maintained, and marked trail?" But after such a big expedition today, an easy hike would just feel like a walk, and I knew we would spend the whole time staring up at the rocks and wondering what it might be like to climb them.

"Well, we could go to Joshua Tree. Or Death Valley... Mojave?"

"Nah." The truth is, I was adventured out. I would need a really long cooling-off period after this one. So we did what we do after all of our road trips: we hurried home to the Stuck House as fast as we could and spent the whole drive trying to think up a way to live on the road for the rest of our lives.

Happy New Year

Even though we were home early, we didn't have to travel far from our Stuck House to find adventure. Mom's sense of direction and my sense of adventure being what they are, we would have no trouble finding a place to lose ourselves, even if we'd been there before.

We decided to celebrate the New Year with a long hike on the mountain that floats between the ocean and the Bay. It was the same mountain where our whole adventure had started nine months before, when we got lost on my birthday. By now Mom had had a lot of practice reading mapps, and after looking at the routes that people had left on AllTrails, she decided that she could put together our own route, different from anything anyone had ever mapped before. Now that you know Mom, you will be just as surprised as I was that we hiked five miles and made it to the first peak without any problems. But that was just the *first* five miles.

Mom had hardly taken any pictures of me on the way up the mountain because the redwood forest had the kind of beauty that you need to move through and feel in your muscles. A camera can't see that kind of charm, even with a charming dog standing in the middle of it. So when we got to the top, Mom was dying to snap a few photos.

We stepped out of the trees and looked around the little paved clearing. "What? Is this it?" I asked. "There's nothing up here but... what are those? Drying racks? Rakes? Torches?"

"I think they're radio antennae."

"And the igloo?"

"Beats me. Probably some kind of public works station. This explains why I never knew that this mountain had a third peak. Why would anyone but the radio repair guy come up here?"

But all was not lost. There was an even better, higher peak just about a mile away. It was the exact steepness and cone shape as the poop emoji, and had an observation tower sitting at the top, so we knew it had to be pretty over there.

We started walking down the trail, and then suddenly Mom held her phone out in front of her and followed it directly into the brush. "Where are you going?" I asked. "Do you need to go potty?"

"The trail is this way!" she said. Then she squawked and almost fell on her butt. Because of Mom's bad habit of walking only on her hind legs, she has a lot of trouble when she hikes down steep trails like this one that are covered in loose rocks, leaves and acorns. If you're new to running, take it from an experienced coach and learn to run on all four of your paws. It may take some adjustment if you didn't start young, but you'll thank me someday. Since Mom never learned to run sensibly, it took us for-ev-ver to get down that short quarter-mile trail, just because it descended eighty stories in that distance. Even though service humans are supposed to stay on leash everywhere on this mountain, Mom dropped the leash so that I wouldn't make her fall by pulling her with my superior speed.

Once we finally got down off the first peak, it was just a short walk to the base of the poop cone where we had to climb up another trail that was just as steep as the one we'd just come down. This trail went through the tightest woods we'd hiked in all day. The brush was so close that the bushes were petting me as I walked through them. This time Mom took the leash off of me altogether so that it wouldn't get stuck on one of those reaching branches and hung it around her own neck instead. I came out of the woods first and stood to wait for Mom, who was crashing like Big Foot through the brush behind me.

"Hi, doggie!" said a man who was standing on the trail.

"Mom, Mom! Come here and look! Quick!" I barked. "There's a man dressed like Smokey the Bear!"

Then Mom came clattering out of the bushes behind me. If she were a cartoon character, she would have had twigs in her hair, hashtags on her cheeks and forehead, and her tongue hanging out, but in real life she just looked like a lost person.

"Um, hi," she said, pulling the leash off of her own neck and hooking it to my collar real quick. "I..." [gasp] "...uh..." [sputter] "...I had him on leash but it got a little..." [wheeze] "...overwhelming in there and I had to..."

"I can see why," interrupted Smokey the Man. "That's why we don't recommend that people hike on closed trails. You know... since they haven't been maintained for years and everything..."

"Right, well... I see that now. And that explains why it was so hard to find the trail at the junction back there... Thanks for the advice."

"You know what I'm about to say to you?"

"Yeah, I'm sorry... I just..."

"Happy New Year," he finished, and started hiking away.

"Wait up!" I said, running up next to him and matching his pace so that we could keep talking, now that we were friends. "I'm Oscar and I'm a very experienced hiker and blogger, who are you? Are you a fan? Want to be my Friend?"

"Thanks for not busting me back there," Mom said after a while.

"Yeah, well, I took in the totality of the situation..." he said.

When he had gone I asked Mom, "What does 'totally of the situation' mean?"

"It means that it's a good idea to pretend that you're a little dumber than you really are around someone who likes being in charge. If they think you're stupid, it makes them feel good to do something nice for you. But if you act like you're smarter than them, then they want to use their power to attack you with a ticket or something."

At the top of the mountain we could see the ocean on one side, turned golden by the sun. On the other side we could see the bright grey sky, the bright grey bay, and The teeny, tiny City with its miniature bridges sticking out into the water. After being alone all morning, suddenly we were surrounded by people who were sharing our beautiful view and harshing our mellow. Worst was a whole family running around and screeching some lost people puppy's name. They must not have had very good treats, though, because the people puppy never came. We stuck around and looked available to help, but the screaming family didn't ask for anyone's help, even though there were dozens of hikers around who could help look for a wandering people puppy, and several four-legged hikers to track his scent. It was distracting, so we left to find somewhere quiet.

That's the difference between people in the wilder-ness and people in The City. In The City, you have to pretend like everyone's invisible, even when someone needs help. And if you're the one who needs help, well, I guess you're just supposed to figure that out alone too. I liked the way of the wilder-ness much better, where everyone says hello, gives each other directions even when no one was lost, and strangers give you an ally-oop without your even having to ask.

Instead of zigzagging down the mountain like we had on the way up, Mom found a trail that bombs-awayed down in a straight line. But it was rocky and steep, and Mom was starting to walk like she had a peg leg, which meant that her knee was hurting. Mom had really slowed down over the past couple of months. She couldn't run anymore, and even hiking was painful for her. I thought maybe she just needed some rest, but the rest wasn't helping. Mom explained to me that when you get older, some parts just wear out. Old things aren't under warranty anymore, which means that they might not get better on their own. If they don't get better, you have to decide whether to try to fix them (which is difficult and expensive), or just give up doing the things that make them hurt. It's called The Old, and Mom was infected with it. So I had to be more patient.

While I was busy being patient, I sniffed a labradoodle up ahead that thought he was large and in charge. He was standing by the side of the trail with his man like he owned the place. I would have to wait for Mom to peg closer to sniff him, so I shouted at him instead, "You wanna say something to me, c'mon and say it to my face, you big galoot!"

"Why I oughta..." he barked back. "Did you learn those manners in the pound, you ugly mutt?"

"Who you calling a mutt, you no-good ball-chomper?!"

Meanwhile, Mom was barking at me because me stepping at this punkerdoodle was pulling on her pegleg. Eventually, Mom got her balance and yanked me over to the side of the trail. "What did I say?! Always pretend that you're dumber and weaker than you are when you meet someone thinks they have a tiny bit of power and wants to use it."

How had this happened? Somehow that half-breed mongrel had forced me into time out, even though he was the snob! I tried to turn my head this way and that to yell at the jerkface how much smarter and stronger I was than him, but Mom made me stare into the bushes until he had passed.

"That guy needed his snout barked in!" I told Mom, once we started walking again. "Why did you stop me?"

"Because sometimes it doesn't matter who's right or wrong. The person who wins the fight is the one who acts the most classy. Losing your cool is never classy."

"But if I can't reach him to sniff him, how am I supposed to tell him that I'm the classier dog? He won't know unless I tell him."

"When you're on the leash you have to live by city rules, which means you have to ignore everyone around you, even if you're on a trail that's so narrow you almost bump into each other. And bragging isn't classy."

"So what am I supposed to do if I can't brag about how classy I am?" I asked.

"You're supposed to judge him," Mom explained. "Judging is how you act territorial from a distance. It's actually pretty effective, see?" Then she stood like a punkerdoodle and looked at me in a way that made me want to bark her snout in. It was tough, but because it was Mom, I kept it classy.

Everyday Adventure

One day Mom dressed up like work and made me put on my tie, but then she walked past our everyday car and unlocked The Covered Wagon, which is our adventure car. We were going on an adventure dressed as busy-ness people! I couldn't wait to see where we were going to hike in our fancy clothes.

But then Mom stopped the Covered Wagon in the same car kennel where we always leave it before work, and we hiked the same three block hike that we always hike to the office. This was very strange. When Mom opened the door for me I ran around the office barking, "You guys, pack your bags, we're going on an adventure!" But then Mom sat down at her desk and started typing.

We worked a very, very long day until I had greeted almost everybody coming in, and also watched almost everybody go home again. When there was almost nobody left, we hiked the three blocks back to the car kennel and got in the Covered Wagon. Finally! Adventure time!

Mom drove a short distance and then put on my leash and let me out into the night. "Yippee!" I said. "Night hike!" Then I dropped my nose and started sniffing around to see what kind of hike we were going to have. "Wait," I said. "But these are just people's front yards. Where's the trail?"

"Do you need to go potty?" Mom asked. I kept sniffing, waiting for the interesting stuff to happen. "Come on, go potty," she urged.

"I'll save it for the trail," I sniffed.

"Fine," Mom said, and turned around.

"What? Is that it? Where's the hike?" Instead, Mom climbed into the back of the Wagon with me and started bedding down. "I don't get it. Is the hike in the morning?" I asked.

"We're trying something new," Mom said. "We're sleeping here tonight."

"But what about our Stuck House? Are we strays now? Like for real?"

"No, of course not. But we spend so much time driving... it's ninety minutes to work in the morning, and an hour back home at night. Just think of all the things that we could do with that time..."

"Well why don't we live in one of these houses here then?" I asked. "They look nice."

"Maybe we will, but moving is just such a pain. And I like where we live. It's quiet, and safe, and the neighbors like you, and the landlord leaves you alone..."

"The who?"

"Exactly. If we moved, you wouldn't see your friend Margo in the driveway, or smell Dan the Cat's pee in the front yard..."

"I do love the smell of Dan's pee..." I said.

The problem with where we were sleeping was that it was on a very steep hill with the pillow-side of the bed facing downhill. Mom asked the Witch in Her Phone to measure the hill, and she said that it was thirteen percent, which means that its great-grandparent was a wall. I tried to sleep like normal, but the blankets I was sleeping on kept sliding into the driving area and I had to climb back up to the bed every few hours.

When we woke up, I thought that Mom would take me hiking for sure, but then she got back in the driving chair and took us somewhere else. "Wait. Where are we going now?"

"To the beach."

"But why didn't we just sleep at the beach?"

"Because the beach is in The City."

"So?"

"Oscar. We must never, ever, ever sleep in The City. In The City meth heads will break into your car for the change in your ashtray."

I knew math heads were very scary and angry ghosts because I had seen one before, but I didn't know that they could see us too. They always seemed like their eyes lived in a different world than the one we lived in. "So why don't you just lock the doors?" I asked. But apparently math heads are the kinds of ghosts that can go through walls. Even though Mom says that math heads used to be human, and we should remember that they're only like that because math ate their brains, they still give me the screaming mimis.

We drove to a dark that smelled like the ocean, sounded like waves, and felt like sand. Then Mom let me off the leash. Behind us in The City there were lights, and cars, and people, and all the human things, but here on the sand there was only dark and the invisible ocean going on and on forever to remind us that even though it feels like the center of the universe, The City is really very tiny. I ran around in big circles until I heard Mom calling my name, then I ran back to check on her before she let me run more circles through the deep sand and waves.

"Mom!" I said, as I ran back to her for the 247th time, "I can see Alcatraz! Look! See the lights in the ocean?"

"Uh, that's not Alcatraz. Alcatraz is that way," she said, pointing away from the water and back toward the lights of The City.

"Can I see all the way to Japan?!" I asked. "Do I have superhero eyes?"

"Well, no. That's just a cruise ship. But it's about the same size as Alcatraz. I made the same mistake when I first moved here."

I ran in all the places while Mom dawdled behind me. I ran until the black air turned grey, and the grey turned blue-grey, and the ocean grew its shapes, and the sky behind us turned sun-colored. Then we got into the Covered Wagon and drove until the beach became a park, and the park became houses, and the houses became churches and stores. Then the churches turned into office buildings and the stores grew into superstores. Finally, when we got to where people piled their homes one on top of the other until they reach the sky, and other people build futuristic things in old drafty warehouses, we turned the Covered Wagon into its kennel.

This was the fancy neighborhood where they like different kinds of decorations. They use parking meters instead of trees as urinals. They decorate the outside of buildings with math heads instead of bushes, and old food wrappers lie on the ground instead of leaves. If we had kept going a little further we would have found The Little Water, and in the middle of it, Alcatraz. The people's proudest things are in the fancy neighborhood because people think that The City is the center of the world, and don't know about the ocean, and the mountains, and desert, and Utah. A few blocks away, at the Little Water, all the rich and famous buildings turned their backs to the hills and oceans, and turned all their windows to look at an abandoned maximum security prison.

I liked being a balanced Oscar, who lives in two worlds. I can put on a tie in The City where they give me jerky, and I'm important and have collies who rely on me. But unlike The City that is obsessed with rules and other human things, I also know about the wilder-ness, and the beauty of rocks and trees and distances. In the wilder-ness I get the different kind of responsibility of an

outlaw doggo who only has to look out for his own pack's safety; where no one will complain that he has no leash, and he can walk and jump wherever his muscles ask him to.

Mom the Weather Jinx

I feel so sorry for all the people who don't know that they can drive an old mailman van to wherever they want and live in it when they get there, because those people always sleep in their stuck houses and so they get stuck too. Mom and I know that we don't need many things or much space, so we can be busy-ness people in The City on Friday, and still wake up in the desert on Saturday. One Friday after work we drove right past our stuck house, and instead of watching a couple of hours of Netflix, we sat in the Covered Wagon and listened to a story while we watched the night go by until bedtime. When we woke up, we were in the desert.

We didn't have enough time in just one night to drive all the way to another desert state, so we went to the Near Desert called the Moon-Havi. The Moon-Havi is named that because it looks like you're on the moon. I don't know what "Havi" means, but it probably means "battleground" or "combat zone" or "octagon" in Martian, because up close it looks like the moon and Mars had a big fight.

They say that it's not supposed to rain in the desert, but whoever said that doesn't know how Mom is the Weather Jinx. It is a well documented (by her) fact that bad weather follows her wherever she goes. For the final driving hour between The Last Starbucks and our hiking spot, the sun lit things up to our right in that special way it does in photos that get lots of likes on Instagram. But to our left everything was grey and angry-looking, like the sky was bruised and swollen from a fight and was looking to get revenge. I sure hoped that our last turn would be to the right, but then Mom turned to the left and drove into the distressed sky until we were smack-jab in the middle of it.

Rain is a funny thing. Sometimes the rain hits the windows like a storm, but when you open the door and stand in it, most of the drops miss you. That's the kind of rain that was happening as we hiked into the desert. Maybe it was just the fashionable rain coat that Mom made me wear that scared away the rain drops, but even though there was rain during our whole hike, it mostly left us alone.

People who don't like the desert just don't appreciate its drama. It's like they are going to the movies expecting to see something with Colin Firth, and instead they get a movie starring Dwayne "The Rock" Johnson. Dwayne "The Rock" Johnson is a very good actor, and his films are always very well written, true to life, and artfully directed. But his movies don't have the over-the-top drama with tea and feelings; they have the kind of subtle drama that uses grunts and blood and gore and pain, so it's not for everyone.

At a sign that told us to be careful of monster-bird attacks, Mom and I turned off of the tire-tracks-trail and walked into the wild desert. The desert is good for walking across, but not good for marking an obvious trail, so I sprinted here, there and everywhere, barking into the clouds while Mom and The Witch that Lives in her Phone navigated. I guess I should have been paying closer attention, because soon a long fence made out of a wire tied to posts blocked our path. "What do we do now?" I asked.

"Well, the sign says 'Foot traffic only.' I think that means we're allowed on the other side..." Mom said, scratching her head. "But how?"

"Where's the door?" I asked.

We looked right and left along the fence, but it went on and on into the desert forever without a break. Mom looked flummoxed, so I had to take control of the situation. "I know what to do!" I said. Then I ducked my head and walked under the wire. Like magic, I was on the other side of the fence. I could almost see smoke coming out of Mom's ears at the magic trick I had just done. Humans are so dumb, they think that a fence is the same as a wall and they never even try to go through. Luckily, Mom was having a brave day and she ducked through the wires herself. Her packpack was feeling less brave and tried to prevent her from trying something new by hanging on to the wire, but after a few tries she convinced the packpack it was safe to let go, and they joined me on the wild side.

We hiked in a dry riverbed, but this one was much nicer than the last dry river we explored because it had no Oscarfalls, just lots of sand and the mess left behind by the fight between the moon and Mars. There were rocks everywhere that were all the colors of grey: jade-grey, red-grey, pink-grey, yellow-grey... In the parts of this desert that the moon had won, there were drip-piles of grey-green cheese covered in matcha dust that dribbled down the cliffs, and slimy bits of cheese curds on the ground in places where the rocks were rotting. In the Mars parts of the desert, the rocks were the color of car accident bruises and the cliffs had big holes in them like they'd been blown up, and the blown-up rocks were flung all over the ground like blood and guts. The moon parts were mostly up-and-down lines like stalagmites, and the Mars lines mostly went side-to-side in stacks, but here and there the moon balanced a stack on top of its drips, or Mars experimented with dripping dribbles down a tall stack.

When we reached the end of the river, we climbed the rest of the way to the top of the mountain and walked along the edge of the cliffs. This hill couldn't decide what it wanted to be. To our right it was Colin Firth – bland, gentle and smooth with only a few rocky or spikey bits to keep it interesting for the eyes. To our left it was Dwayne "The Rock" Johnson where the ground was ripped away in a cliff that would *KILL* you! We walked on the edge between the two until finally The Rock won and we had to pick our way down Colin Firth back to the Jeep trail.

Colin Firth is not without danger, it's just a slower, less sensational kind of danger. We weren't risking falling off a cliff, but the wet, sandy ground liked to be slippery and could sag down the hill with you on top of it if you weren't careful where you stepped. Some spots looked solid like smooth rocks, but when we stepped on them they dribbled and smeared into sticky mud that was slick like ice, and we skied down six inches with each step.

A little further down the Jeep track, the trail that we were following turned off into the wilder-ness again. Whenever we had left the main trail it had shown us a fun adventure, but it was also harder to find our way through the fences, and battle grounds, and trick mud, and Colin Firth that slowed us down. We had been hiking for more than seven miles and the rain had eased its way through my rain jacket. Mom's front paws were so cold that sometimes The Witch didn't recognize her as a living thing when she poked to ask for directions. So we decided to stay on the main Jeep trail and skedaddle back to the Covered Wagon as fast as we could. I wished very much that Mom could run on her bad knee so that we could get to the Covered Wagon faster. Instead, I bounded around in the brush beside the trail and tried to dig to China to keep myself warm.

The heat in the Covered Wagon felt wonderful, and I snuggled deep into all the winter blankets, wiping all of the wet desert off of my lustrous fur and into the warm bedding. We had to drive five hours to get back to our stuck house, and we enjoyed relaxing in the sauna that the Covered Wagon becomes when Mom turns on the heat. And guess what? In all the three hundred miles between our hike and our stuck house, there was not one drop of rain!

Work

If you've never had a job before, you really oughta try working. It's the funnest way to spend a day indoors. Now that I was a busy-ness dog in The City, I was responsible for lots of people at work. When I got to the office, I could barely wait for Mom to open the door, and as soon as she did, I blasted off to take attendance and screech hello to everyone. I was usually one of the first busy-ness people to arrive, so once I'd done my roll call, I would check in individually with everyone on my team to see how they were doing and let them scratch my butt. As people walked up the stairs toward my desk, I sang them a little welcome song, and then escorted them to their desks so that they didn't get lost along the way.

I really loved my job, but having all that responsibility meant that Mom and I couldn't just hop in the Covered Wagon and drive into the wilder-ness. We had to be busy-ness people by week, and adventurers by weekend, which is called "balance." I think balance was harder on Mom because humans aren't pack animals and so sitting inside all day, surrounded by other humans is unnatural for them. That's why work needs to provide them activities to do all day so they don't get bored and aggressive. There's quiet Play on the Computer time, and private Practice Busy-ness Talking with the TV time, and my favorite: Meetings! Meetings are when everybody gets together in one room to let one person show off their barking while everyone else looks bored and watches jealously as I make the rounds and my collies take turns scratching behind my ears.

"Isn't it a drag that we have to go to work today?" Mom said one morning on our drive to The City. "I wish it were the weekend already."

"What??? A drag? Work is my favorite thing ever! I get to see all of my Friends and herd them into meetings and have my butt scratched..."

"Well, that last one's a dogs-only perk. Humans can't touch coworkers' butts..." Mom's always complaining about how no one can touch her butt at work, and how she can't kiss anyone either. But I think that she's got a loser's attitude, because she didn't even try it before deciding that it wasn't for her.

"...and do important things like greet guests and show them to the conference rooms..." I went on.

"...yeah, I wish you wouldn't do that. Not everyone appreciates a big stranger-dog that just barked at them following them everywhere they go."

"...and meetings! Oh how I LOVE meetings!"

"...I'm pretty sure that's just you..."

"...everyone's hands are bored because they don't have their laptops or phones, so they give me massages to soothe their boredom. Meetings are the best!"

"Again, I think you should check your doggo privilege..."

"And in between meetings I get to lie on my bed at our desk and nap. Really, what could be better than working, I ask you?"

"Working is okay, I guess. But wouldn't you rather be out there adventuring, and hiking, and exploring?"

"Exploring is grand and all, but frankly I find it a little stressful sometimes," I said. When we travel I never know what to expect, and there are all of those unfamiliar smells and sounds. "If *you* like exploring so much, why don't you do it full time?"

"Well, because if I didn't work, I wouldn't have the money to pay for the things we need on our adventures, like food and gas and campgrounds with showers..."

"Hang on a second. They give you *money* to come to work???"

"Well, yeah. That's the deal."

"You get free food, clean indoor people bathrooms, screens to watch, and a warm place to relax all day where nobody bites you... they help you pay for the vet if you're sick, and then they give you money *on top of all that*???"

"Well, when you put it like that..."

"Wait, do all humans have this arrangement at work? With such awesome and friendly collies, and free food and gourmet coffee, and their vet bills paid for?"

"Not the free food and health insurance, but yeah. We all get paychecks and bathrooms. And almost nobody gets bitten in the line of duty."

"But at least their dogs get to come to work with them, right?"

"Well no, that's not really standard proce..."

"*Then what do their dogs do all day long?!*" I asked, alarmed.

"The same thing you do when I'm not home, I guess: Nap and eat through the bottom of all the pockets in the laundry looking for treats while they wait for their families to come home."

"But that's horrible! Don't the humans even worry a little bit about making their dogs so anxious that they seek a life of crime?"

"Speaking for myself, yes, I miss you every day when I'm at work without you. That's why I have someone bring you to the dog park to play with your friends, and let you go to the bathroom, and give you kisses and butt scratches and something to do during the day."

"Mom, I hate to break it to you, but I think you need to fire that lady."

"Why? I thought you loved Grecia."

"Well yeah, I do. But that was before I knew that she was supposed to be PAYING me for all the stuff we do together. Every time she comes, she takes that money you leave out on the counter for me and puts it in her pocket."

Oscar the Volcano Beast

I don't want to brag or anything, but I've hiked inside a volcano.

One day we packed up the Covered Wagon with a few days' food and clothes, and after work we drove a long, long way. Then, when we woke up, we drove for even more whiles. When Mom finally let me out to sniff around, I was expecting something really awesome like mountains, or Dr. Seuss trees, or rocks that looked like they were wrapped up in fancy paper. But when I looked around, all I could see were naked mountains in the distance, and all around us was ugly, empty sand, black sponge-rocks and a great, big, ugly, black pile of dirt hundreds of feet high. "We drove all that way for this?!" I asked, sniffing around for pee, or food, or a critter, or anything interesting at all.

"We're going to hike to a crater!" Mom said.

"A crater?! Like from a meteor from space?!" I looked around at the flatness around me with new eyes. Maybe this was where the crater that bombed the dinosaurs hit! Maybe we were standing in it, and this crater was *so big* that the edges of it looked like mountains.

"No, not that kind of crater. A volcano crater."

"Well that sounds exciting too!" I said, still looking around for where the excitement was hiding in all this boringness. "I can't wait to know what lava smells like! Do you suppose it smells like camping? Where's the volcano? It must be very far away, because I can't see it."

"It's right there," Mom said, pointing toward the humongous pile of black dirt.

"What? Behind the dirt?"

"It *is* the dirt pile. Well, it's called a 'cinder cone,' so I guess they're cinders."

"Trapezoid, Mom," I corrected her. "That shape is called a trapezoid. But where's the lava?"

"There is no lava. It turned into these black rocks a long, long time ago. That's why we get to go inside the crater without burning up like Gollum at the end of *Lord of the Rings*."

This all sounded like a bunch of nonsense to me, but we'd come all this way, and when the leash comes off after a long Wagon ride, I'll run around anywhere, even somewhere as boring and spongy as a kitchen sink.

After no time at all we came to a bus stop in the middle of the sand. The bus stop had a bench and a sort of roof, and a sign warning me that because of the extreme heat, hiking wasn't recommended. "Mom, when we get into the lava in the middle of the volcano, how are we going to not catch on fire?" I asked.

"I told you. There's no lava in the volcano. The volcano hasn't erupted in ten thousand years."

"This must be the world's oldest bus stop then," I said with new respect for the ancient bus stop architects. It was in very good shape.

"This isn't a bus stop, it's for people who are too hot and need to sit down. It gets very hot here during the summer."

"Do you think it gets hot because the lava is coming back and it's getting ready for another eruption?" I asked, noticing that it was much warmer here than it had been at home. But Mom said it didn't work that way.

We hiked all the way to the tinder trapezoid, which was less than a mile but had three bus stops along the way. The black sponge-rocks were everywhere, and in between there were nothing but sand and those wiry desert bushes. Seriously. **Nothing** else. I sniffed around in all the places until I figured out that they all smelled the same. From then on, whenever I waited for Mom to catch up, I stood with my nose in the air smelling the scenery and letting the wind flap through my ears and my grin.

As we got closer to the tinder trapezoid I was surprised to find that it wasn't made of dirt, but millions and millions of the black sponge-rocks piled up and stuck together. They were stuck so hard together that we could climb up the trapezoid without them wobbling or rolling away under us. We climbed until we got to a notch, and stepped into what seemed like a huge stadium for rocks, and I was the rock star. All around me, the sides of the stadium swooped up to make a bowl taller than a medium-sized building.

"This is it," Mom said. "You're inside a volcano."

"Volcano? This is more like a bull ring. Where's the lava?"

"I told you! It turned into all of those spiky rocks..."

Mom has such an active imagination, but sometimes I wonder if it is really good for her to live in such a fantasy world all the time. "You're full of it, Mom. Everyone knows that lava is light-up, and that it looks like the melted chocolate in Willy Wonka's chocolate factory, not all spiky like a Ferrero Rocher."

We climbed up to the top of the stadium, and walked around the lip of the bowl until we had walked in a circle around the whole volcano. Sometimes it kind of looked like we were on a big tinder balance beam, but luckily I have stupendous coordination and terrific balance so we weren't in danger. All around we looked down on where the sponge-rocks were waiting outside the tinder trapezoid to get into the stadium, and behind them was the sandy desert, and then Route 66, and beyond that the mountains at the end of the world.

In the woods you always see the same stuff: trees, rocks, dirt, water... over and over in lots of different combinations. But the desert has so many different surprises that woodland dogs couldn't even imagine; like striped rocks, and mitten gods, and canyons, and volcanoes. "Mom, can we stay in the desert for just a little longer before we drive all the way home?" I asked.

"Actually," Mom said, "I have a little surprise for you..."

"We're moving to the desert?!" I squealed mannishly.

"No, I don't think you would appreciate that in the summertime." Oh yeah, the volcano eruptions. "But we're going to stay in the desert a little longer. We're going to explore the desert all the way to New Mexico."

OMG! We were going to travel through the desert in a car-house and be outlaws just like my favorite superhero: Walter White!!!

Baked Potato Beast

Before we got to New Mexico, we had to travel through Arizona. I had been to Arizona before, but that time we had been further up in the canyon country, where Arizona, Utah, New Mexico and some other state crashed together so hard that it left giant cracks in the ground. This time we were in the bottom, Colin Firth half of Arizona where the desert was lumpy and the danger slow. Actually, I didn't know what this part of Arizona looked like yet, because it was dark when we got there, and it was dark when we got up. The dark is supposed to be for sleeping, but if you want to see the sunrise in a place more beautiful than the back of a stinky mailman van, then you need to wake up and make your poop juice in the dark.

Where we went hiking seemed like the desert's idea of a forest, with tons of trunks for us to hike past, except that desert trees have spines instead of leaves so the sun still shines through. Cacti that looked like human beefcakes making muscles for the mirror were all around us. Among the cacti there were just as many cactupi, which is what you call a bunch of cactupuses, and a cactopus is a cactus with too many arms. The cacti and cactupi were so crowded together that it looked like they were standing between two mirrors to make a muscle, and the mirrors were copying them over and over forever into infinity.

It wasn't just the big cactupi that had spines. The bushes did too. There were round Oscar-high poofs that looked like something you could sit on... if you wanted to get poked in the butt. And there were bushes that looked like they were made of spiny ping pong paddles. And other bushes had tiny little delicate spikes that looked almost like floofs of cotton until you touched them and found out that they were made out of the same murder-cotton as kittens.

As we walked through the hills of spiky trunks, the first sun reflected off my incandescent butt fur. I don't know why, but this morning the sunrise didn't make Mom stop and take a gajillion pictures. Humans have a very keen sense of sight, and sometimes Mom can see colors in the sunrise that I can't even imagine, but today it was dark, and then it was bright with nothing in between, like someone had switched on a light. Luckily, today Mom had dressed me in foil wrap, and the sun gleamed off my jacket in a very flattering way.

I should explain what I was wearing, because Mom had to explain it to me. You see, my name is Oscar, but I also answer to Dummy, Puppy Drums, and Potato Beast. Mom calls me a potato beast because I'm the exact shape and density of a raw potato. "...So you'll be a baked potato... get it?!?!" Mom said, holding up my shiny jacket and smiling like she thought she was very clever.

"No. What's a baked potato? Is it ferocious?"

"A baked potato is probably the least ferocious food. Never mind. It will keep you warm. Let's go," Mom said. She seemed mad at me because her joke was dumb.

We kept hiking until, out of nowhere I heard a squeaky toy. I whipped around and Mom was holding a brown blob. I know a toy when I see it, so I jumped around higher and higher, and screeched higher and higher while she waved it around. "GIVE IT!!!" I squealed. When she finally threw it, I chased it until it landed on the ground, and then pawed at it before I ripped its guts out. "What is it?" I sniffed.

"It's a stuffed potato... get it?!?!" Mom said.

"It looks like a turkey leg."

"It's a potato."

"No, look. The rope is supposed to be the bone, and this lighter spot is supposed to be where it separated from the bird. It's a drumstick. What are you doing carrying a Thanksgiving squeaky toy into the desert in January anyway?"

"It was on sale and you're no fun," Mom said, and stormed off down the trail, putting the drumstick in her pocket.

We hiked through all the spikes in the forest, watching how the light changed on the mountains as the sun got higher. There are all kinds of history people who walk across deserts through danger, and risk death to get to a special place, or understand a special thing. But nowadays because there are freeways and Chevron stations in the desert, the stories about walking across it don't have the same sense of danger. But Mom explained that in this part of the world there are still people who walk into the desert hoping to find a promised land. These people are called furry-ners, because they don't have dogs, they follow coyotes. But coyotes aren't loyal like dogs. Sometimes the dirty coyotes lead them into the desert and leave them there, and they have to walk and walk and hope someone will find them.

"I don't like furry-ners," I said. I had just met my first Canadian this week, and he spoke to me in a scary way where the words swished and sloshed in his mouth. So I barked at him.

"Don't be such a fuddyduddy, Oscar. You were only scared because you'd never heard French before. Some of your favorite people are from other countries." Mom said. Then she reminded me of all of my Friends and collies that were born in other countries. The list was very long.

"Well they can't be furry-ners if they're mine. You just listed a bunch of my Second Favorite People."

"Or maybe strangers are just Friends you haven't made your own yet. We have a lot in common with those people wandering in the desert, you know..."

"Nuh uh!"

"Yuh huh! You know how we drive a long way from our home every day to go to work, because The City is where the best job was?"

"Yeah..."

"Well these people are doing the same thing. They just want to work for awhile and then go home to their families. They want balance, just like us."

"This is even worse than our commute!" I said, looking at the spiky cactupi and the mountains the cactupi were climbing.

"Exactly..." Mom explained. "If it were easier to go back and forth, they'd come up and work, and then go home to be with their families. But because it's so hard, once they get here they stay longer, even though they'd rather go home. It's just like how we sleep in the Covered Wagon if we have a late day at work, rather than coming all the way to the Stuck House. It's not worth the effort to go home."

I thought back to the time that Mom had walked me into the desert in Death Valley and I thought I was going to die. I had barely lasted four miles, and there had been a cool waterfall at the midway point. I don't think that I would commute home if I were a furry-ner either.

When we finished hiking we had another long drive to our next stop: NEW MEXICO! New Mexico is my new favorite state because of what happened when I got there. You see, Mom had loved the sunset in Arizona the night before so much that she drove looking behind her instead of where she was going. So when we got to New Mexico and she saw the waves of rocks lined up in neat rows, she insisted that we stop to watch the sunset. She pulled off the freeway and chose all the turns that would take us to the edge of town where there was nothing but open nature all the way to the cliffs. Because towns aren't very big in New Mexico, that meant that all we had to do was make one turn off the freeway and drive past the couple of buildings that were there. When we reached a place with no buildings, we got out of the Covered Wagon and walked onto the wilder-ness. And do you know what was there?!?!

White dirt!

...And horse poo!

I rolled around and around in the white dirt and horse poo until I was so tangled up in my leash that Mom had to free my paws. Then I found a fresh patch and made some more snow/poo angels. Then some movement caught my eye.

THERE WERE HORSES!!!!

And best of all, the horses weren't even in a horse-yard, they were standing on the same grass as I was! I barked at them, but they must have been deaf horses because they only made a farting noise with their lips and went back to eating grass. Then we got closer, and I showed them my snow angels. I guess they were blind too, because they kept on eating like they had hardly noticed the impressive performance happening right under their snouts. Well, two could play at this game. I got even closer, and right when they were about to ignore me again, I barked, "Hey! You guys!"

They all turned and slowly walked away except one. He was smaller than the other horses, so I think he was a horse puppy. I could see in his eyes that he thought that I was one impressive dog, so I showed off all of my moves: I made a snow angel, and dug a hole, and play-bowed and barked all in one move. "Bet you can't do that, can you?" I barked.

Then he took a step closer and I ran and hid behind Mom. Now that I had his undivided attention, I went back to doing very impressive things and pretending like I hadn't noticed that there were any horses there at all. I think it worked, because the horses worked very hard to ignore me until the sun was gone and Mom and I got back in the Covered Wagon to find a place to sleep.

To Heisenberg!

Do you ever have one of those adventures that you just know that you're going to remember forever? So many exciting and interesting things happened on my first day in New Mexico that it's going to be hard to tell all the important parts without writing a whole new book about it.

After my sunset show for the horses the day before, Mom and I drove a few miles up the twenty-mile dirt road that led to tomorrow's trail. We drove until we were tired of the wobbling and swaying, and then we pulled over. Then I tried to keep warm in the Covered Wagon while the moon watched Mom make dinner. I could tell that we were near the sky because the moon looked so close that I could practically look up his nose and count the boogers. It was also cold in the attic of the world. After thinking about it all night, The Witch would figured out that it was twenty-three degrees cold. But we were wearing our warm clothes and cuddled together under our two sleeping bags and two blankets, so Mom and I were comfy, warm and snug as mugs in hugs.

In the morning we still had another fifteen miles to drive up the dirt road, which took almost an hour. And then, when we were almost at the end, *Huzzah!* A paved road. I don't know how no one thought to pave the nineteen miles that led to that road, but we were glad they hadn't, because places that are hard to get to don't get crowded!

We turned a corner and found... a gate across the road. This was fantastic! Gates really make it hard to get somewhere, and guarantee that it won't be crowded. Mom read the sign, "The park is closed due to the government shutdown. For your safety, no entry past this point." She sat in the driving chair, trying to figure out what this meant. Then she pulled the Covered Wagon to the side of the road and got our hiking stuff.

"How long do we have to hike to get to the trailhead, Mom?" I asked.

"Four miles," she said.

"And then how long is the trail?"

"Five miles."

"And what happens when we finish the trail?"

"We have to hike four miles back."

"Mom, what's 4 + 5 + 4?"

"Thirteen."

"And what's that rounded up for getting lost?"

"More than fifteen."

Fifteen miles was a long distance to run, but walking it would take all day. Mom and I walked dejectedly away from the sunrise and down the paved road beyond the gate, staring longingly at the cliffs that we wished we were hiking on. Then Mom stopped. She looked back at the gate. She looked at the Covered Wagon. She looked at the desert next to the gate. And then she started walking back to the Covered Wagon. "Wait! Where are you going?!" I thought after her as I watched her go. "Aren't we hiking?"

But no, Mom put me back in the Covered Wagon and turned it on. Then she drove right off the paved road and into the bushes and sand next to the gate, just like Walter White did when he was being an outlaw.

"Towanda!" Mom hooted.

"To Heisenberg!" I howled.

Neither of us actually said those things, but when we drove back onto the pavement on the other side of the gate, Mom did laugh a crazy, evil, triumphant laugh. She would have rubbed her hands together evilly if she hadn't needed them to drive. We had just broken bad!

The place that we were visiting was called Choco Canyon, but they weren't serving hot cocoa that day, probably because of the government shutdown. Joke's on them, though, because dogs can't drink chocolate, and I got to hike with my leash off and live by wilder-ness rules because no one was there to catch me. Another thing that I got to do because no one was around was to go into the crumbly old building that was next to the parking lot. Mom wouldn't let me actually touch any of the walls because she said there's a difference between breaking the rules and being disrespectful, but as we walked through what was left of the building, she told me that people had built it a thousand years ago. Even though it was a lot of work and they built a lot of big buildings in this canyon, modern people who dig through their old trash think that almost no people actually lived there. That seemed like a big waste of effort for a sometimes-home, but I guess that Mom and I work hard so we can spend a lot of money for a stuck house when

378

we could just live in a mailman van, so maybe someday somedog will dig through all the ripped up toys and poop bags in my dog bathroom and wonder why I had a stuck house so far from my work just for sleeping in.

Behind the tumble-down building we found the trail climbing straight up the cliff. Standing at the bottom you wouldn't even be able to see that there was a way up, but the trail showed itself to us little by little as we climbed. This climb was a lot like our adventure scramble in Las Vegas, only less scary because I didn't have to jump as high; but more scary because if I missed, I would fall right off the cliff and might land on one of those walls I wasn't allowed to touch. Then, the trail turned and went into an enormous rock. Inside the rock there was a secret passageway about two Oscars wide whose walls were the rock and whose roof was the sky. When we got to the other side, we were on top of the cliffs looking down at the Covered Wagon.

We hiked around on top of the cliffs, letting the Karens show us the way so that we wouldn't walk off a cliff into thin air like Wile E Coyote. A bunny who was also outsmarting the government shut-down hopped out from behind a bush, and when he saw that he was sharing the park with a confident and wiley outlaw, he fled. I barked, "Tally-hooooo!" and sprinted after him along the cliff's edge at a million miles an hour. I chased him pretty far before he got away, and when I came back around the corner to find Mom, she was screaming my name and looking frantic. "Don't you ever sprint like that along a cliff!" she told me in her cracking, shaky voice. Like I would ever run off the cliff and leave her alone in the desert like dumb old Wiley E Coyote!

Mom was so in love with the different rock shapes and views off the cliffs that she wanted to take a picture at each one. I was running out of ways to avoid looking at the camera, so I was glad when the trail turned and walked onto the big open grassland that you could only see if you turned your back to the cliff. We followed some kind of hoof tracks left in the soft sand until they veered off the trail and into nothing. Sometimes I even saw paw prints about the size of my own, which was funny because the park had been closed for a long time, and whatever hefty critter had left these mandog-sized paw prints hadn't been traveling with their service human.

We came over a rise, and to our surprise we found two more of those little tumble-down castles, way up here on the roof of the world. "A thousand years ago, this was the center of the most advanced society for a thousand miles around," Mom told me. "People came here from all over the desert to trade things. They've found artifacts from as far away as Mexico… although I guess Mexico isn't all that far from this spot, depending on which part of it you're talking about."

I looked around. It sure seemed like an empty place to me. "Weren't people scared to wander through the desert without coyotes or service humans to get here?"

"Back then they had roads that were as wide as our roads. There were hundreds of miles of them, and the longest one didn't end for thirty miles. That's longer than a marathon."

"Wasn't anyone upset that the furry-ners were coming up here to work?" I asked.

"Well, this was hundreds of years before Mexico was a thing. They had different international relations back then."

This was so confusing. How could people from a place share everything and trade artsy facts with each other in one millennium, and their great, great, great, great... great grandpuppies be so territorial, just when we'd invented cell phones and cars and Google Translate to make it easier for people to go back and forth and talk to each other?

We hiked on and on through the flat spot in the sky until the trail led us back to the top of the cliffs. We were still walking away from the Covered Wagon, and I was starting to worry about how we'd get down when the trail disappeared into another rock. When I looked at where we had to go, I thought for sure Mom had gotten us lost again. The trail-crack was shaped like a V, and at the bottom where the hikers go it was only about 0.8 Oscars wide. No way this was the trail! But there were Karens and signs all around the big rock that had swallowed the trail saying we were in the right place. When I peeked through the crack, there was another sign at the bottom that said "TRAIL." I was just trying to figure out how we were going to walk around this huge obstaple when, to my dismay, Mom disappeared into the crack.

I followed her cautiously, but about half way down, the crack got so narrow that my muscular chest simply would not fit through. I tried to go forward, but I just got wedged in tighter. Mom tried to urge me to squeeze through, but I said, "Nah, let's find another way," and backed out of the crack. She came back to the top with treats and convinced me to try one more time, but I got stuck again, even tighter this time. Now I was starting to panic. What if there was no way down? What if I was stuck up here forever? What if Mom decided not to wait for me, and went back to the Covered Wagon without me? Is this what happened to the Choco people and why they never came back to live in their big houses; because they got wedged into a rock and couldn't get home?

Then, to my horror, Mom walked away from the bottom of the crack. I kept watching the place she'd disappeared from until much to my relief, she came back with a rock the size of a stack of frisbees. Then she climbed up the crack, and stuck the rock in the narrow spot. Then she called me down again.

"Heavens no!!" I whined. "Let's just go back the way we came."

"I don't want to have to walk four miles back. Plus, I want to see what's this way. Come on, you can stand on the rock and go through the V higher up where it's wider."

"I'm not going down there again," I whimpered. "I'll be stuck there forever." I was in an outside-of-Starbucks-level panic, and there was no way I was going back in that slot to die. Mom tried treats, and she tried clapping and snapping, but every time she did, she took a step closer to the top of the crack. I was winning! Maybe I could convince her to come all the way to the top and we could walk back the way we'd come.

Finally I won, and she climbed all the way up the slot to where I was standing... and took out the leash. *Cheater!* I was too scared to fight the leash too much, so I followed her, and when her plan worked and I squeezed through the narrow part by standing on the frisbee rock, I didn't wait for Mom to lead me the rest of the way down, but knocked her legs out of my way and bolted to safety, not even waiting to make sure Mom was okay too.

As we hiked along the cliffs, we looked down at the tumble-down houses from above. Each one was bigger than our Stuck House and had lots of circle rooms and square rooms and windows, and walls, and holes where they could put tree trunks. I think I was supposed to feel something like curiosity or something when I saw them, but really the landscape was much more interesting. Even the tumble-down houses seemed to think so, and had been busy trying to turn back into the landscape for a thousand years.

Once we got back to the Covered Wagon we had to get out of the park somehow. We drove down the long one-way road down the canyon toward the Exit Only. When we got there, Mom said, "Uh oh." Not even Heisenberg could drive around this gate. There was a big ditch on both sides, with lots of Wagon-proof bushes and rocks blocking the way through the desert. Luckily, we were wild west outlaws, and also luckily we knew we

were the only ones in the canyon so there was no one to
run us over for driving the wrong way up a one way road.
We turned around and drove eight miles the wrong way
to break back out of the park and mosey on down the
trail to our next adventure.

Oscar the Trespasser

The story of the next adventure started when we left Choco Canyon and thought we were leaving our life of crime behind with it. Mom and I held our pee for as long as we could so that we would make it to our last stop in time for sunset. All of our hurrying paid off, and we got to White Dirt, New Mexico right as the sky was starting to get wistful. But as we got closer, we could tell that there was something wrong in White Dirt.

First, there were signs that said that the park was closed. Everyone knows you can't close nature though, and signs never stopped us in the past when we wanted to do something that wouldn't hurt anyone. Next we saw a sign that said that we couldn't park within three miles of the entrance. Clearly, other less sneaky outlaws had been there before us and the jig was up. Mom and I had no problem sneaking into the park, but we also needed to protect the Covered Wagon against parking certificates and wagon-nappings. At the entrance itself, instead of a little gate that we could drive around, there was a serious-looking stone wall. On the other side of the wall, a pack of matching trucks that looked like The Law were lounging in the car kennel. We didn't see any coppers inside of them, but unlike Choco Canyon, White Dirt is only a few miles away from a McDonald's and a Starbucks where The Law might be hiding and waiting for two nature lovers like us to try to illegally look at things. Being a victimless outlaw only works in the wilder-ness where no one knows what you're up to. Once someone sees you breaking the rules, you're no longer Schrödinger's Dog, and right and wrong get more important, and less certain.

"What's this all about?" I asked. "Did we do something wrong? Do they know that we snuck into Choco Canyon, and now they're coming to arrest us and throw us in the pound?"

"No, it's not just us, Oscar. This is because the President is mad that he's not allowed to build a wall to keep the Mexicans out, so he shut down the whole federal government to try to get his way."

"So he's building a wall around all the nature to keep the people out of their own country? Are we grounded because we won't help him build the wall?" I asked.

"This sort of thing is a strategy in business to make the other side submissive. He's just using the tools he learned in his old job to try to solve problems in his new job."

"I don't get it. Forcing someone to be submissive when they don't want to be is what you do to your enemy. Does the Alpha Puppy think we're an enemy?"

"Nah. He's just trying to look busy so that when he fails he can say he tried and blame someone else."

"Oh, I get it," I said. And I did. It's like when I bark at someone that I don't really care to bite, just so that they'll *think* I'm ferocious. Then the frienemy leaves me alone *and* Mom stops what she's doing and tells me to "sit," so that I get a treat and some attention. That way I get to look tough *and* look like a good boy. That's called win-win.

Anyway, the park entrance fortification was a problem. Now that we were a thousand miles from home with nothing to do and no time to go somewhere else, we were committed to crossing into public nature illegally. Outlaw experience had taught us that if a park won't let you in, sometimes there are back ways, or similar but wilder off-brand landscapes nearby and outside the park boundary. Mom studied and poked at the mapps and found a service road that went through the white desert outside the park. "Let's just Google what this road is for, shall we?" Mom said. Then she was quiet for a minute while she read. "Well… it says here that it's a missile range. So let's not hike there after all."

We spent the night in a dump off the highway where people stacked up dead branches and broken sidewalks into piles taller than the Covered Wagon. We stayed up late eating junk food that tasted like disappointment and watching something called an eclipse, which is supposed to be exciting, but turned out to just be the moon getting eaten by the darkness until it was just one more thing that we couldn't see.

The next morning we woke up and discovered, much to our surprise, that we were camping next to a beautiful lake, and the lake was copying the sky, and the sky was doing that thing that makes Mom not watch where she's going because she's got her head tilted back like a baby bird. We found a dry dirt basin that looked kind of white, and Mom said this would have to do. When we climbed in and looked at it closely, the basin was filled with regular sand that someone had sprinkled shredded coconut all over. The shredded coconut was actually some kind of teeny-tiny rocks the size of snowflakes. It was cool, and it was weird, but it wasn't something worth driving a thousand miles for, like white dirt piled high into dooms.

We walked around and around in circles in the coconut ditch for a little over a mile — barely more than a potty break — and then we went back to the Covered Wagon and asked The Witch how to get home. On our way out of town we drove along the fence holding in the park. We stared longingly out the window at the sands that looked like a beach vacation advertisement had gotten lost and wandered into the middle of Walter White's desert.

Then, like a miracle, one of the huge waves of sand banded into a rebel tsunami big enough to climb over the fence and spill onto the highway on the freedom side of the fence. Silly Alpha Puppy, you can't hold in nature!

We left the Covered Wagon by the side of the road and climbed up the Rebel Hill. When we got to the top, we could see doom after doom of white sand rolling out in front of us for miles. The way the sand looked and felt, it was like something you only find in magic or the movies. There was no trail, but we didn't need a trail to tell us how to enjoy an open ocean of sand as far as the nose could smell. I dug in it. I rolled in it. I barked at it. I sprinted on it. I chased sticks over it. And the whole time Mom followed me around taking my picture so that the scenery would have someone stunning to stand behind.

When we were finished exploring, we went back to the Coverd Wagon and continued west through Walter White's desert. Several times along our drive we had to go through big toll booths with angry spotlights and The Law inside. In most of them, Mom rolled down her window, showed The Law a friendly smile and her privilege, and we didn't even have to stop. But the last toll booth waver signaled us to stop because he wanted to ask Mom some questions.

"THEY KNOW! THEY'VE COME FOR US!" I barked in Mom's ear so loud that my voice cracked. "BE COOL!"

"Are you from around here?" The Law asked.

"No, I'm from the Bay Area."

"WHERE'S YOUR WARRANT?!" I yelled at him, using Mom's ear as a megaphone.

"Where are you coming from?" he asked.

"White Sands, New Mexico."

"NO! NEVER ADMIT YOU WERE AT THE SCENE OF THE CRIME!" I yelled to Mom. Then, because I wasn't sure if they taught geography at the police academy I told the man, "THAT'S WHITE DIRT, *AMERICA*!"

"Is this your vehicle?" he asked, looking at the mailman decorations that never came all the way off.

"THE COVERED WAGON IS INNOCENT! IT STAYED OUTSIDE THE FENCE THE WHOLE TIME!"

"Yup!" Mom said.

Then he waved us through. Once we were moving again, I said, "Geez, Mom. You almost got us caught!"

"Calm down, Oscar," Mom said. "Border Control doesn't enforce park borders."

Oscar the Flying Pooch

For our final act on the way back from New Mexico, we stopped for a last hike in a place near the Salted Sea. We got there in the dark, but when we stopped the Covered Wagon for the night and got out to stretch our legs and have dinner, the moon was bright like a street light and we could see without using flashlights. I know we have the moon at home too, but I don't notice how great it is there like I do when we're traveling. A lot of other things are only great when we're traveling too, like driving, and rocks, and hard boiled eggs, and public people bathrooms.

The road to the trailhead wore a sign at the bottom that said "Four Wheel Drive Only." Luckily the Covered Wagon has four wheels, so we kept going. The road was made of dirt that shook us like a machine gun, but the Covered Wagon is tough just like me, and knows how to climb much steeper and rougher wagon trails than this. When we got to the trailhead after only six miles of machine gun fire, there were other four-wheeled cars there too, like a Prius, an antique camper van, and a Winnebago.

As is our custom, we hiked into the canyon just as the sun was starting to rise. Mom called the landscape "biblical," which means that there are so many things to look at that you start drooling because you forget to close your mouth, so you should hike with a bib. All together the canyon was very pretty, but if you looked at each thing on its own, it was kind of a mess. From close up, all the rocks looked like they were each part of a different story. There were some that had zebra stripes, and some with Charlie Brown stripes, and some that looked like they were made of shiny plastic, and some that looked wet even though they were dry, and some that looked like rocks but turned out to be just sand if you tried to stand on them, and some that looked like a bunch of pebbles held together with tar-flavored chewing gum. When I watched the canyon, I felt like it had an important story to tell me that I couldn't quite understand; like I was listening to the radio from outside the car.

For two and a half easy miles we walked up the empty river canyon with our heads tilted back: me sniffing and Mom looking for the story that explained how so many different kinds of rocks found their way into one place. When we reached the top, The AllTrails route showed that we should turn around and walk back the way that we had come. But the mapp also showed that the trail continued around in a loop, taking a different canyon back to the start. The loop was called Painted Canyon Loop (Easy), so we weren't too scared of it. In the middle of the loop there was a trail called the Ridge Trail that cut the loop in half like the crack in a coffee bean, and there were little cross trails all along the way so you could get back and forth from the ridge to the two canyons. "Let's walk back on the ridge," Mom said. Mom likes ridges because you can see where you're going, where you've been, and they make good backdrops for hunky dog modeling shoots.

We climbed up a steep trail that hardly looked like a trail unless you were a goat. When I stood at the top, I could look out across the whole valley. I looked down into the canyons right below me that were gashed into the mountain like the mazes that scientists use to feed rats. Mom looked into the distance at the ragged mountains looking like crumpled up brown paper. We walked along the ridge like Legolas and Aragorn walking to Rohan (I'm Legolas, remember?), and the camera in my mind zoomed out to watch us from a distance to better tell the story of all of the kinds of emptiness we were adventuring through.

Some people think that we hold our land inside of us, and those people are territorial and bark angry words when other people come on their land. Other people like to let different lands flow through them, and be a part of different homelands at different times. Mom and I are the second type, but that doesn't mean the territorial humans are wrong. I bet it's a hard job to decide how much of a land is inside each human that comes from there, because each human is different. I wouldn't even know where to start trying to figure out what things are true about every single human from a land that aren't true about humans from your land too. But you need to figure those things out to make laws, which is why law making is a hard job. I just want to make sure that no human gets their feelings hurt because of the land that's inside of them. The hills and mountains of The West are something that Mexico shares with us, so Mom and I share a kinship with them. We also appreciate the Mexicans' fondness for cheese. So Mom bought me a sombrero while we were in New Mexico so that our Mexican friends could see that we're friendly.

But I did not like wearing my sombrero. Whenever Mom put it on my head, I slowly let my head sink lower and lower until the hat toppled onto the ground like an accident. Mom tried to make me pose with my sombrero on the ridge, but I was lucky. A strong wind came along and threw it into the canyon. We watched it roll down the steep slope until it fell off a cliff and disappeared. One of us was very disappointed.

After a mile or so, we took a steep almost-trail off the ridge and into the canyon to get away from the wind. The rocks in this canyon were a little different, but then again the rocks in the last canyon were different everywhere you looked, too. We were most of the way back down to the Painted Canyon Loop (Easy) when we came around the bend and the trail fell into a hole. We looked into the hole to see where the trail had gone, and found that it had fallen about two Mom-lengths below us, with the trail's two parts held together with a rope leash. You could use the rope leash for climbing down, but only if you had the sort of paws that could grab onto it. I had the wrong sort of paws. "Well this isn't going to work," Mom said.

We looked around for an Oscar-friendly way down, but there was nothing but smooth rock walls for a hundred feet above us on both sides. We were trapped. The only way out was to walk back up to the ridge and find a different way down. Mom looked closely at the mapp and found another trail higher up the mountain that crossed from the ridge to the Painted Canyon Loop (Easy). Because we're learning from experience, Mom looked closer at the stripes that tell her how steep a trail is. In a spot right above the Painted Canyon Loop (Easy), a whole bunch of lines came together in one place, and the trail went straight across the spot without so much as a squiggle. "That," Mom said, "looks like a cliff." Instead of investigating to find out what the cliff looked like, Mom decided that our best option would be to walk all the way back up the ridge to the top, and then walk all the way back down through the second canyon. Basically our route would look like a big McDonald's M, and we still had to walk the whole second arch.

The wind was in our faces now that we were walking up the ridge instead of down. This was the kind of wind that only blows in stories where something really interesting happens. People don't return library books, or buy more poop bags in wind like this; they go on quests or save the world. Colin Firth would blow away in wind like this. Mom hiked with her paw on top of her head so that she wouldn't lose her sombrero, and I walked behind her so that she would block my wind.

After hiking almost two miles into the wind, we were excited to go back into the shelter of the canyon for the second half of Painted Canyon Loop (Easy), and the final leg of our canyon arches. We were back in a big, wide, sandy, dry river and all we had to do was hike some easy miles back to the Covered Wagon, so Mom stopped being grouchy and laughed at all the delightful things that exploring made me do.

After awhile, I started hearing a strange "plunk, plunk" noise further down the canyon, like something hitting metal. "What's that noise?" I asked.

"I have no clue..." Mom said, looking confused and curious.

Then we came around the bend and saw that the trail had fallen into another hole. In the spot where it disappeared was a rickety metal ladder that had fallen in and was trying to climb back out again. I peeked over the edge, and saw that the drop was almost two Moms tall, so I backed up real quick so the hole couldn't suck me down like it had the ladder. Mom stayed at the edge inspecting the rock. Then, to my horror, she held out her arms and tried to scoop me up like a fork lift! Luckily, I am very fast and The Old won't let Mom run, so I got away and stood just outside her reach.

Then something even scarier happened. Mom turned away from me and climbed down the ladder without me. I stood at the top of the hole and watched her go with growing panic. Then I watched her move the ladder out of the way. Then she called me and told me to come.

"I can't! I can't fly!" I whimpered. But she seemed to have her doggie telepathy turned off, because she kept cheerfully calling my name like I was being a big baby by not jumping off of a cliff. I looked around for another way down, but there wasn't one. That's when I started manly crying. I was as scared as I've ever been waiting outside the Starbucks or wedged into a slit in a rock, and any other brave adventurer would have bleated and mewled if they'd been in the same position of despair.

Mom was still standing at the bottom of the hole calling me like nothing was wrong. Maybe she knew something I didn't. I put my front paws on the edge, and tried to see if an eagle would swoop down and let me ride on its back to safety, but the only thing that happened was that Mom's voice got even more excited. Mom had never let me get dead before, and despite her bumbling, she had always figured out how to get us out of our adventures. Even though it seemed like a bad idea, she obviously wanted me to jump off a cliff. And you know what they say, "If everyone is jumping off a cliff, then you should definitely jump off a cliff too." I inched forward until I felt the ground sucking me into the hole. Then the hole grabbed all of me and I went over the edge.

The hole that had eaten the trail wasn't straight up and down. It leaned just a little bit, like the steepest slide you've ever seen. So even though I was falling, I kept moving my legs like I was running and it kept me from falling butt over ears. When I got to the flat bottom, I kept running on the sand like a truck on a runaway ramp until finally the falling wore itself out several yards beyond the Oscafall.

I was okay! Mom was already throwing a party, cheering and telling me what a good job I'd done and how brave I was (as if I didn't know). Her whole body lit up with pride and love. Now that I knew I could fly, I couldn't stay stuck to the ground and jumped and pranced around doing my happiest happy dance and squealing along with her.

"You did such a good job! I was so scared," Mom said, grabbing me in a head lock so that she could kiss the special spot on my forehead.

"What? But this was your idea! I wanted to go back!"

"I know you did..."

"You *knew*?!?! Then why didn't you come up out of the hole and walk back with me?"

"I knew you could make it. But the only way to do it without getting hurt was if you didn't hesitate. You couldn't doubt yourself for a moment."

"Because I thought you knew what you were doing!"

"When have I ever known what I was doing?" she protested. "Anyway, it worked, didn't it?"

Can you believe that a little while later the trail fell down into a hole one more time?! If there hadn't been a way down this one, we would have been trapped with no way up the cliff behind us, and no way down the one in front of us. Luckily, Mom found a way that I could climb down lower, and only jump from 3/4 of a Mom high. So this time I was only medium-scared and survived without much whimpering at all.

When we were almost back to the Covered Wagon, we reached the place where we would have come out if we had taken the trail that went over the spot where all the steepness lines came together. We expected to see something horrible, like a hundred-foot-long leash dropping off a cliff, or a fire truck ladder stretched all the way out, but instead we saw a big crack in the canyon wall filled with lots of big rocks we could have climbed down easily. If we had come down this way, we would have been finished three miles, two ladders, and a sombrero ago.

In this last half mile, we also started seeing other hikers. One lady stopped and asked us if it was this way to the ladders. "I tried to do the ladders last year, but I didn't make it," she said.

"I almost didn't make it either," I told her so that she would know that failure doesn't mean you're not brave.

Workday Adventure

Do you ever wonder where the adventures rest during the week while everyone's at work? One morning Mom and I went to find out. We left The City after work and drove along the smell of the ocean until the lights went away and were just tiny twinkles in the distance. Then we stopped the Covered Wagon and slept with the sound of the ocean cheering for me like a million far-away fans, and the rain falling on the Covered Wagon like a million tiny drummers.

We woke up in the dark like a normal work day, but instead of our normal boring routine, Mom opened the Covered Wagon door and we walked into the dark unknown. Humans like to "multitask," so Mom usually looks at the far-away when we hike because that way she sees the most things at once. But how can you enjoy the subtle fragrance of a week-old rabbit turd, or the tangy scent of a vine of poison oak if you don't stop and sniff it closely? If you try to smell all the pee spots, crotches and dropped trash for miles around in one giant sniff, you're going to miss something. Because we couldn't see, I followed my nose from one sight to another, and Mom followed me wearing my spotlight on her head. Just like me, she could enjoy only the things within smelling distance, because everything farther away was gone in blackness. Down below us we could hear the beach, and in the air we could feel the fog that was snuggling up to the mountain above. We could smell the ocean mixing with the rain, and the rain pulling out all the other smells.

But except for what was in my spotlight, we couldn't see any of it.

"Do you mean that this has been hiding tucked under The City for all these years, while we've been running in The Fart hundreds of mornings?!" I asked.

"Yeah," Mom said. "Makes you feel like a bit of a fool, doesn't it?"

"I'm not the fool," I said. "I'm just the coach. The route planner is the fool." Then I had a brilliant idea! I asked The Fool, "Mom, can we do more work day adventures?"

"Well, that was the plan. Except after just a couple of runs I hurt my knee. And starting next week we're not even going to be able to hike for at least two months."

Two months is like... 527 days! "What?!?!" I barked. "Why?!"

"Well, I need to get my knee put back together if I ever want to run another step again. A surgeon is going to tie the pieces back where they belong next week, and then I can't put any weight on it for a few weeks while I heal, or else I could rip it apart again. I'm going to have four legs, just like you!"

"That's the dumbest thing I've ever heard!" I said. "You don't get four legs just so you don't have to walk on one of them. You're doing it wrong. What's a surgeon anyway? Sounds like a scam to me..."

"A surgeon is a person who puts you to sleep so that he can move things around inside of you," Mom explained. It sounded to me like one of those ghoulish stories that you tell a puppy when you want to scare them into behaving.

As the ground started to make enough light that I could see where we were going without my spotlight, I looked skeptically at Mom's knee. It looked like it was already connected together, even if it was a little floppier than usual and hung a bit like a puppet's leg when she walked. "Are you sure that the vet isn't just having you on so that he can sell you a surgery?" I asked. "Those psychos really can't be trusted."

All Mom said was, "I'm so sorry..." as if that answered anything at all.

"But, Mom! What about my fans?! That one time I stopped writing for a couple of months everyone thought we were dead."

"Well, you can write about what it's like when you can't run," Mom pointed out. "There are lots and lots of other runners out there that are injured and feel like the whole world is going to pass them by if they can't run for a little while. You can be a life coach again!"

I thought about what Mom said. What advice would I give to another runner that just found out that they were going to miss 527 days of adventures? How would I respond to their hopelessness? I started to compose my inspiring blog post...

"Dear Friends," I would write.

Then I thought about what they might want to hear. Probably the truth. "...you may feel like life is passing you by," I'd tell them. "It is."

Then they would probably want to hear if there was any hope of living a fulfilling life without running for 527 days. "Abandon all hope," I would tell them frankly. Then, because people sometimes think that things are going to turn out okay no matter what, I would add: "You're doomed."

Encore

I decided to take Mom on one final adventure before the vet tied her knee back together. Mom hates the rain, and I didn't want her to spend her last hike suffering from the cloud sickness, so I had to find somewhere dry. I hoped we wouldn't have to drive all the way back to the desert to find a dry place to hike, but unfortunately I was traveling with the Weather Jinx. It was going to rain all over California that weekend, even Death Valley, but finally we found a place where it was going to stop raining on Sunday. The problem was that the place we found was almost all the way to Nevada, in the Moon-javi desert.

We did everything that Mom wouldn't be able to do once she was four-legged before lunchtime on Saturday, and then spent the rest of the day driving to the desert. We camped the Covered Wagon in the sand next to a lonely desert road where the wind blew so hard that it blew the heat out of Mom's soup, and the rain beat on the roof of the Covered Wagon like it wanted us to come out and fight. But some dark hours later when I got out of the Wagon to take my morning potty break, I could see more stars in the sky than I had ever seen in my life. The more I looked at the sky, the deeper it got and the more stars sprinkled into my eyes. Then, out of nowhere a star popped out of the dark, sprinted across the sky, and disappeared again like a bunny under a bush. Mom said that was a shooting star and that I should make a wish. I'm not supposed to tell you what I wished for because then it won't come true, but my wish had long ears and a fluffy tail. Also, I wished that Mom wouldn't have The Old anymore and we could have more good years together.

The trail we found wasn't very adventureful. Instead of walking over the top of the mountain, it walked around the outside of it. I wasn't bored for long though, because suddenly I saw something in the corner of my eye. It moved fast, and appeared and disappeared, just like the shooting star. *Yippee-kai-yo-kai-yay!* This desert was hopping with jackrabbits! I spent the next hour sprinting forty or fifty miles chasing one bunny after another while Mom watched the trail to make sure it stayed where it was supposed to be. I came back every now and then to have her pick the cactus spikes out of my butt and paws, or to let her take my picture. Sometimes when I found her she was spinning around holding out The Witch in front of her to divine which sandy spot between the bushes was the trail, and which was just a sandy spot between some bushes; the difference matters more to humans than it does to dog runners and bunny runners.

Under the skeleton of a tree that had been barely bigger than a bush, I found something sort of loaf-y with pointy parts, and holes in it. It smelled like the frozen beef bones Mom gives me as a treat when it's hot out, only not as smelly. If this was my wish coming true, then I was confused. It had long ears, but where was the fluffy tail? "What is it?" I sniffed.

"It's a cow skull. Or maybe a bull? Do cows have horns?"

"What happened to its beefy bits?"

"Well, it's dead. This is what happens when something's been dead for awhile."

"How did it die all the way out here?!" I asked, alarmed.

"Ummmm... I don't know. Maybe it was watching cowboy movies on Netflix and got so absorbed it forgot to get up and have a bowl of water."

"Oh no! Do you think it died before the last season of Breaking Bad?"

"I don't think it's been here for that long," she said. "Maybe it just died of old age..."

"Wait, you can die of being old?!" I asked. Suddenly things were falling into place. Mom had The Old, and now that she couldn't live a fulfilling life doing the things that she enjoyed, she was going to a vet who would put her to sleep. I never wanted Mom's and my story to end, but if it had to, it's supposed to be the *dog* that dies at the end, not the Mom. The idea scared me so much that I had to put it out of my mind.

We continued walking through rivers of sand and fluffy cacti to the other side of the mountain. I was having fun chasing bunnies and discovering dead cows, but I was afraid that this wouldn't be enough adventure for Mom's last expedition. We had hiked almost five miles and she hadn't had to figure anything out yet, and I hadn't had to be brave and use my brawny muscles to get me out of danger. What kind of memories would I be leaving Mom with if this was our last adventure before she was put to sleep?

At this part of the trail I saw that the mountain wasn't shaped exactly like a big 0, it had a smaller mountain holding its hand so that it was shaped more like an 8. As we got closer, I realized that we weren't headed around the top of the 8, but right for its waist. The rock columns around the collar of the mountain looked like a bunch of guards standing shoulder to shoulder, and the closer we got, the more they closed in on us and leaned over us menacingly. When Mom talked, the rocks talked back to her so that they would have the last word.

By now I could recognize when I was in a dangerous place. In places like this I had gotten wedged tight in the rocks like Winnie the Pooh, I'd learned to fly, and at least one time I'd thought I'd be stranded forever. I could smell adventure and I couldn't wait to see what kind of thrilling fix Mom had gotten us into this time.

Finally the rocks crowded in so close on each side that they closed ranks in front of us. In the place where they met was a rounded slide that was curved like a taco shell, and someone had pierced a line of giant earrings into the inside of the taco. "How the heck are we going to get up this?" I asked.

"Don't worry! I have a plan!" Mom said, reaching into her packpack. She pulled out my ugly safety harness and my Kona leash. "See? It's rock climbing equipment. We'll use the harness like a sling and I can help hoist you up!" Mom said. "That's called belaying."

"Wait," I said. "Did you know this was here?"

"Yeah. Sorta. I mean, I saw a picture. But I didn't know if there would be another way around."

Mom used her front paws to hold the rings, and her back paws used the studs as stairs, and that way she got to the top of the Oscarfall, taking her end of the leash with her. When she got to the top, she threaded the leash through one of the rings and pulled on it until the harness pulled on me and I had no choice but to climb up the pile of rocks at the bottom of the Oscarfall. The harness kept pulling, so I had no choice but to stand up tall on my hind paws like a human, using my front paws against the wall for balance. But Mom still kept pulling. "I can't!" I whined like a tough guy. "I can only fly down, not up!"

"Come on! Jump!" Mom encouraged me, tapping the top of the rock, which was several Oscars above my head. I tried jumping to show her that it was too tall, but I must have had Chuck Norris in my legs, because I felt myself lifted by a magic force and I jumped higher than I've ever jumped before. I landed with my front paws over the top, and then my back legs ran up the wall with such force and speed that once I was back on level ground I kept flying with purpose like a bowling ball in the gutter; barreling right past Mom and continuing through the canyon with my leash dragging on the ground behind me.

Before long we reached another set of giant earrings. This one was taller because it didn't have as big a pile of rocks at the bottom to help me get closer to the top. Mom climbed the earrings like she had before, but this time my leash wasn't long enough to get all the way to the top earring. Instead bullying me with the rope like she had at the last Oscarfall, this time she just tried to hoist me straight up like a yoyo. I still have my pride, and

I had had enough of this nonsense, so when the irresistible force tried to make me jump like Chuck Norris again, I turtled my head into my shoulders until I had backed out of the harness and Mom dropped the empty leash back to the ground. "Well you've got to figure out some way up," she called down to me. "If you turn back then you're going to have to figure out how to get *down* that last set of rings and that seems scarier and more dangerous to me."

We looked at the empty harness and leash lying on the sand. Then I smiled up at Mom because I knew that this meant that she had to come back down and help me figure out another way. I couldn't wait to see what she came up with, because we really seemed to be in a jam now.

She climbed down the rings and explored the rock next to the Oscarfall. The rocks had big cubbies in them where giant woodpeckers had tried to peck their way out. On one side there was a set of ledges and woodpecker holes that looked like Mom and I could climb. Mom went ahead of me, and patted all the places where I should jump. But then she put her hand on a spot that was way, way above my head. "How do I get up there?" I grinned.

"You come up here where I'm standing, and then I give you a boost."

"You're in my way."

She climbed out and I jumped up to where she was, then she patted the rock where she wanted me to go. "It's around the corner," I said.

"Um, okay I'll carry you."

"No way, José," I said, backing into the hole. She reached for me, and the rock under her wobbled.

"Aw, come on. You can make that jump," she said, patting the rock that was now above her head. "Then you can just walk up to the top. It'll be so easy."

Instead, I jumped back down to the bottom. "Nope, let's try something else."

Mom studied the Oscarfall again. "Alright, fine," she said finally. "I'll give you a boost." She scooped me up by my chest and butt, using both arms like a shovel, and stepped onto the lowest and most stable rock at the bottom of the Oscarfall. I was so close to the side of the taco shell that my nose was touching the rock. Then Mom poked me in the ribs with the beak of her hat. I waited patiently for her to turn so that I'd be facing the correct wall. Seeing the problem she said, "Well I can't turn. I'd lose my balance and then we'd both go tumbling down." I waited and stared at the rock at the end of my elegant snout while she pecked me some more and her persuasive voice got squeakier and squeakier. "Okay, fine," she grunted finally. She dug her knuckles into the rock next to my butt so that her arm would be more stable, and shifted my whole butt onto that arm. Then she used her free paw to hang onto an earring for better balance, and stepped up on a higher rock. "Okay, now use my arm like a step and climb up the wall. I'll grab your butt and give you a boost," she gasped.

I stayed sitting on her arm like pirate's parrot. "Mom," I explained patiently, "I'm a dog. I can't pull with my front paws. I can only push. How am I supposed to pull myself up? That's your job: to bully me. Remember?"

"Okay, fine," she growled, panting like a handsome pooch on a hot day. She adjusted her feet, pulled her knuckles out of the wall to grab my butt, and squatted down underneath me. Now I was standing on her shoulder with her paw under my butt like she was a waiter holding a tray made out of dog butt. Then she leaned forward so that I had to put my front paws on the wall for balance. My paws were just under the top of the Oscarfall, but not quite there yet, and my back paws were still on Mom's shoulder.

"Now you've done it," I said. "I can never get back onto your shoulder like a gargoyle without losing my balance now. And if I fall, I'm going to take your legs out on the way down."

"Well you'll just have to use me like a step stool then," Mom said, pushing on my butt without lifting me even a whisker closer to the top. "That way" (grunt) "you can" (gasp) "use those strong back legs of yours." Gingerly, I put my hind paw on the highest part of Mom, which just so happened to be the middle of her face. Then I put my other hind paw on the second highest part of her, which was her throat. Then, with one powerful push of my legs, I jumped off of Mom's head, and she pushed on my butt, and I managed to get my front paws on flat enough ground that I could push myself up and, with a little more pushing from Mom, scramble my back legs over the top.

When Mom climbed out of the hole, she looked like she had squeezed all of the stress out of herself like a sponge and now she was floppy with tiredness and relaxation. I was already doing my happy dance, sprinting back and forth in the little sandy area at the top of the Oscarfall. "Did you see that, Mom?" I squealed. "That was called rock climbing, what I did. And what you did was bullying. That's what rock climbers do. They help each other and bully each other. We did it as a team!" Then I bounded to the place where the sky spread the rocks apart again.

When we were back in the sun, we sat on a rock looking into the hole that we had just climbed out of. "See? That was fun." Mom said. "Aren't you glad that we didn't take the easy way around?"

"There was an easy way?!"

"Oh sure. I learn from my mistakes, you know. This time I made sure that there was an alternative route, and I brought your rock climbing equipment. See? We're getting better at this."

Saying Goodbye

The day had come for the vet to put Mom to sleep. It was possible that she would recover and we would run again someday, but it was also possible that The Old would stay for good, and we would never run together again.

When The Witch wakes us up in the morning, Mom always makes sure to spend a couple of minutes kissing and hugging me, scratching behind my ears, and rubbing my belly. I used to call this "making love," but then Mom said that I should absolutely *not* call it that ever, and wouldn't tell me why. It's a pretty clever expression, I think, so I guess it's probably trademarked by somedog else. The morning Mom was getting put to sleep, we spent longer than usual heavy petting™ before she got out of bed.

Mom showered like we were going to work, but then she put on sweatpants like she was staying home. Then she opened the door, and I ran out into the yard and waited for her to open the gate. "No, bud. You're staying home for this one..." Mom said.

"But don't you want me there when they put you to sleep?" I asked.

"Of course I do. But it's not like at home, they can't let you in bed with me."

"Why not?!"

"In case someone in the next operating room makes a noise and you run around screaming your head off. They don't like it when you do that in surgery." So she

413

gave me a pig ear to soothe my anxiety, and walked out the door alone.

Since Mom and I lived together, worked together, and adventured together, I almost never did anything alone anymore. It felt strange to be home without Mom to stare at. What did I used to do all day before I was a busy-ness dog, when Mom wasn't there to call my name to give me a treat, or take me somewhere exciting like a meeting or the ATM? More time passed than it takes to go to the grocery store, and so I got depressed thinking that getting put to sleep might be exciting, and Mom was doing it without me. So I took a nap hoping that it would be like I was put to sleep too; and since Mom and I do everything together, when I woke up, she would probably wake up with me.

When I woke up, Mom still wasn't home and I started to wonder if maybe she had forgotten about me now that her knee was fixed. I wandered around the house sniffing for laundry or backpacks with food in them, but Mom had cleaned the house from top to bottom before she had left. What would I do if she never came home to open the food fortress, or let me out for a potty break and recess? I went to the toy bin and took out one of my dinosaurs to put it back on the floor where it belonged, but there wasn't much sense in ripping it up without Mom dropping what she's doing to tell me to stop and give me a kiss as she took it away. So I listened out the window until another nap overtook me.

I had a great dream where Mom and I were chasing bunnies and barking at them together, like in the good old days. For a groggy moment I was happy again, because I knew that Mom would never go bunny hunting without me. But as I woke up more, I remembered that Mom is scared of bunnies, and that she *never* chased them when she was off leash, only when she was tied to me. All this time I thought that bunny hunting was something fun we did together, but maybe it was something she did only because *I* liked it. I stared at the door, waiting for it to open and wondering why she would take me to all those trails where she might get attacked by a roving bunny rabbit?

The more I thought about it, the more I realized that Mom *never* had as much fun as me. Most of her smiles at work happened when someone came to give me butt scratches. She also seemed like she was "working" on our runs, and never smiled unless I showed her something fun like how to tip over and roll around in fresh grass. Even on our hikes she was sometimes tired and grouchy. Why would she do all those things if it wasn't fun for her? Except... maybe just like I needed Mom to be my service human to open the food fortress, or drive me on our adventures, or smile and tell people that I bark (like they couldn't figure out themselves what the commotion was), maybe she needed me for something she couldn't do alone. There are humans whose eyes don't work so they have dogs to see for them. But Mom's eyes work just fine, so what couldn't Mom do that I could?

Then it hit me: all this time I had been trying to teach Mom not to be so sad and grumpy, but I hadn't taught her what she was supposed to be feeling instead. The thing that Mom couldn't see without me was joy. No duh! I had been giving her more and more services to do for me rather than letting her off the leash so that she could cut loose.

I had been staring at the door for at least a dog hour and Mom still hadn't opened it, so I got even more worried. What if something had happened to her?! I knew she wouldn't leave me here alone on purpose, but what if The Old was worse than the vet thought, and she had died of old age right there on the operating table while

they tied her leg back together? My life passed before my eyes then, and I saw all the times that Mom had put herself in danger to save me, like when she stood between me and the chopping cart. Or how she had loyally walked off the trail and into the desert with me when she could have easily climbed alone back to safety at the top of the Oscarfall. And now she was getting put to sleep just so that she could run with me. I had never really noticed how I never noticed all the things that Mom had done for me.

I finally heard a car in the driveway, my friend Margo's voice, and a strange clacking sound. Then I heard someone opening our gate. "I'm here! I'm in here!" I shouted through the door so that whoever it was would open up and I could look for Mom. "Let me out quick! I think that Mom might be in trouble."

"Back up, Oscar," Margo called through the door. "Calm down!"

I heard the sound of the key in the lock. "Calm down?! How can you expect me to be calm at a time like this?!" I screeched. "Mom could be in danger and only I know about it! Do you know they put her to sleep today???"

Then the door opened, and I forced my way outside faster then the door could open. I pushed Margo out of the way and made for the open gate, where I stopped short. There was Mom, looking older than I'd ever seen her. She had a hideous contraption made of sticks and straps holding her leg together from the outside. There was no way that that ghastly thing they'd

built could do leg things, so they had given her two more
fake legs to move around with. But her prosthetic legs
were clacky and stiff, and wouldn't be any good for any
of the things that legs like to do, like jump, or dance jigs,
or run, or hike. I had always wished Mom had four legs,
but not like this!

"Okay, Oscar. You take care of her," Margo said
when Mom had clacked her way inside and lay down in
bed.

Take care of her! I'd never thought of doing *that*
before. I thought that it was Mom's job to take care of
me! "What have they done to you?!" I asked, kissing
Mom's face without taking my eyes off of the horrible
monstrosity that she had dragged into the bed with us.

"I'll have a bum knee for a few months," Mom
said. "But when I recover, hopefully we can go back to
the life we used to have when we explored the mountains
and deserts and had the world all to ourselves."

"They sewed a bum into your knee?!" I said,
horrified. "That's not where a bum belongs!"

"I did it for you, so we could run together again."

"This isn't what I meant when I told you that you
should run on four legs!" I said, snuggling my head into
her chest so that she could feel me pushing out all the
space between us. "You were perfect just the way you
were! Now look what they've done to you..."

Once I had recovered from the shock, I cuddled in
as close to Mom as I could get while still staying out of
range of the bum in her leg. "Don't worry, Mom," I said.
"I'll keep you company until you're feeling better again.

And when you're back in one piece, I'll teach you how to feel joy."

"But Oscar, don't you see? Taking care of you *is* what gives me joy! The world is full of unpleasant and hurtful things, and I can't stop bad things from happening in the world, but I control almost everything in *your* world. I can create a life for you that is made up of nothing but good experiences, and when I'm with you I live in a world without suffering. When I see that you expect love from every person you meet because you know no different, and every experience is an adventure because you have absolute faith that you're free from danger, that *is* what makes me happy. You make me happier than you could possibly imagine."

I hope you enjoyed following me on my adventures. I certainly loved having you along with us. If you want to read more of my adventures, come visit my blog at dogblog.wf. If you want to share your adventures with me, I'd love to hear from you! You can write to me at oscar@dogblog.wf. You can also follow me on Facebook (facebook.com/poochoscarthecoach) and Instagram (@poochoscarthecoach). I can't wait to meet you!

-Oscar the Pooch

Made in the USA
Monee, IL
25 May 2021

69494233R00246